Thomas More
A Portrait of Courage

Thomas More
A Portrait of Courage

Gerard B. Wegemer

SCEPTER PUBLISHERS
PRINCETON

Nihil obstat: Msgr. William Maguire, S.T.D., *Censor Deputatus;*
Imprimatur: ✠ John C. Reiss, D.D., J.C.D., Bishop of Trenton,
April 12, 1995

Scepter Publishers, Inc.　　　　　Published in Europe by:
P.O. Box 1270　　　　　　　　　　Four Courts Press, Ltd.
Princeton, NJ 08542　　　　　　　Fumbally Lane
E-mail: general@scepterpub.org　Dublin 8, IRELAND
Phone: 609-683-8773　　　　　　　E-mail: info@four-courts-press.ie

Third printing, 1998

Library of Congress Cataloging-in-Publication Data

Wegemer, Gerard B., 1950–
　　Thomas More: a portrait of courage / Gerard B. Wegemer
　　　　p.　cm.
　　Includes bibliographical references (p.　).
　　ISBN 0-933932-84-7
　　1. More, Thomas, Sir, Saint, 1478–1535. 2. Great Britain—
History—Henry VIII, 1509–1547—Biography. 3. Statesmen—
Great Britain—Biography. 4. Christian martyrs—England—
Biography. 5. Humanists—England—Biography. I. Title.
DA334.M8W44　1995
942.05′2′092—dc20
[B]　　　　　　　　　　　　　　　　　　　　　95-15747
　　　　　　　　　　　　　　　　　　　　　　　　CIP

ISBN 0-933932-84-7 (hardback)
ISBN 1-889334-12-X (paperback)
ISBN 1-85182-425-1 (Four Courts Press edition)

"Courage is not simply *one* of the virtues, but the form of every virtue at the testing point, which means, at the point of highest reality."
— C. S. Lewis's *The Screwtape Letters*[1]

"This is a book about that most admirable of human virtues—courage. 'Grace under pressure,' Ernest Hemingway defined it."
— John F. Kennedy's *Profiles in Courage*

For permission to reprint extensive excerpts from the following material, grateful acknowledgment is made to these publishers:

Confraternity of Christian Doctrine, Washington, D.C.: Excerpts from the Psalms are taken from the New American Catholic Edition of the Holy Bible, © 1961.

Everyman's Library, David Campbell Publishers, Ltd.: Excerpts from *Lives of Saint Thomas More*, ed. E. E. Reynolds, © 1963.

Sheed and Ward: Excerpts from *A Dialogue of Comfort against Tribulation*, ed. Monica Stevens, © 1951.

University of Toronto Press: Excerpts from *The Collected Works of Erasmus*, vols. 2–8 (Letters nos. 142–1251, dated 1501–1521), © 1975–1978.

Yale University Press: Excerpts from *The Complete Works of St. Thomas More*, vol. 4, *Utopia*, ed. Edward Surtz and J. H. Hexter, © 1965; vol. 14, *De Tristitia Christi*, ed. Clarence H. Miller, © 1976; *Selected Letters*, ed. Elizabeth F. Rogers, © 1961.

Contents

Illustrations

Following page 118.

Sir Thomas More's Coat of Arms, 1995, by Peter Drummond–Murray, Slains Pursuivant of Arms. Courtesy of W. David Holliday.

Thomas More, 1527, painting by Hans Holbein the Younger, © The Frick Collection, New York.

Thomas More at the Opening of Parliament, 1523, engraving by an unknown artist for Richard Fiddes' *Life of Wolsey* (London, 1724); based on a painting done *c.* 1523 (Windsor Castle). Courtesy of Bridwell Library, Southern Methodist University, Dallas, Texas.

Sir Thomas More, 1527, sketch by Hans Holbein the Younger, The Royal Collection, © Her Majesty Queen Elizabeth II.

Thomas More, His Father and His Household, 1527, sketch by Hans Holbein the Younger, Kunstmuseum, Basel.

The Thomas More Family, 1995, painting by Gary Chu Kar Kui, Dallas, Texas.

Sir Thomas More, 1984, bust by H. Reed Armstrong, Silver Spring, Maryland.

Annotated page from Thomas More's prayer book and psalter, Beinecke Rare Book and Manuscript Library, Yale University. (See also Appendix 6.)

Thomas More, 1969, statue by L. Cubitt Bevis, Chelsea, London. Photograph by Ben Kobus.

Maps

Thomas More's London: Endpapers (hardback edition only)

Thomas More's Travels: Appendix 1

Thomas More's Travels near London: Appendix 2

Introduction

THOMAS MORE LOVED LONDON DEEPLY, but unsentimentally. There he was born and raised, there he fell in love, there he married. There he practiced law, told a thousand jokes, and judged as many cases—sometimes in a single year. There he raised his family, served his country, and wrote about the particular controversies of his day. There he achieved fame as an outstanding judge, scholar, educator, and statesman. There also he was condemned and executed by men who were his friends.

More knew London well—so well that he seriously considered leaving it. As a young man, in one of the earliest letters that have come down to us, he lamented:

> In the city, what is there to move one to live well? But rather, when a man is straining in his own power to climb the steep path of virtue, it turns him back by a thousand devices and sucks him back by its thousand enticements. Wherever you take yourself, on one side nothing but feigned love and the honeyed poisons of smooth flatterers resound; on the other, fierce hatreds, quarrels, the din of the forum murmur against you. Wherever you turn your eyes, what else will you see but confectioners, fishmongers, butchers, cooks, poulterers, fishermen, fowlers, who supply the materials for gluttony and the world and the world's lord, the devil?[1]

1

Yet in London, imperfect as it was, More—imperfect as he was—achieved by the end of his life what he earlier had said was laughable even to consider.

At forty-three, More wrote an angry and biting reply to certain accusations by a French poet and courtier named Germanus Brixius. For the sake of peace among their circle of international scholar friends, Erasmus urged More not to publish this Juvenalian diatribe. More took Erasmus' advice, but in his own defense he wrote:

> It may well be that my own sense of injury makes a statement seem not at all bitter to me which someone who is not so involved in the matter will find rather harsh. Even if this should happen, I have enough confidence in my readers' fairness, Erasmus, to be hopeful that even in me (although your love assigns me so grave a demeanor, just as it always looks for great things in me)—to be hopeful that even in me, while I still dwell in this mortal abode, and have certainly not yet been entered in the number of saints (let me laugh at a laughable notion), humane readers will exhibit some tolerance for those human emotions which no one has ever been able to banish entirely.[2]

To become a saint in a terribly imperfect world, while being terribly imperfect oneself, is the challenge of every person. So More believed. Such a challenge More knew to involve difficult trials which he saw as the forge needed to fashion genuine strength and refinement of character—a character that would be capable of serving in any and all seasons. No wonder he disliked most "lives of the saints." They substituted foolish, superstitious fables for human realities as they were.[3]

Did More have faults? Of course. The most obvious ones went hand in hand with his most obvious strengths. He was, for example, a sensitive poet with a vivid imagination and an intellect of rare genius. But he was a dreamer in his younger days,[4] and he had to work hard to use the sharp blade of his wit to heal and construct, rather than to injure and dominate.[5] He was keenly aware of his tendency to neglect concrete duties in favor of his passion for philosophy and the arts. In fact, he indulged this passion to such an extent that he angered his good-natured father, to the point that Sir John actually threatened to disown his unfocused son.[6]

In addition, More was a great talker and a constant joker.[7] Such qualities can endear, but they can often irritate. When moderated they can become virtues, but when indulged they necessarily cause strife. More also recognized the inordinate strength of his attachment to the comforts and pleasures of life. Even shortly before he died, he commented that "I am of nature so shrinking from pain that I am almost afraid of a fillip."[8] Furthermore, his sharp-sighted realism gave rise to a Chaucerian earthiness that frequently shocked, then as now. But the fault that worried him the most was pride.[9]

In confronting these weaknesses, More did not try to excuse his faults by calling them virtues. This clarity of judgment led him to decide early in life to train himself with great diligence and care. Otherwise, he realized, he would stand to lose the battles that mattered most. At an early age, he sought out extra training, and he persisted in that training throughout his life—right there in the heart of London. What he did and how he courageously conquered, that is the focus of our story.

A note on quotations: To make More's sixteenth-century English easier to read, I have often edited sentences to conform somewhat better to contemporary usage. In all cases, however, references are given so that the original can be consulted.

Chapter One

Family Foundations in the Heart of London

> *Children should have honorable people for parents, since in this way, to speak metaphorically, a seedbed of good nature and virtue is secretly fostered in these children [from the time] they are born.*[1]

GREAT PERSONS often have at least one great parent, grandparent, or childhood guardian. Thomas More considered his father a great man. Of his mother, Agnes Granger, he recorded no memories, since she died when he was still a child.[2] But he deeply loved his father.

Thomas described his father as an "affable man, charming, irreproachable, gentle, sympathetic, honest, and upright."[3] He gave far greater praise, however, by imitation. "Young More," as he was commonly known in the city, had, like his father, a good sense of humor, a strong work ethic, and keen judgment. Without possessing the known virtues of his father, young More could not have achieved such rapid success in law and politics. As one early biographer noted, "It is difficult to say whether the son was more worthy of such a father or the father of such a son."[4]

Not much is known about John More, as is often the case with those concerned with duty, not glory. What we do know, however, shows that his was not an easy life. As the oldest of six children, John felt the full force of his father's premature death. In the course of later life, he would also suffer the deaths of three wives. He witnessed the bloody Wars of the Roses, from beginning to end, and he saw England beset by major plagues and famines.

John was born in 1451, to William and Johanna More, both from "respectable though not distinguished" London families.[5] We know nothing about William's parents, but Johanna's were successful brewers who had grown quite prosperous. William's own hard work as a baker also brought a fair degree of prosperity, if the size of his business in London is any indication.[6] But in 1467, when John was only sixteen, William died, leaving Johanna, and John as eldest son, with the care of the five younger children and the family business. In those early years, John experienced firsthand the value of difficulties and sufferings in forging character and testing mettle—lessons he would soon pass on to his talented son.

An immediate consequence of his father's unexpected death was John's greater immersion in family and business concerns. Although we do not know the specific role he played in these matters, we do know that it was another eight years before he entered Lincoln's Inn, the best law school in England. John married Agnes Granger the year before that, in 1474, and their first child was born during his first year in law school. Two years later, near the end of John's time as a student, Thomas was born: on February 7, 1477.[7]

John's father-in-law was a lawyer actively involved in London politics. He served for a time as an alderman and eventually became the sheriff of London. These family connections probably helped John secure his first legal work, since much of it was connected with such civic projects as the maintenance of London Bridge and the construction of sewers, which were then badly needed to control the flow of the Thames River. But John's early financial stability was surely rooted in the family business. Thomas was, after all, born on Milk Street, one of the more fashionable sections of London.[8] In a few years, young Thomas would also attend London's finest grade school, St. Anthony's.

In this busy period of studying, working, and raising a family, John made important connections in high places, as evidenced by his friendships with King Edward IV and with Lord Chancellor and Archbishop John Morton. His friendship with

Morton was to have a far-reaching impact upon young Thomas. This family friend was destined to be the greatest influence of Thomas's adolescence.

At the age of twelve, Thomas began a two-year period of service as a page to Morton at Lambeth Palace. Here England's leading civil and ecclesiastical statesmen met and worked along with the most important foreign envoys. Here was a place where few aspiring politicians could ever hope to be, even at the height of their careers. Yet More was there at twelve, because his worldly-wise father knew the importance of properly challenging his unusually gifted son—and so did Morton. Chancellor Morton, old and battle-worn, delighted in young Thomas's "wit and towardness." He once said to the nobles that dined with him, "This child here waiting at the table, whosoever shall live to see it, will prove a marvelous man."[9]

One famous example of Thomas's "wit and towardness," one that old John must have repeated at many a family gathering, is reported by Thomas's son-in-law William Roper. At Christmastime, in Morton's palace theater, young Thomas would "suddenly sometimes step in among the players and, never studying for the matter, make a part of his own there presently among them, which made the lookers-on more sport than all the players beside."[10] Such spontaneous love for acting, wit, and good fun explains why young and old alike found him endearing.

Recognizing the boy's extraordinary talents, Morton was especially "careful to have him well trained up."[11] He even persuaded Thomas's reluctant father to send his son away from London to receive what John More considered a questionable education at Oxford.

Thomas's greatest educational debt to Morton, however, surely arose from within the halls of Lambeth Palace. To be able to see on a daily basis the leading men and women of the realm, as they conducted business and enjoyed their leisure, would alone have added a wealth of experience to a youth of More's intelligence and sensitivity. But his years with Morton were not simply years of observation. The fundamental purpose of serving as a page in such a household was to learn how to conduct oneself and, more specifically, to develop the virtues and abilities that would be needed for assuming leadership responsibilities. In addition, this arrangement began a friendship and an undisclosed number of conversations that were destined to continue for ten years, until Morton's death in 1500.

Morton received the greatest tribute More ever bestowed upon any of his teachers. In his two most celebrated works, he made it clear that Morton had left a profound impression. In his *History of King Richard III* he described how Morton "had gotten by great experience (the very mother and mistress of wisdom) a deep insight into politic, worldly drifts."[12] He credited this shrewd and learned doctor of laws with having brought "infinite benefit to the realm" by craftily arranging an end to the Wars of the Roses. Morton was "a man of great natural wit, very well learned, and honorable in behavior, lacking no wise ways to win favor."[13] Significantly, these same qualities would later be attributed to More himself.

Morton also received high praise in *Utopia*, from the highly critical Hythlodaeus. Here again, the qualities of the teacher, at least most of them, would later be attributed to the student:

> He was a man . . . who deserved respect as much for his prudence and virtue as for his authority. . . . His speech was polished and pointed. His knowledge of law was profound, his ability incomparable, and his memory astonishingly retentive, for he had improved his extraordinary natural qualities by learning and practice.
>
> The king placed the greatest confidence in his advice, and the commonwealth seemed much to depend upon him when I was there. As one might expect, almost in earliest youth he had been taken straight from school to court, had spent his whole life in important public affairs, and had sustained numerous and varied vicissitudes of fortune, so that by many and great dangers he had acquired a statesman's sagacity which, when thus learned, is not easily forgotten.[14]

One great difference between teacher and student was that More stayed away from the royal court for a long time. Unlike his teacher, More waited almost fifteen years after the end of his formal education before allowing himself to be persuaded to enter the royal service. These years were his most productive in terms of literary output; they were also the years of reflection and study that formed the foundation of his later career. In conjunction with his study and practice of law, More joined with some of the best minds in Europe to pursue the humanities, especially history and philosophy, together with biblical and patristic studies.

But here we have gotten ahead of our story.

From roughly 1491 to 1493, More attended Oxford, a federation of colleges that were mostly for boys interested in the priesthood. John was probably reluctant to send his fourteen-year-old son there, away from their home in London, but he prudently ensured frequent contact, as well as good behavior, by giving him very little money. As a result, even to get his shoes repaired, Thomas had to ask his father for the money he needed.[15] Although he would not use this exact method with his own children, he would praise his father's astuteness in having kept an inexperienced teenager on a tight budget to dispel distraction and discourage vice.[16]

After two years, however, John insisted that his son attend the New Inn of London. This school provided the preparatory education needed for both law school and the social life expected of those who would be the leaders of English society.

Besides providing a broader education than the Oxford of that time, the New Inn probably allowed John to supervise his son's overall development more closely. As history was to prove, John knew his son's talents and temperament quite well, and his close attention to Thomas's early development greatly helped those talents to flower.

Thomas was sixteen at this time. Twenty-five years later, he would write a poem attesting to his father's parental wisdom. In this poem, he reflects upon his first experience of adolescent love, for a fourteen-year-old girl named Elizabeth. "I was helpless," he says, "as though stunned by a lightning stroke, when I gazed and continued to gaze upon your face. Then, too, my comrades and yours laughed at our love—so awkward, so frank, and so obvious. Thus did your beauty take me captive."[17] Overcome by "the stirrings of adolescence and the ardor which accompanies the approach of manhood," More experienced emotions he found to be irrepressibly strong. In his lighthearted comments on their parents' reaction to this infatuation, one detects gratitude for their wisdom. "On this account," he writes, "a chaperon was imposed upon us, and a door strong enough to thwart our very destiny kept apart a pair whom the stars wished to bring together."

Along with that "door," one can also imagine the frank, manly, down-to-earth conversations that the worldly-wise John had with his adolescent son. That this worldly wisdom was successfully passed on from father to son was soon to become evident.

Chapter Two

Vocational Trials in Revolutionary Times

YOUNG MORE WAS RAISED in exciting and revolutionary times. The Renaissance was just beginning in England, and he would play a major role in its development. As a young university student, he heard about the discovery of the New World; later, his own brother-in-law would set out to explore that wilderness of promise and adventure. Printing had only recently been invented, and Sir Thomas More would be one of the most celebrated Englishmen of his day to use that new medium. When the Protestant revolt suddenly erupted, both king and clergy turned to him for help. All these developments would have a dramatic effect on the culture and the politics of his day, and More was closely involved in every one of them.

As a young man, however, he faced a personal conflict that proved as difficult and rending as any he would later have to face. In fact, it may have been the most wrenching of all. Although the later conflicts were to shake the very foundations of English culture, More was able to maintain his serenity throughout. In contrast, this early conflict shook him to the depths of his soul, at a time before that uncommon serenity was secured. The challenge he faced was a simple choice, but one that would affect his entire life: was he to marry and live amid the dangers of the city, or was he to become a priest and withdraw from them?

Since marriage was a mere concession to weakness, it was certainly not a path to perfection—or so held the cultural prejudice of More's age. Therefore, when this young, brilliant, idealistic youth struggled to accept what eventually emerged as a clear call to marriage, he was brought almost to the "very gates of hell."[1] Nonetheless, his humility and legendary integrity led him to become "a chaste husband rather than a licentious priest."[2]

Many of lesser character did not have the strength to resist the power of this prevailing orthodoxy about marriage and the priesthood. Lacking self-knowledge and experience, many of the young were lured by romantic images of the grandeur and glory associated with priestly and religious life. As More would later point out, Church leaders often neglected their responsibility to test adequately those who thought they had a vocation to the clerical state. Therefore, many entered without the necessary vocation or virtues. More considered this a grave problem. Indeed, he judged that half of the Church's problems in those days could be traced to the fact that there were too many priests. "If the bishops," he said, "would only take into the priesthood better and fewer laymen, all the matter would be more than half amended."[3]

Chaucer and Shakespeare agreed. If all good people were encouraged to enter the monastery, how should the world be served? So Chaucer had asked several generations before More's birth.[4] Several generations after More's death, Shakespeare dramatized the same problem in *Measure for Measure*. In that play, Duke Vincentio is the reluctant ruler of a city that has suffered the ravages of war, famine, civil strife, and plague. He needs to rebuild his city, but good people are reluctant to serve something so worldly. Earlier, the Duke himself had withdrawn from the affairs of Vienna in order to pursue a life of study and contemplation, but he came to realize that this choice only led to the city's further degeneration. Once he realized his grave error, he began looking for others who might help repair the damage. Much to his dismay, however, his most virtuous and gifted subject—the one he wishes to marry—has just withdrawn from the world to join the strictest convent. As a result, much of the play revolves upon the Duke's plan to persuade this young lady, Isabella, to help him rule his land and strengthen the institution of marriage within it.

In choosing a path in life, neither Duke Vincentio nor young More had attractive or compelling models of people who consciously set out to achieve Christian perfection in and through marriage and worldly responsibilities. They did, however, have many outstanding models of priests who achieved sanctity by renouncing that world and its human attractions.

At that time the prevalent view of marriage and secular life was well represented by More's friend and early spiritual advisor John Colet. Indeed, Fr. Colet's opinion of marriage must have been a major stumbling block for More. Colet considered marriage to be permitted merely "as a remedy for passion" and "for the avoidance of evil." He also said of marriage that "he who cannot be in the first rank is mercifully allowed to stand in the second, and to have one wife if he cannot do without any."[5] If such a learned and cultured leader could hold this negative and condescending view of marriage, then one can certainly understand why the humanism of the Renaissance became such a powerful force in the centuries to follow.

Although Colet, like More, loved the company of women and greatly enjoyed joking and engaging in witty conversation, he considered these inclinations to be temptations that must be fought. For this reason, "he usually abstained from the society of the laity, and particularly from dinner parties."[6]

Colet held these views until the end of his life—alongside others which were incompatible with them. After years of experience and education, notes his early biographer, Fr. Colet actually came to the conclusion that married couples with many children were the "class of people in whom he had found the least corruption." Therefore, when he founded St. Paul's School, he took the unprecedented step of entrusting it not to "priests or the bishop or the chapter, as they call it, nor eminent laymen," but to "a certain number of married citizens of approved reputation."[7] Nevertheless, the prevalent negative attitude toward marriage was too deeply ingrained in him for it ever to be completely eradicated.

More himself never shook completely this prejudice against marriage and involvement in the world. His own home was compared in some ways to a monastery, and at the end of his professional life, he longed for monastic solitude. He also believed that the laity could not achieve the level of spiritual perfection that priests and religious could, though he did recognize the value of marriage and work in the development of human and supernatural virtues.[8]

He did, however, have the indispensable example of his own father, a man known to be "very virtuous, and of a very upright and sincere conscience."[9] John More was married four times in his seventy-nine years. He was highly respected for his personal character and professional integrity, and he was well loved for his affability and good humor. Especially known for his prudence "in giving counsel and judgment," John passed on this wide-ranging experience to his son.[10] He also passed on the stability of character that often comes from growing up in a strong home, and the clear self-knowledge achieved in such a home. Without his father's help and example, young Thomas might not have been strong enough to shoulder the responsibilities that he would face in the course of his life.

John More attended closely to his son's personal and professional development. As John saw it (and history proved him right), young Thomas was a born lawyer. Indeed, had it not been for the vigilant guidance of his father, Thomas would never have become a lawyer. Left to his own preferences, he would have restricted his studies to those he found most interesting: the liberal arts and theology. His father, however, insisted that he combine those liberal studies with the practical skill of common law—a body of experience in which he saw expressed the deepest aspirations of England.

Thomas studied law for roughly five years before being called to the bar. During these years, he also deepened his study of literature, history, philosophy, and theology. He wrote poetry, comedies, and even a response to Plato's notion of a community of wives. After law school he began a serious study of Greek and soon set up translation competitions with William Lily and the great Erasmus, two of the best translators of the day.

In addition to language and literature, More immersed himself in the fundamental questions of political philosophy. So advanced were his studies in this area that William Grocyn, one of England's leading scholars, invited him to give a series of public lectures on Augustine's difficult, thousand-page book,

The City of God. These lectures attracted "all the chief learned of the city of London,"[11] even though More was only twenty-three at the time. The focus he gave these lectures indicates the depth of his reflection upon the way of life he eventually chose. He approached *The City of God*, "not from the theological point of view, but from the standpoint of history and philosophy."[12] This same preoccupation with the deepest questions of politics and law is also seen in his early poetry and literature.

In comparison with these all-absorbing subjects of history, philosophy, and literature, More did not find the study of law itself all that interesting. He must have wondered whether law could possibly be the whole of his life's work. After all, he showed extraordinary promise in the humanities, which he loved, and he was receiving encouragement from some of the best intellectuals in England and throughout Europe. Pace, Colet, and Grocyn all recognized his genius and encouraged his development. Later, Erasmus would complain that More had been "lost" to the intellectual life when he decided finally to immerse himself in civic affairs.[13] Yet More would hardly be lost. Like Cicero, whom he knew and admired, he was to use civic involvement as a way of deepening his reflections on the most important issues of life.

Young More was also well aware of the impact that revolutionary ideas in philosophy, theology, and literature were having on the cultural makeup of Europe. The Renaissance was just beginning to enter England, with all the promises and threats which genuinely radical ideas always present to the highest levels of culture. These ideas would, before More's death, change in unforeseen ways the very character of England and all Christendom.

More's hesitation to throw himself into law caused great tensions between father and son. Erasmus tells us that More's decision to "devote himself to Greek literature and philosophy [received] so little support from his father, a man in other respects of good sense and high character, that his efforts were deprived of all outside help and he was treated almost as if disinherited, because he was thought to be deserting his father's profession."[14]

Part of this being "deprived of all outside help" apparently meant that More had to leave home. Finding the positive side of adversity, he went to reside near the London Charterhouse, a Carthusian monastery, where he participated in the monks' life of prayer and learned their ways of austere living. For roughly four years, More learned from some of the best spiritual masters of Christendom. Many of these Carthusians later joined him in suffering death (some of them first suffering torture) rather than reject their Christian faith.

During these years, More worked at developing his prayer life and achieving self-mastery, struggling especially to discern his vocation and to prepare himself for whatever that was. In these four long years, he discovered the need for grace, and not for his own talent and effort alone. As a result, he began the spiritual practices he would maintain for the rest of his life. Until the time of his imprisonment, he started each day with private prayer, study, and Mass. Recognizing the importance of personal effort, he also began the practice of extensive mortification. During this period, for example, he began wearing his famous hair shirt, a penitential practice he continued until his death. He also limited the number of hours he slept, fasted regularly, and strove to teach his quick tongue to seek charity rather than victory. Such age-old methods of self-mastery and "prayer of the senses" did not become outmoded during the Renaissance; if anything, the rediscovery of Roman valor, toughness, and virtue acted as yet a greater spur to their use.

After these years of soul-searching struggle, More thanked his spiritual advisor John Colet for having helped him escape "almost from the very gates of hell."[15] Yet even after realizing that marriage was his vocation, he still felt himself occasionally "falling back again into gruesome darkness."[16] This rather dramatic description of his anguish may have been somewhat exaggerated, but it does express well More's youthful anxiety in facing an unknown future and the unknown forces within himself. It was such wrenching experiences that he drew upon when he wrote the profound spiritual handbooks of his youth and old age.

By 1503, rapport was once again established between father and son. More's position as a teacher of law at Furnivall's Inn and his election to Parliament showed a real commitment, to the legal profession and to the city, that John More could approve. Around this time, Thomas wrote his "Merry Jest," probably as a way of honoring his father and making up for the tensions that had existed between them during the previous years.

This witty narrative, about a bumbling sergeant who uses rather unorthodox methods in collecting debts, is made up of 430 lines of dimeter and trimeter verse—an undertaking ambitious enough to suggest that it was motivated by some special occasion. This occasion was probably the feast that took place November 3, 1503, at the Lambeth Palace, where More had served as John Morton's page over ten years before. At this feast, his father was honored, along with the other new sergeants-at-law. Also honored was his maternal grandfather, Thomas Granger, the newly elected sheriff of London. This dual celebration before all the notables of London, including his future father-in-law, would certainly have provided sufficient motive for the composition of this entertaining piece.

More begins his "Merry Jest" by praising those who are wise enough to stick to their own business:

> Wise men always
> Affirm and say
> That best is it for a man
> Diligently
> To apply
> The business that he can,
> And in no wise
> To enterprise
> Another faculty,
> For he that will
> And has no skill
> Is never likely to thrive.[17]

This simple lesson, More goes on to say, has been verified "here by a sergeant late, / That thriftily was / . . . Rapped about the pate."

The sergeant in question was not one of the distinguished judges of the highest courts of the land whom More was addressing. The sergeant of this poem is a petty officer charged with arresting a crafty character who has ingeniously evaded his creditors. Supposedly sick in bed, this clever fellow will admit no one into his house. As a result, our peerless sergeant decides to enter dressed up as a friar. After lying his way past the lady of the house, the sergeant takes the sick man's hand and speaks gently—until they are all alone. Then out comes the mace, and the fight begins.

> They rent and tear
> Each other's hair
> And cleave together fast,
> Till with lugging
> And with tugging,
> They fall down both at last.
> Then on the ground,
> Together round,
> With many a sad stroke
> They roll and rumble,
> They turn and tumble,
> As pigs do in a poke.

Unfortunately for the sergeant, reinforcements for the thief arrive, and the impostor friar gets the soundest beating of his life. The poem then concludes with the same lesson that was given in the beginning:

> In any wise
> I would advise
> And counsel every man,
> His own craft use,
> All new refuse.

Taking his own advice, young Thomas became heavily involved in his own craft. By 1504 he had decided that his fields of expertise would be law and politics, and he soon became heavily involved in both. That same year, at the age of twenty-seven, he served in Parliament as a burgess, representing the London merchants his family knew so well. And in 1505 he married Jane Colt. His vocational and professional choices were finally made; but the great adventure of seeing them through still lay ahead.

Chapter Three

More's First Handbook on Spiritual Combat

DURING THE TRIALS OF HIS YOUTH, More did what every talented author does. He wrote. In fact, at every stage of his career he wrote, both to clarify his own thoughts and to help others in struggles he saw as universal and perennial.[1]

These early years of study, reflection, and struggle yielded the material for his first book on the spiritual life. He would write other books of this kind, at different stages of his life, but this first one contains the fundamental themes that he developed in all the others.

The Life of John Picus has been rather neglected, in comparison with More's other writings, partly because of the unusual character of the book and partly because of the difficult questions it raises.[2] Why, for example, did More choose the biography and writings of this particular man as the basis for his first spiritual handbook?[3]

The standard answer is that Pico was an outstanding layman and intellectual whom More saw as a model for his own life.[4] As we have seen, More had no role model for lay sanctity as such; that much is true. But to mistake Pico for such a model is to overlook the subtleties of More's work.

At first glance, Pico would seem a likely candidate for any Christian humanist to imitate. A man of immense learning, he was a descendant of that great civic leader Charlemagne, and a person of piety well known for his penitential practices, good works, and prayers. Not only did Pico share in the Renaissance predilection for the pagan classics, but from early manhood onward he also "gave himself day and night most fervently to the study of Scripture."[5] He prayed at set hours each day. He "gave alms of his own body" in the form of austere mortifications. He despised worldly possessions and glory; what he had, he distributed freely, even lavishly, to the poor. He loved to meditate on the Passion of Christ. He devoted his life to studies pertaining to the defense of the Church, and he was even said to have received a visit from the Blessed Virgin Mary.[6]

What a surprise it is, therefore, that after presenting these many spectacular accomplishments, *The Life of John Picus* concludes with the rather shocking revelation that, upon his death, Pico does not go to heaven.

Such an unusual ending forces the reader to reflect more deeply on this famous humanist of reputed holiness. The ending is typical of Thomas More, whose quick and subtle wit found ingenious ways to pose issues, moving others to stop and wonder.

Another puzzle involved in More's selection of Pico is the marked difference in their situations. By the time More published this book, he had four children and a large law practice; he had also served twice in Parliament. Pico, in stark contrast, had been a scholarly recluse, shunning both civic involvement and marriage as obstacles to true liberty of soul.[7] A second major difference had to do with the nature of their vocations. Pico, at the end of More's book, is burning in purgatory largely because he had a clear vocation to be a friar but never accepted the call. More, on the other hand, recognized his vocation to be a layman "tossed in the flood and rumbling of worldly business."[8]

Why, then, did More choose to write about a layman who should have been a monk? How could such a person serve as a fitting model? To answer this question requires considerable reflection, not only on the biographical section of the book, but also on the many materials which More appends to it. A first-time reader should be cautioned that the value of this book, its title notwithstanding, does not lie primarily in the account of Pico's life. That biographical section establishes the context for a highly selective collection of Pico's spiritual writings, excerpts which More goes on to comment upon, amend, and expand.

Yet the biographical element is important. What is true of good tragedy can also be true of good biography: one can learn much from witnessing a great person's failings. In fact, it was precisely Pico's awareness of his need to struggle, together with his prudent advice about what was required to win in such battles, that More found to be of greatest value in Pico's life and writings.

The story's surprise ending invites the reader to ask where Pico went wrong. After reviewing the story, one discovers three failings which explain why the book ends with him crying from the fires of purgatory: he was negligent in his duties, he was ungrateful for the many gifts he had received, and he was slow in fulfilling God's will.[9] More must have reflected a great deal on these failings, for he was never accused of them himself. (Except, that is, when King Henry VIII later accused him of ingratitude and treachery for not having repaid his many gifts with compliance to his will.)

One striking example of these failings was the way Pico performed his duties as head of his household and as earl of Mirandola. Out of contempt for "base, abject, and vile earthly trifles," Pico refused to give personal attention to his household accounts or to household business, thus providing "his servants occasions for deceit and robbery."[10] At the age of twenty-nine he also set aside "all the charge and business of rule" by virtually giving away "all his patrimonies and dominions" to a nephew. In contrast, More took unusual care in managing his household, promptly and genially putting right whatever went wrong,[11] paying close attention to everyone and everything related to his home.[12]

Another example of Pico's failings was the way he responded to his vocation to be a monk. Although he saw this calling clearly, he "deferred it for a time," little imagining that he was to die at thirty-one. What caused this early death is not revealed; all we are told is that Pico "was suddenly taken by a burning fever which crept so far into the inner parts of his body" that no medicines could help. (According to other accounts, however, Pico was poisoned by servants who were eager for his money.[13])

What, then, is the lesson of this unusual story? In the introduction, More makes it clear that his purpose is to stir the reader to an "increase of virtue." But how, one might well ask, can such a story accomplish this end?

For many, the story might lead to discouragement about the very possibility of achieving virtue. After all, if a person as learned and pious as Pico fell short of the mark, what is the prospect for the rest of us? As this biography reveals, Pico did take extraordinary steps to counter his vices, as soon as he became aware of them. If his generous prayer and penance were not enough to send him straight to heaven, what would have been?

Just this type of question leads the attentive reader to turn with keen interest from the biographical section of this book to the later sections dealing with the basics of spiritual combat. Because the opening story has shown the extreme difficulty of waging such combat successfully, the reader is well motivated to pay close attention to what follows.

As paradoxical as it may sound, the essence of the spiritual life as presented in this first handbook is to fight to love—that is, to fight vigorously to love God with ever greater tenderness and ardor. As long as this effort is foremost in one's life, success in the battles against temptation is assured. Since God is not only all-powerful but also "a very tender, loving father,"[14] he will not refuse whatever his children sincerely ask of him. Nor will he ever allow his faithful children to be tempted beyond their powers.

Yet such trust, such a "heavenward mind," is achieved only through active cooperation with grace, a cooperation that requires the greatest personal effort[15]—though not an effort to achieve proud success in worldly competition or in stoic self-mastery.

All of the prayers, letters, and poems appended to *The Life of John Picus* were chosen to "stir thee to prayer," a prayer consisting not in many words, but in personal and deeply affectionate conversation with God. Such a "prayer of contemplation not only presents the mind to the Father, but also unites it with Him by unspeakable ways which only they know who have tried it."[16] In this handbook, More exhorts us to develop this type of prayer.

> I care not how long or how short your prayer is,
> but how effectual, how ardent, how interrupted
> and broken with sighs rather than drawn out at
> length with an endless number of words. If you

> love your health; if you desire to be secure from
> the snares of the devil, from the storms of this
> world, from the hands of your enemies; if you
> long to be acceptable to God; if you covet everlast-
> ing happiness—then let no day pass without at
> least once presenting yourself to God in prayer,
> falling down before Him flat on the ground with a
> humble affection and a devout mind; not merely
> with your lips, but from the innermost recesses of
> your heart, crying out these words of the prophet:
> "The sins of my youth and my frailties remember
> not, but in Your mercy remember me because of
> Your goodness, O Lord" [Ps 25:7].[17]

This kind of prayer is a humble and confident appeal to a good
and merciful God who is "a very tender, loving father" to his
faithful children.

Such confident prayer is a result of love. One of the most
original features of this handbook is the section entitled "The
Twelve Properties of a Lover."[18] This long poem is a thirteen-
part love ballad. Each part has two sections. The first describes a
quality of ardent youthful love, and the second applies that
quality to the love of God.

The ardent lover, for example, not only bears willingly some
trial or pain for the sake of the beloved, but actually longs to do
so. In fact, he "thinks himself happy that he may take / Some
misadventure for his lover's sake."[19] After vividly describing
this quality of human love, More then offers a parallel on the
supernatural plane:

> Thus should you who love God also
> In your heart wish, covet, and be glad
> To suffer for Him trouble, pain, and woe.

Another quality of lovers is their desire to be with each
other constantly: "The perfect lover longs to be / In the presence
of his love both night and day." When this is not physically possible, the two nonetheless remain together "in mind and
thought." In the same way, lovers of God should also "be present with God and conversant always."

Throughout this poem, More shows that the spiritual life consists in treating God as the spouse of one's soul. Anyone who loves God should cultivate the same affections toward this beloved as the greatest human lovers have cultivated toward each other:

> Here should the lover of God example take,
> To have Him continually in remembrance
> With him in prayer and meditation wake
> While others play, revel, sing, and dance.
> No earthly joy, sport, or vain pleasance
> Should him delight, or anything remove
> His ardent mind from God, his heavenly Love.

All genuine love takes attentive and painstaking cultivation, and the love of God is no exception. Therefore, the whole secret of the spiritual life is summarized in those words of the psalmist, "I set the Lord ever before my sight; with him at my right hand I shall not be disturbed" (Ps 16:8).[20] As Pico expresses it, "If a person had God always before his eyes as ruler of all his works . . . , he would soon be perfect."[21]

Here "perfect" refers to the union of our will with God's will. To achieve this unity, a person "should abstain not only from unlawful pleasures but also from lawful, so that he might have his mind wholly heavenward . . . unto the contemplation of heavenly things."[22] In this one brief sentence lies the rationale for the life of mortification that More practiced from the age of eighteen or twenty.[23] His hair shirt and his fasting served as prayers of the senses, physical reminders he employed to stay united to God.

Setting the Lord ever before one's sight is a difficult enterprise, especially when many things demand attention. For this reason, More says, active mortifications and set times of prayer are needed to keep the "heart afire" with the love of God.[24] Indeed, keeping the fire ablaze takes the greatest perseverance. To help in this enterprise, More offers two additional poems, "The Twelve Rules of Spiritual Battle" and "The Twelve Weapons of Spiritual Battle." These poems are meant to "partly excite" and "partly direct" a person's efforts in the battle to stay "in the presence of his Love both night and day," regardless of what else is happening.

More uses battle imagery to emphasize what is obvious to any experienced lover: in this world as it is, one must be courageous enough and virtuous enough to defend what one loves.

The first three rules of spiritual battle are reminders that all ways of life—whether of virtue or of vice—involve pain. Even the most vicious persons, intent on getting all the material goods they can, must be prepared to battle long and hard and to bear much sacrifice. But how foolish it is to endure so much pain in this world, only to suffer even greater pain in the next. Besides, why should we "look for heaven with pleasure and delight," when "Christ our Lord and sovereign captain / Ascended never but by manly fight and bitter passion"?

After arguing in these first three rules that we *must* fight, whether for virtue or for vice, More shows us in the next six sections of the poem *how* the virtuous should fight. First, they should be joyful, since they imitate the most generous and valiant of captains. After all, Christ is the most courageous soldier who ever fought in the spiritual combat, so anyone who follows him should "be glad and joyful of this fight."[25] They should also trust only in his power, not in their own, and they should be vigilant always. Finally, even when a battle is won, the virtuous should know the importance of keeping themselves in shape, ready to fight again at any time.

In the next two rules, More gives several other important points of advice: good soldiers never think themselves invincible in the face of temptation; they always resist temptation from the first moment; they think of the joy of victory, not the passing pleasures missed in achieving that victory; and, aware that a clear conscience is the greatest of earthly joys, they gladly put up whatever "manly defense" conscience may require.[26]

Finally, the last rule cautions that the good soldier should not lose heart on account of being tempted, since everyone is. All should be concerned about their own pride, however, since it is the "root of all mischief" and the greatest peril any good soldier faces. Temptations can actually be of great help in fighting pride. The great St. Paul was tempted, even after his vision of

God; indeed, God wisely allowed these temptations, precisely "to preserve His servant from the danger of pride."[27]

The most effective way of countering temptation is to "consider how Christ, the Lord of sovereign power, / Humbled Himself for us unto the cross." Such a vivid recollection of God is, as we have seen, the single most important element of the spiritual life. Recalling "Christ's ineffable Passion" is "a strong defense against all adversity."[28] The victorious combatant is admonished never to forget "that the Son of God died for you, and that you yourself will also die."[29] Frequent contemplation on Christ's Passion will act as an impetus to a love that will "spur forth your horse through the short way of this momentary life to the reward of eternal happiness."[30] More would repeat this same idea many times later in his life, and he followed this practice until the moment of his death.

The next set of poems, "The Twelve Weapons of Spiritual Battle," makes the same basic points as "The Twelve Rules." But now these points are expressed in short, memorable phrases that can be ready "at hand when the pleasure of a sinful temptation comes to mind."[31] Even their titles—"Eternal Peace, Eternal Pain," "The Painful Cross of Christ," and "The Witness of Martyrs and Examples of Saints," for example—reduce large issues to simple ideas that can be readily recalled, even at times of great stress.

After each of these aphoristic counsels comes an explanatory seven-line poem. The first ones, again, put earthly pleasures in perspective. Since even the greatest of earthly pleasures is "little, simple, short, and suddenly past," why should one act like a mad merchant and sell one's soul for "foolish merchandise"? This life passes so quickly that it is like "a dream or a shadow on the wall"—a mere moment, to be followed by an eternity of joy or an eternity of pain. Why, asks More, would any sane person buy a momentary pleasure for an eternity of pain? Furthermore, if we would compare all the pleasures of this world, we would discover that the greatest by far is a clear conscience, that "inward gladness of a virtuous mind."

Central to his argument is that "God has made thee . . . unto His image and figure, / And for thee suffered pains intolerable."

Remembering who we are and what Christ has suffered for each one of us, "How mayst thou then to Him unloving be / That ever hath been so loving unto thee?" To drive home this fundamental truth, More continues with rhetorical flourish:

> When thou in the flame of temptation friest,
> Think on the very lamentable pain,
> Think on the piteous cross of woeful Christ,
> Think on His blood beat out at every vein,
> Think on His precious heart carved in twain,
> Think how for thy redemption all was wrought—
> Let Him not lose thee, whom He so dear has bought.

More concludes by pointing out that "God will thee help if thou do not refuse," insisting that victory always depends on genuine trust in God.

The final section of this spiritual handbook is a lengthy prayer that dwells upon the goodness and generosity of God—a God who, besides being an all-powerful Creator, is also the most tender and loving of fathers. This poem is filled with a sense of awe and gratitude, a sense of wonder at how a God of such dreadful majesty could treat sinful humanity with such mercy and goodness.

In short, More's first spiritual handbook shows the importance of keeping God ever before one's eyes, and it passes on practical advice to the lover who wants to remain "in the presence of his Love both night and day." Maintaining this ardent love was, as we will see later, the ultimate foundation of More's legendary courage.

Chapter Four

Husband and Father: New Joys, New Sorrows

*Only a person of intelligence and foresight,
whose guide is reason, can enter upon true love.*[1]

IN HIS EARLY POEM "How to Choose a Wife," More emphasizes the singular importance of virtue in choosing a spouse for life. "True love," he says, "is inspired, with happy promise, by respect for a woman's glorious virtue—a noble gift which endures, does not fail in sickness, does not perish with the years."[2]

More then gives a number of practical suggestions. First and foremost, the man should "observe what kind of parents the lady has," since much of virtue is acquired through imitation. "See to it that her mother is revered for the excellence of her character, which is sucked in and expressed by her tender and impressionable little girl."[3]

Other important traits are also given. "Next, see to this: what sort of personality she has; how agreeable she is. Let her maidenly countenance be calm and without severity. But let her modesty bring blushes to her cheeks; let her glance not be provocative. Let her be mild-mannered, not throwing her slender arms wantonly around men's necks. Let her glances be restrained; let her have no roving eye. Let her pretty lips always be free of pointless garrulity and also of boorish taciturnity."[4]

Unlike most men of his day, More considered the ideal wife to be a "lifetime companion" who could support her husband with "pleasant and intelligent conversation" while helping him raise their children according to "right principles" which she

27

herself had been striving to practice.[5] This presupposed an education that provided both the learning and the practiced virtue whereby "she would not yield to pride in prosperity, nor grief in distress—even though misfortune strike her down."[6] Such a virtuous disposition More considered the richest dowry and the greatest beauty that a bride could bring to her husband.

Following his own advice, More chose his wife from a family noted for good character. As his son-in-law Will Roper tells us, More "resorted to the house of one Master Colt, a gentleman of Essex who had often invited him there, having three daughters, whose honest conversation and virtuous education provoked him there specially to set his affection."[7] (These three were the daughters of marriageable age, but there were actually eighteen children in all, eleven of whom were girls.) Out of consideration for the good of the family as a whole, More made an unusual sacrifice. Roper is the source for this family secret: "Although his mind most served him to the second daughter, for he thought her the fairest and best favored, yet when he considered that it would be both great grief and some shame also to the eldest to see her younger sister in marriage preferred before her, he then of a certain pity framed his fancy towards her, and soon married her."[8]

More did not follow his own advice in one important respect, and he suffered considerably as a consequence. "Let her," he had said, "be either just finishing her education or ready to begin it immediately."[9] Jane Colt, however, had little education and was used to the many leisurely amusements of a country home. As a result, this seventeen-year-old girl had none of the intellectual habits of her twenty-seven-year-old husband, who was already an accomplished scholar, lawyer, and writer.

More undoubtedly thought that Jane's "lack of sophistication recommended her, because he would fashion her to his tastes the more readily." He thereupon "undertook to teach her literature and music and gradually to accustom her to repeating what she had heard in a sermon, and by other devices to train her in what would be of later use."[10] Young Jane, however, strongly opposed her husband's plans to "mold her character to match his own."[11] As a consequence, More learned one of his first great lessons about the reality and force of human freedom.

His friend Erasmus wrote a fictionalized account of what happened. According to him, since serious study "was all new to the girl, who had spent her time in her own home in complete idleness and been brought up amidst the chatter and pranks of servants, she began to grow bored. She became balky, and when her husband became insistent she would cry and cry, sometimes throwing herself down and dashing her head against the floor as though she wished she were dead. Because there was no end to this, her husband, hiding his vexation, invited his wife to accompany him on a visit to the country, to his father-in-law's house, for a holiday. She accepted eagerly. When they arrived there the husband left his wife with her mother and sisters; he himself went hunting with his father-in-law. Then, when they were out of hearing, he told his father-in-law he had hoped for an amiable partner but now had one who was forever weeping and tormenting herself and could not be corrected by any reproofs. He begged for help in curing the daughter's fault."[12]

Thinking deeply (as usual) to arrive at a real solution to this problem, More wisely went to someone who knew his wife well, and asked for advice and help. The father-in-law, not wishing to get personally involved, told More just to use physical force. More, however, did not want to use coercion. Instead, he persuaded his father-in-law to exert the thought and effort needed to help him find the real solution to this pressing marital problem.

Erasmus gives his own detailed account of the story: "The father-in-law replies that he gave him his daughter once for all; that if she refused to obey his commands, he should exercise his rights and correct her by blows. 'I know my rights,' says the son-in-law, 'but rather than resort to this desperate remedy I'd prefer to have her cured by your skill or authority.' The father-in-law promises to attend to the matter. A day or so later he seizes an opportunity to be alone with his daughter. Then, putting on a stern look, he begins to recall how homely she was, how ill-mannered, how often he had feared he would be unable to find her a husband. 'But,' he said, 'with the greatest difficulty I found you a husband such as any girl, however favored, would long for. And yet, not recognizing what I've done for you, or realizing that you have such a husband—who would scarcely think you

fit for one of his maidservants if he weren't the kindest of men—
you rebel against him.' To make a long story short, the father's
speech grew so heated that he seemed barely able to keep his
hands off her. (For he's a man of marvelous cunning, capable of
playing any comedy without a mask.) Moved partly by fear,
partly by the truth, the girl promptly went down on her knees
before her father, begging forgiveness for the past and swearing
she would be mindful of her duty in the future. He pardoned
her, promising to be a most affectionate father if she carried out
her promise."[13]

After this dramatic father-daughter scene, "the girl went to
her bedroom, met her husband privately, fell on her knees before
him, and said, 'Husband, up to this time I have known neither
you nor myself. Hereafter you shall see me a changed person;
only forget the past.' Her husband received this speech with a
kiss and promised her everything if she kept her word."[14]

Afterwards, "there was nothing, however lowly, that she did
not do promptly and willingly when her husband wished. So
strong was the love born and confirmed between them."[15] The
strong love that was "born and confirmed" between Thomas
and Jane stemmed in large part from their mutual commitment
to grow in virtue. And great virtue was needed in their busy
home. Within about five and a half years of marriage, they were
blessed with three daughters and a son. Despite the rapid
growth of his law practice, More immersed himself in studies
that would later become indispensable to him. Jane was not only
a happy and busy mother, but also the manager of a large home
in the heart of London—an enormous change from her leisurely
life in the country. With Thomas's encouragement, she also
became "skilled in music of every kind" and, contrary to custom, even learned Latin.[16]

Just when their life seemed happiest, however, death unexpectedly visited young Jane, in the sixth year of their marriage.
Apart from his deep grief, Thomas also had the pressing difficulty of caring for his four young children. What to do?

The solution he chose went against friends' advice and common custom. Within thirty days, he married the best woman
available. Given his wide circle of friends, More was acquainted

with many eligible women. He knew Alice Middleton well because he had worked with her late husband, who was a prosperous merchant. Nonetheless, so unusual was the quickness of this marriage that he had to get a dispensation of the banns. This he easily obtained, being a man whose life and ways were well known. His pastor, Fr. John Bouge, had already been serving as his confessor and spiritual advisor for some time. Years later, Fr. John wrote down a few of his remembrances of "Sir Thomas More . . . my parishioner at London." He tells us: "I christened two of his goodly children. I buried his first wife; and within a month after, he came to me on a Sunday at night, late, and there he brought me a dispensation to be married the next Monday without publishing any banns. . . . This Mr. More was my spiritual child; in his confession to be so pure, so clean, with great study, deliberation, and devotion, I never heard many such; a gentleman of great learning in law, art, and divinity, having no equal among laymen living today."[17]

In choosing his second wife, More once again did not follow all of the advice he had set forth about choosing the perfect wife. Realist that he was, he simply chose the best and most virtuous of existing possibilities. Alice Middleton differed greatly from him in age, temperament, and interests. He was thirty-four; she was forty. He loved music and playful jest; she did not. He was extraordinarily learned; her one accomplishment in this area was the ability to read. So unlike were they that Erasmus marveled at how well they came to love each other. This was his explanation for the close friendship that developed between them: "Few husbands secure as much obedience from their wives by severity and giving them orders as he did by his kindness and his merry humor. He could make her do anything: did he not cause a woman already past the prime of life, of a far from elastic disposition, and devoted to her household affairs, to learn to play the zither, the lute, the monochord, and the recorder, and in this department to produce a set piece of work every day to please her exacting husband?"[18]

More had realistic expectations about marriage, and about human nature. In a letter to a close friend, Francis Cranevelt, he wrote, "I do not think it possible to live, even with the best of wives, without some discomfort." He also admitted that "generally we make our wives worse by our own fault."[19]

Fortunately, we have a few examples of how More handled potential conflicts between Lady Alice and himself. One had to do with something as fundamental as their clashing ambitions and expectations. Lady Alice was quite intent upon improving the family's position in society, and she became cross with Thomas's hesitancy to rise and to assume greater authority. His sense of history reminded him that the highest often fall the quickest, and he knew well that greater authority brings with it issues and problems that are often far outside of one's control. As More colorfully wrote, it is impossible to please everyone, since "even in one house the husband would have fair weather for his corn and his wife would have rain for her leeks!"[20]

More records one of their lively exchanges over their disagreement about positions of authority. In a conversation that probably took place shortly after their marriage, Alice scolded More for his lack of ambition.

> "What will you do since you do not wish to put yourself forth as other folk do? Will you still sit by the fire and make designs in the ashes with a stick as children do? Would God I were a man— look what I would do!"
>
> "Why, wife, what would you do?"
>
> "What? By God, go forward with the best! Because, as my mother liked to say—God have mercy on her soul—it is always better to rule than to be ruled. And therefore, by God, I would never be so foolish as to be ruled when I might rule."
>
> "Here I must say that you have said the truth, because I never found you willing to be ruled yet!"[21]

Given their fundamental differences on this issue, More understood that his wife would not accept well his eventual resignation from the King's service. Indeed, she never accepted it at all. This factor must have been a significant one in those late-night hours which he spent thinking through all the consequences that would follow upon this resignation. As we will see, he took great care to prepare his family for what he knew would happen.

When he actually resigned, he used his good humor to soften the blow for his wife. Although this story is brief, it nonetheless shows More's great concern for his wife and his sensitivity to detail.

The family had the custom of going to church together on holy days. While he was Chancellor, More sat in one part of the church, and his wife in another. When services were over, one of his attendants would always go to Lady Alice's pew, bow as a sign of respect, and announce, "Madame, my Lord is gone." After he resigned, More went himself to Lady Alice's pew, made a low bow, and announced, "Madame, my Lord is gone."[22] Lady Alice at first thought he was joking—as usual. She therefore responded somewhat gruffly—as usual. "No doubt," she said, "it pleases you, Master More, to joke in this way." She was quite surprised when he replied, "I speak seriously, and it is as I say: my Lord Chancellor is gone and is no longer here." As Thomas Stapleton tells the rest of the story, "In great astonishment she rose at once, and when she had learned the whole truth of the matter, she was in great distress at her husband's loss of position." The family acknowledged, however, that "by this humorous way of making the announcement, More wished both to soften the blow for his wife and to show what little account he made of his high honor."[23]

Another clash between husband and wife had to do with general attitudes towards dress and other everyday affairs. More was known for his indifference to what he wore, and to what he ate, and for his extraordinary flexibility and serenity in the face of unexpected change.[24] In contrast, Lady Alice was highly meticulous about dress and domestic arrangements; she lacked her husband's flexibility and serenity; and she was known for her nagging persistence. More responded with his usual humor and equanimity, and, in fact, her manner became a joke between them. In time, Lady Alice was able to joke about it herself. One day, for example, after she returned from confession, she told her husband to be merry because she had just got rid of all her ill temper—and could now begin to harass him anew![25]

How More achieved such harmony in his home was basically a matter of attentiveness and consideration. First, he gave close attention to the overall running of the household—and, as we will see, especially to the ongoing education of all. His attention to household affairs was so vigilant and genial that he generally avoided major troubles and disputes. As Erasmus describes it, "If anything should go wrong, he puts it right promptly or makes them agree; nor has he ever dismissed anyone as a result of ill feeling on either side. In fact, his household seems to enjoy a kind of natural felicity, for no one has ever been a member of it without bettering his fortune later, and no one has ever earned the least shadow on his reputation. . . . His affection for his kinsmen, his children, and his sisters is such that his relations with them are never oppressive, nor yet does he ever fall short in his family duties."[26]

Placing such an emphasis on his family duties was a distinguishing characteristic of More as husband and father. Yet, as we will see, he also respected Lady Alice's role as day-to-day manager of their busy household.

As a man who had long reflected on the demands of justice and the needs of human nature, More was absolutely clear that his family was his first responsibility. So important to him were his family duties that he was willing to change his career rather than neglect them. This he writes explicitly to his oldest daughter: "I assure you that, rather than allow my children to be idle and slothful, I would make a sacrifice of wealth, and bid adieu to other cares and business, to attend to my children and my family."[27]

One important sacrifice he had to make early on was his love for writing literature. As his early work *Utopia* shows, More was a man of exceptional literary talent, yet that work was one of the few he wrote while his children required his closest attention. To write even that one book, making sure that his family duties did not suffer in the process, took heroic effort on his part. More himself speaks of this difficulty, in a letter which he writes as an apology for the lateness and unpolished character of *Utopia*:

I am almost ashamed, my dear Peter Giles, to send you this little book about the state of Utopia after almost a year, when I am sure you looked for it within a month and a half. . . . Yet even to carry through this trifling task, my other tasks left me practically no leisure at all. I am constantly engaged in legal business, either pleading or hearing, either giving an award as arbiter or deciding a case as judge. I pay a visit of courtesy to one man and go on business to another. I devote almost the whole day in public to other men's affairs and the remainder to my own. I leave to myself, that is to learning, nothing at all.

When I have returned home, I must talk with my wife, chat with my children, and confer with my servants. All this activity I count as business when it must be done—and it must be unless you want to be a stranger in your own home. Besides, one must take care to be as agreeable as possible to those whom nature has supplied, or chance has made, or you yourself have chosen, to be the companions of your life, provided you do not spoil them by kindness, or through indulgence make masters of your servants.

Amid these occupations that I have named, the day, the month, the year slip away. When, then, can I find time to write? Nor have I spoken a word about sleep—nor even of food, which for many people takes up as much time as sleep—and sleep takes up almost half a man's life! So I get for myself only the time I filch from sleep and food. Slowly, therefore, because this time is but little, yet finally, because this time *is* something, I have finished *Utopia* and sent it to you, my dear Peter.[28]

More's clear sense that his family duties should "count as business" and should be placed even before his professional work is best illustrated in an incident recounted by his son-in-law Will Roper. Shortly after entering King Henry's service, More came to find that his new job was preventing him from

spending enough time with his family. What is one to do when
the king is your boss and the cause of the problem? As Roper's
account shows, More's solution was ingenious—and also courageous:

> Because [More] was of a pleasant disposition, it
> often pleased the King and the Queen . . . at the
> time of their supper . . . to call for him to be merry
> with them. They delighted so much in his talk that
> he could not once in a month get leave to go home
> to his wife and children (whose company he most
> desired). When he was absent from the court for
> only two days, he was sent for again. Much dislik-
> ing this restraint upon his liberty, More began to
> dissemble his nature somewhat. Little by little he
> so changed from his usual mirth that he was not
> so frequently sent for.[29]

Such clear-sighted and courageous action reveals a level of
virtue and a sense of personal responsibility that few achieve.
What accounted for this achievement will be revealed in the
chapters ahead.

Chapter Five

The Laughing Philosopher: Early Writings

THROUGHOUT HIS YOUTH, More was well known not only for the brilliance of his wit but also for the charm of his humor. His contemporaries marveled that he never descended to sarcasm, to bitterness, or to silliness. We hear from Robert Whittington, for example, that More "is full of wit and pleasant humor, but his jests lack the bite of cynical Momus; for this More, this censor of our city's mores, has banished all sarcastic and scoffing expressions."[1] Erasmus, too, considered More's special blend of the comic and serious a rare phenomenon. "From boyhood," he says, "[More] has taken such pleasure in jesting that he might seem born for it, but in this he never goes as far as buffoonery, and he has never liked bitterness. In his youth he both wrote brief comedies and acted in them. . . . Hence his trying his hand as a young man at epigrams, and his special devotion to Lucian. . . . You would think him Democritus reborn. . . ."[2]

Richard Pace, who knew More well, likewise compared More to Democritus, the pre-Socratic thinker known as the "laughing philosopher." According to Pace, "Whenever the occasion demands, [More] imitates good cooks and pours sharp vinegar over everything. . . . He likes . . . in particular . . . the school of Democritus. Naturally I'm speaking of the Democritus who laughed at all human affairs."[3]

Two generations later, five London playwrights—including Shakespeare—collaborated on *Sir Thomas More*, a play highlighting these same characteristics. Their More is a statesman who laughs, improvises his own part as Prudence in "The Marriage of Wit and Wisdom," and is presented as the only leader in London who is capable of quelling the riot of 1517.

Such a character is arresting. Who normally pictures a philosopher laughing? And who would imagine a laughing philosopher as an effective judge and ruler? Yet it was precisely the rare blend of such elements that led his contemporaries to marvel at this "man for all seasons."[4]

More was the one who encouraged Erasmus to write his best and most famous literary work, *The Praise of Folly*. Together they translated Lucian's comic dialogues, making them available for the first time to a wide audience. Together they also helped to recapture the classical understanding of irony, thus contributing in a major way to the Northern "renaissance of good letters." This renaissance included a plan for social reform based on the gradual development of education and law, a plan cut short by Luther's more violent and revolutionary approach.

Like other Renaissance humanists, More and Erasmus considered comedy, especially satire, a major force in bringing about social reform. Understanding the place of comedy in this plan for social reform may help us appreciate not only the enthusiasm which these humanists had for the classics, but also the staunch opposition which they later mounted against the angry approach of Luther and his followers. A central issue over which they differed was the status of reason and its relative power.

In More's view, comedy had always been a powerful means of social reform and personal betterment. Why? Because comedy strongly appeals to reason and can therefore defuse passions that would otherwise prevent reason's engagement.

More shared the classical assumption that good social order depends upon the rule of reason over passion and self-interest. To bring about such order, literature and law play special roles—not only as products of reason, but also as its support. Of these two, More considered literature, not law, to be the primary civilizing force, though he recognized law to be indispensable. From his student days, he was an active participant in the "renaissance of good literature"[5] which the humanists saw as the foundation for a larger project of reform aimed first and foremost at strengthening the use of reason over superstition, prejudice, passion, and provincialism. As he would later explain, he considered literature to be the most effective means for achieving "a good mother wit," that "one special thing without which all learning is half lame."[6] That literature could play such an important role in civilization was a commonplace among Renaissance humanists, a commonplace inherited from the ancients. More adopted, for example, Horace's maxim that literature is meant to instruct and delight,[7] and he understood literature as an important means for developing reason and bringing about justice.[8] As we will see, an important assumption behind his work and writings was that personal and civic harmony can be achieved only if it is reason, not passion or pride, that rules. And in order for reason to rule, he saw the absolute need for literature and law to reign as well.

The three Lucian dialogues which More translated show the role of art in fostering reason. All three satirize proud pretensions and passionate excesses. The "antidote to such poisons," according to Lucian, is found "in truth and sound reason brought to bear everywhere"—which, of course, is the principal objective of classical comedy.[9]

So well does Lucian succeed in this objective that More praises him as holding, in this respect, the highest rank among the world's writers. "If," he says, "there was ever anyone who fulfilled the Horatian maxim and combined delight with instruction, I think Lucian certainly ranked among the foremost in this respect. Refraining from the arrogant pronouncements of the philosophers as well as from the wanton wiles of the poets, he everywhere reprimands and censures, with very honest and at the same time very entertaining wit, our human frailties. And this he does so cleverly and effectively that although no one pricks more deeply, nobody resents his stinging words."[10]

More cultivated just this kind of comic wit throughout the rest of his life.

Comedy rests upon the clear-sighted grasp of the ironies or discrepancies of a situation. As such, it is both the mark and the product of reason. Thus it was that More's intellectual abilities were manifested to his contemporaries in a special way through a comic sensibility that enabled him to grasp things as they were. Like Chaucer, he seemed to appreciate the whole range of life, from the earthy to the celestial. (Erasmus discreetly acknowledged this earthy quality in his first biography of More, in his comment that "only his hands are a bit coarse."[11])

More's favorite literary form in these early years was the epigram, a short poem with an unexpected twist. His collection of 281 epigrams is a marvel of variety and comprehensiveness. As one scholar put it, More's "vivid interest in life in all its aspects" makes this collection "the best book of Latin epigrams in the sixteenth century."[12] Some he translated from Greek, others he composed in Latin, but all helped him reflect deeply on the human condition.

A majority of the poems are comic sketches, sympathetically ridiculing human folly. Like the Roman comedian Terence, whom he loved, More was deeply concerned with the problems of those around him. In his very last work, he quotes Terence in reference to people's responsibility towards one another. "Certainly," he says, "if that saying of the comic poet is so highly approved, 'Since I am a man, I consider nothing human foreign to me,' how could it be anything but disgraceful for Christians to snore while other Christians are in danger?"[13]

More's comic epigrams are capable of arousing those who slumber in the face of vice. They also show that he did not consider anything human foreign to his concerns.

Some of these poems make fun of physical characteristics, like being short or having a big nose. (More himself was rather short, and he had a big nose.) One epigram celebrates a certain Gellia's heroic victory in getting up before noon—a miracle never seen before, and likely never to be seen again.[14] Another shows a guest at a banquet bantering with his waiter about the flies in his drink.[15] A dozen or so poke fun at lawyers, doctors, and priests who perform their duties in a less than edifying fashion.

Another series deals with animals. A cat toys with a terrified mouse, which then happily escapes.[16] A fly experiences the same relief when a bird consumes its captor—a spider—in the nick of time.[17] Bees are praised for their generosity and industriousness.[18]

Other poems focus on the contingency of life and the certainty of death. One is about a sailor who joyfully escapes the raging waters of the sea, only to be killed by a snake on the shore.[19] The fickleness of fortune,[20] the shortness of life,[21] and the prevalence of suffering[22] all show that life itself is but "a journey towards death."[23]

Several poems have an earthiness to them that might catch one by surprise, but no one who appreciates Chaucer will take them amiss. They serve to deflate the incongruous pride of us creatures who emit bad breath[24] and foul-smelling wind.[25]

One of the longer poems is a charming account of More's first adolescent love.[26] Another is a tender and playful poem to his children in which he declares his love for them, gives his reasons for loving them so much, and ends by telling them what they can do to make him love them even more.[27]

In the midst of this vibrant celebration of humanity arises More's largest and most distinctive group of poems, those on political life and rule. In a sense, these poems give unity to all the rest, because they force us to question how diverse and free human beings can be ruled harmoniously in a fallen world. The answer is, as one would expect, subtle and complex. To discover it requires long and deep consideration about all 281 of these poems and how they fit together as a whole.

One of the most surprising and original of these political poems is about two beggars, one lame, one blind. The English prose translation, unfortunately, does not communicate the subtlety and artistry of the Latin poem.

> There can be nothing more helpful than a loyal friend, who by his own efforts assuages your hurts. Two beggars formed an alliance of firm friendship—a blind man and a lame one. The blind man said to the lame one, "You must ride upon my shoulders." The latter answered, "You, blind friend, must find your way by means of my eyes." The love which unites shuns the castles of proud kings and prevails in the humble hut.[28]

This thought-provoking poem draws attention to the radical insufficiency of our fallen human nature. More seems to suggest that only a loving and graceful acceptance of human limitations, along with a conscious attempt to strengthen the bonds of human solidarity, can give rise to true harmony. The proud are their own worst enemies, and everyone else's.

Chapter Six

Coming to a Statesman's Understanding of Life: *Richard III, Utopia*

ONCE THOMAS MORE SAW CLEARLY that he was to serve the city, he carefully and conscientiously prepared himself for the task.

From 1501 to 1506, he immersed himself in Greek studies, convinced that the wisdom found there would be "most useful in the government of the state and the preservation of civic order."[1] He also studied with great care Augustine's *City of God*, a book that has always served to moderate expectations about building a city of heavenly justice while on earth. By exploring More's choice of these foundational classics, one can come to appreciate better the deepest aspirations of the Renaissance which he helped to lead in England.

The Renaissance exploded with dreams of an earthly city that would be truly just and strikingly beautiful. The awe-inspiring empire of ancient Rome, the cultural growth that had flourished during the *pax Romana*, the nobility of civic self-rule—all these fired the imagination of citizens, poets, and statesmen tired of warfare, poverty, and political intrigue.

Great dreams must be moderated by realism, however, and for this reason More turned to the historians of old. From roughly 1506 to 1518, he "studied with avidity all the historical works he could find,"[2] especially the Greek historians Thucydides and Plutarch, the Roman historians Sallust, Tacitus, and Suetonius,[3] and that great Christian philosopher of history, St. Augustine.

After reflecting deeply on these matters for at least fifteen years, More wrote his own history of England, and his own philosophical investigation of social justice: *The History of King Richard III*, and *Utopia*.

More began writing *The History of King Richard III* around 1513, but was still working on it when he entered King Henry's service in 1518. That he put his best efforts into composing it can be easily seen in the eloquence of his language,[4] the many classical allusions he incorporated, and the simple fact that he wrote two different versions of it, one in Latin and one in English. (The Latin version was evidently meant for an international audience, since More gives explanations of English institutions such as the Parliament and eliminates details that would interest only the English.[5])

But is it true? That is the first question usually asked about *The History of King Richard III*. Some historians now claim that Richard was not actually a bad king; after all, he was a good administrator, and no one has ever proved that he actually killed those two young princes. These same historians therefore tend to conclude that More was guilty of spreading propaganda in support of the Tudors—as was Shakespeare, who based his play largely upon More's account.

More, however, makes clear early on in his *History* that many facts about Richard simply cannot be known with certainty. If Richard was the master of deception More says he was,[6] he would have made it his business not to let others know of his actions. But be that as it may, there is one point on which More had no doubt whatsoever: Richard III was the quintessential tyrant.

Like the classical historians he imitated, More never intended to write a factual account of all the events and circumstances surrounding Richard's movements and actions. His intention was to portray the true nature of Richard's motives and character. If Richard was the deceptive and cunning tyrant More claimed he was, then how could anyone know with any real accuracy the particulars of his strategies? Richard was, according to More, such a master of deception that he could in one moment assure someone of his unfailing friendship, and in the next moment order that same person's execution.

More's information about Richard had come to him from eminently reliable witnesses, whom More knew intimately. His own father had lived through Richard's reign; so had many other relatives, teachers, and older friends. Of special importance was his childhood teacher and longtime mentor Lord Chancellor Morton, who had worked closely with Richard over many years. In other words, through his many London and court connections, More had access to the best information available at that time.

More's *History* explores the nature of tyranny. But, perhaps more importantly, it also explores how it was possible for a tyrant to come to power in England despite the many laws and institutions that had been developed over the centuries to prevent this from happening. The lesson More sets forth is one of interest even today. He points out that, oddly enough, Richard did not come to power by force; he succeeded "not by war, but by law," and by the simple fact that no statesman stood up to stop him.[7]

To appreciate the theme of *Richard III*, one must take seriously More's convictions that tyrants do exist in the world and that they can arise whenever enough people believe that they cannot. (The rise of Hitler and Stalin in our own day shows that More was correct.) Given these convictions, More uses every literary device at his disposal to impress upon the mind and imagination of the English nation the reality and magnitude of the danger.

Richard's hunchback, for example, may have been a theatrical device to give memorable form to what all the English leaders discovered too late: that Richard was morally deformed. This spiritual deformity was not visible to them, but it should have been.

At first view, Richard seemed good, generous, loving—and yet he was the opposite. Why did no one see through this deception in time to prevent civil war and the permanent disappearance of the two legitimate heirs to the throne? How could an entire generation of leaders, both civil and ecclesiastical, be blind to what was actually occurring? More's *History* yields one simple answer to both of these important questions: these leaders were blinded by self-interest. In their eagerness to curry favor with their new, powerful lord, they did not bother to find out what kind of ruler he was.

The political and ecclesiastical leaders were clearly at fault; but so were England's lawyers. In fact, suggests the narrator in More's *History*, the person most responsible for the nation's downfall was a lawyer well respected for his knowledge of the law. This learned Catsby began the whole chain of events by prostituting his legal prestige and position in hopes of preferments and advancement.[8]

In contrast to the *History*'s world of tyranny is the tyranny-free world of its companion piece, the famous *Utopia*. Utopia is presented as a society that has accomplished the incredible feat of eliminating all the terrifying upheaval and political strife that marks *The History of King Richard III*.

Utopia boasts, for example, a peace that has lasted 1,760 years. How can this be? The answer, we come to find out, is a combination of several factors: no private property; popular elections (in the fourteenth and fifteenth centuries!); few laws (supposedly); and one of the oddest social arrangements imaginable.[9]

This odd social arrangement constitutes one of the most distinctive intellectual puzzles ever devised in the history of literature. So complex and surprising is this puzzle that scholars have not reached any critical consensus about *Utopia*, except to acknowledge its brilliance. It is, therefore, small wonder that *Utopia* remains one of the most frequently read and debated classics of all time. To appreciate the depth and difficulty of the problems this book was designed to explore is to appreciate why no consensus has been possible, even among those who know *Utopia* best.

In a sense, the whole puzzle of *Utopia* is capsulized in the name of the one who tells the story of Utopia, Raphael Hythlodaeus. Does this character represent "the healing of God" ("Raphael") who can reveal the secret to political peace and justice here on earth? Or is he a mere "speaker of nonsense" ("Hythlodaeus") who deceives us about the true character of peace and justice? Or is he some combination of both?

By provoking such questions, More has engaged us in the type of deep reflection that all great literature invites. Indeed, the model he chose for this book is itself one of the greatest and most thought-provoking works of all time: Plato's *Republic*. Both books force attentive readers to ask the deepest of questions about human nature and its personal and political needs. What do human beings need in order to be happy? What form of government is most conducive to the satisfying of those needs? Are laws and private property really necessary? If so, why?

In thinking through such basic issues, More was preparing himself for a life of statesmanship. In the process, he also succeeded in creating a literary classic that could help prepare others in generations to come.

Chapter Seven

Achieving Professional Success

MORE'S PROFESSIONAL PREPARATION, thanks in large part to his father but also to his own hard work and prudent planning, offers many important lessons for our own day. Then, as now, expertise in any particular field came from serious training, careful planning, and diligent study. This was equally true of a scholar's ability to translate, a lawyer's command of the law, a rhetorician's mastery of language, a diplomat's knowledge of his country's traditions and social graces, and a philosopher's understanding of human nature.

Mastery in all these fields More achieved before entering the royal service at the age of forty-one, because already at age twenty he had set his sights high. His command of these diverse but related fields would eventually help him achieve an eminence and an influence rarely seen in history.

More knew that his success as a lawyer and politician would depend on much more than a thorough command of the law. Acquiring full competence in this field was itself a project that took over ten years of study and effort on his part. Yet he well understood that law, like most other professions, requires for its proper execution the philosopher's understanding of human nature, the rhetorician's art in directing the emotions, the diplomat's skill in counsel and negotiation, and the historian's understanding of tradition. More realized early on that he would need competence in each of these fields if he was to serve his city well.

This vision of a well-rounded and complete education was the one that inspired More and his fellow Renaissance humanists to return to the classical writers of Greece and Rome. There the arts of rhetoric, diplomacy, philosophy, history, and politics were seen to be interrelated and necessary if one were to lead a country that aspired to be just, free, and self-governing. More finished law school and was called to the bar around 1501, at the age of twenty-four. From 1501 to 1503, he presumably practiced enough law to make a living, but his first priority was to complete his education. Only then would he commit himself wholeheartedly to his professional work.

During this period, he attached himself to the Charterhouse, the Carthusians' monastery, to see if he had a priestly vocation. Here he learned to "fast and watch and pray."[1] He would continue these practices of prayer and self-mastery throughout the rest of his life.

At the same time, he also studied Greek, under several of the most eminent scholars of his day, so that he could read the classics in the original. Not only had the Greeks developed rhetoric, philosophy, and literature to an unprecedented degree, but they had also reflected most deeply on those capacities needed for self-government and peaceful political rule.

Rhetoric, the art of eliciting free assent, is itself a fundamental element of the art of governing. Erasmus tells us how hard More worked to achieve a rhetorical power that would match the brilliance of his wit. "His early years," he says, "were exercised principally in poetry; after that came a long struggle to acquire a more supple style in prose by practicing his pen in every sort of writing. . . . He has taken delight especially in declamations, and, in that department, in paradoxical themes, as offering more lively practice to one's ingenuity."[2]

More's "long struggle to acquire a more supple style" lasted for at least twenty years. His earliest poems date from roughly 1496, about the time he left Oxford to study in London. By 1504 he had partly translated and partly composed his first prose work, *The Life of John Picus*. Right up until 1518, when he joined the royal service, he continued writing and translating. In 1518, of course, practice had to come to an end. For over twenty years, however, More had worked on developing his powers of expression, powers that would acquire more value as he rose to positions of greater responsibility.

So intent was More on achieving a mastery of rhetoric that he set up friendly contests with some of the most talented writers of his time. He and Erasmus, for example, competed with one another in translating Lucian's witty dialogues from the Greek. Earlier, he and William Lily competed in translating epigrams. Erasmus, one of the greatest rhetoricians of all time, maintained that eloquence can be achieved only through long study, effort, and practice. "If we were to follow," he says, "the precepts of Cicero and Quintilian, and also the general practice of antiquity, and carefully train ourselves from boyhood onwards in exercises of this kind, I believe there would be less of the poverty of expression, the pitiful lack of style, and the disgraceful stammering we see even among public professors of the art of oratory."[3]

More's proficiency in speaking and writing was one of the major reasons for his rapid advance. Yet he saw these skills as inseparable from a deep understanding of human nature and the issues of the day, an understanding that would come primarily from the study of what he called the *bonae litterae*: philosophy, theology, history, and literature. As will become clearer later on, when we look at his educational plans for his children, More considered these studies the heart and soul of a good education.

After devoting several years to the *bonae litterae*, More was elected to his first official position in the tough world of politics. In 1504 he served as a member of Parliament, elected by the London merchants whom he and his father knew so well. He soon learned a lesson that was both surprising and sobering, since he almost lost his life in the process—and just for speaking his mind clearly. In light of that experience, it should come as no surprise that twenty years later, when he served as Speaker of the House of Commons, the first request he made was for freedom of speech. It should also come as no surprise that he would, in the meantime, immerse himself in further study and reflection about the life of civil leadership he saw to be his vocation.

That incident of 1504 unfolded in this way. In the parliament of that year, young More proved to be the most outspoken and persuasive opponent of a subsidy proposed by Henry VII. He was so persuasive, in fact, that Henry did not get what he wanted. Angered that this "beardless boy" had thwarted his will, Henry sought double revenge. First he imprisoned More's father, on trumped-up charges, and ordered him to pay the exorbitant sum of one hundred pounds. Then he watched and waited for an opportunity to get direct revenge on young More himself. So serious did this hardened opposition become that More visited the universities of Louvain and Paris around 1508, just in case he should have to leave England suddenly. Roper tells us that More was concerned for his life. This problem disappeared, however, in the following year, when Henry VII died.[4]

Between his wedding in 1505 and his appointment as undersheriff for the city in 1510, More's reputation as a lawyer gradually spread. He was elected financial secretary of Lincoln's Inn in 1507, and he became quite involved with London's commercial interests, especially through the Mercers' Guild. This guild was the most powerful association of merchants in London at that time. They made More a member in 1509, and they were highly influential in his reelection to Parliament in 1510. Later they chose him as their ambassador for two major commercial embassies in 1515 and 1517—missions he greatly disliked.[5]

As a lawyer, he acquired a reputation for honesty and integrity. One early biographer reports that "to his clients [More] never failed to give advice that was wise and straightforward, always looking to their interests rather than to his own. In most cases he used his best endeavors to get the litigants to come to terms. If he was unsuccessful in this, he would then show them how to carry on the action at least expense. He was so honorable and painstaking that he never accepted any case until he had first examined the whole matter thoroughly and satisfied himself of its justice. It was all the same whether those who came to him were his friends or strangers . . . : his first warning was ever that they should not in a single detail turn aside from the truth. Then he would say: 'If your case is as you have stated it, it seems to me that you will win.' But if they had not justice on their side, he would tell them so plainly, and beg them to give up the case, saying that it was not right either for him or for them to go on with it.

But if they refused to hear him, he would refer them to other lawyers, himself giving them no further assistance."[6]

Erasmus gives a similar account of More's conduct as a lawyer. More, he says, gave all of his clients "helpful and reliable advice, thinking much more of their advantage than of his own; the majority he used to persuade to settle their actions, on the grounds that this would save them expense."[7] This emphasis on the money these litigants could save was probably another shrewd and diplomatic way of addressing a more fundamental problem, one that every lawyer has to face: "Some men are so made that they actually enjoy going to law."[8] Wise lawyer that he was, More recognized that the passion for justice, like all other passions, has to be moderated in this fallen world. And, as usual, he found an indirect, subtle way of achieving what would be next to impossible to accomplish in a direct, blunt way. His ability as a counselor and diplomat owed much to his deep appreciation of the frailty of human nature and the hardening effects of pride.

Testimonies to his honesty and integrity are abundant. When, for example, it came time for Bishop Cuthbert Tunstall to dedicate his book on mathematics to someone, he chose More, because "from all my friends . . . you seemed to me the most fitting of all, both on account of our intimacy and on account of your frankness; for I know that you will be pleased at whatever good it may contain, warn me of whatever is imperfect, and forgive whatever is amiss."[9]

More lived up to Bishop Tunstall's expectations, even when Tunstall himself would have preferred otherwise. Towards the end of More's life, for example, Tunstall and two other bishops sent him twenty pounds, asking him to accept the money for a gown and then to join them in attending Anne Boleyn's coronation. The response he gave them shows how forcefully and yet humorously he could express himself in an effort to get others to face the full truth of a situation. A brilliant piece of rhetoric, this response was designed to shock through its earthy directness while appealing to reason through its comic vividness. It runs as follows: "My lords, in the letters which you lately sent me, you asked two things of me. Since I am so well content to grant you the one, therefore I thought I might be the bolder to deny you the other. As for the first, because I took you for no beggars, and myself I knew to be no rich man, that one I thought I might fulfill. But the other reminded me of an emperor that had decreed a law that whoever committed a certain offense (which I now do not remember) should suffer the pains of death—unless the person were a virgin, since he had such a reverence for virginity. Now it so happened that the first offender was indeed a virgin. When the emperor heard this, he was greatly perplexed since he wanted an opportunity to have that law executed. When his council had sat and solemnly debated this case, suddenly there arose one of his council, a good plain man, who said, 'Why make so much ado, my lords, about so small a matter? Let her first be deflowered, and then after may she be devoured.'"[10]

Lest the bishops miss the point of this little tale, More went on to draw out its meaning. "And so," he continued, "although your lordships have in the matter of the King's marriage so far kept yourselves pure virgins, yet take good heed, my lords, that you continue to keep your virginity. For some there are who, by first getting your lordships to be present at the coronation, will then get you to preach for its legitimacy, and finally will get you to write books to all the world in defense of it. These desire to deflower you, and when they have deflowered you, then will they not fail soon after to devour you. Now, my lords, it lies not in my power if they devour me, but God being my good Lord, I will provide that they shall never deflower me."[11]

There are few better examples in all of More's writings than this one to show his courageous and artful way of expressing the truth as he saw it, of challenging others to confront issues before the tribunal of conscience.

This fearless ability to challenge and test others in a pleasant and even humorous manner gave More an unusual effectiveness in diplomacy, even in the most difficult negotiations. These qualities he learned especially from his own humorous father and from his beloved teacher Chancellor Morton. Both as chancellor and as archbishop, Morton constantly tested people—necessarily, given his position as a ruler of both church and state. Morton served as Lord Chancellor under two kings; he was arrested and tried for treason under a third. He had been bishop of Ely, a diocese with all the usual problems that arise when the faithful fail to remain so. Later he became Archbishop of Canterbury and therefore the primate of England, responsible for taking care of all the greatest problems. These were often highly unusual problems that called for uncommon prudence and wit.

With such a wide range of experience, it is no wonder that Morton developed the habit of judiciously testing those who might serve under him. In fact, he did not hesitate to use a harsh manner in these tests. As More tells us, "Of those who made suit to him, [Morton] enjoyed making trial by rough address, but in a harmless way, to see what mettle and what presence of mind a person might manifest."[12]

More would himself devise a much different approach for proving the mettle of another's character. Having learned the value of lighthearted irony from Plato, Lucian, and his own father, More found that he could discover all he needed to know by way of pleasant jest rather than gruff confrontation.

Often a person can most effectively tell "the full truth in jest"—it was Horace who taught him this valuable lesson.[13] More used this lighthearted approach so effectively that even members of his family could not always tell if he was speaking seriously or in jest. In this way, he would lead them to reveal their own thoughts on the matter at hand. This playful irony was the dominant characteristic of his artful way of engaging the minds and hearts of all. Yet his approach was not simply playful; it proved to be a highly effective means of appealing to conscience and of enjoining reflection. It was perhaps the most important and original element in his work as a counselor of law and as counselor of King Henry. It surely accounted for much of his charm and effectiveness as a diplomat and as a kind but demanding father. It was even an important element in his work as a judge.

More's career as a judge began in 1510, when, at the age of thirty-three, he accepted the modest position of city undersheriff. In this capacity, he advised the sheriff and the mayor on any and all legal issues that arose from their dealings with sixty thousand Londoners from all trades and walks of life. (Our equivalent would be the office of city attorney, except that

More's position also involved the responsibility of presiding as judge in the sheriff's court. This court dealt with nearly every kind of case except the type reserved to the king.) Besides providing him with an unusually broad range of legal experience, this job as undersheriff gave More the opportunity to provide a practical and much-needed service to the people of his city while at the same time advancing his own career.

More carried out his work as judge every Thursday morning. Erasmus reports: "No one ever determined more cases, and no one showed more absolute integrity. Many people have had their money returned to them which according to precedent must be paid by litigants; for before the action comes into court, the plaintiff must deposit three drachmas, and the defendant the same."[14]

As a result of such expeditious, fair, and even generous action, More's "native city held him in deep affection."[15] Londoners seemed to love him most, however, for his legendary good humor.

Londoners' loving admiration for "merry More" is evidenced by the daring portrait which Shakespeare and his fellow London playwrights presented some sixty years after his death.[16] *Sir Thomas More* dramatizes him as the Londoners remembered their fellow townsman—that is, as "the best friend that the poor ever had," and as the pleasant and wise wit who could always, even at his own execution, find matter for jest.

More's impartiality as a judge is also well documented. When, for example, one of his sons-in-law complained that his position was "nothing profitable" to his family and friends, More gave an answer that has become famous: "Son, I assure you on my faith that, if the parties will at my hands call for justice, then, even if my father stood on one side and the devil on the other, his cause being good, the devil should have right."[17]

Another son-in-law, Giles Heron, brought an action before Judge More, and he was "warned . . . to cease litigation, as his cause was not just." When he went ahead anyway, More gave "a flat decree against him."[18]

In a case dealing with "a declared enemy of his," More was "strictly impartial." He explained that "however bitter an enemy to me a man may be, or however much he may have injured me,

I will not allow this to prejudice his case in court, where justice must be administered impartially to all."[19]

Because of his reputation for integrity and prudent judgment, More's law practice grew enormously. However, growth itself was clearly not his objective. During this period, he continued his studies in history and philosophy. He also refused pay from the King, because he did not wish to compromise his impartiality in cases dealing with the city and the crown.[20] Nevertheless, he became involved in every major case in London during this time, because his good judgment and command of the law were so widely recognized and respected.[21]

This preeminence in the law did not come without effort. Along with everything else he did, More worked hard at continuing his own legal education and helped with the legal education of others. He was appointed reader (professor) of law at Lincoln's Inn in 1511, and a governor of the same law school in 1512. By 1515 he was given the highest honor conferred by the inns of court: he was asked to deliver the Lenten lectures in law, an honor reserved to the very best and most experienced practitioners.

Meanwhile, his law practice developed in many different directions. He was appointed to the commission in charge of sewers and to the one in charge of maintaining London Bridge—important positions because of the problems which resulted from the periodic flooding of the Thames. He was counsel to the chancery. In 1514 he was elected to the Doctors' Commons, an association of the realm's leading lawyers, legislators, and foreign emissaries. In 1511 an important court official reported that More saw the Chancellor of England every single day; in 1516 the same official added the revealing detail that, by then, More not only saw the Lord Chancellor each day, but was always the first one to do so.[22]

Throughout these years, More made quite a bit of money. Roper says he made four hundred pounds a year—a substantial sum, considering that the ordinary artisan lived on ten pounds a year.[23] Once he entered public service, however, he would not make that kind of money again for many years to come.

Though his primary concern was never money, More was both ingenious and enterprising in acquiring resources for the

social, educational, and spiritual projects he considered necessary for the good of his family, city, and nation. Some recent
biographers have been surprised that such a reputedly pious
man would have shown so much interest in acquiring money.
They conclude that he must not have been pious at all during
this early stage of his life—as if the pious were not to be
worldly-wise as well.

Yet More was a genius, he worked exceptionally hard, and
he had the humility to seek out good advice. In his own education, for example, he did not simply follow the set curriculum of
whatever school he was attending, good as it might be. He
sought advice from those he most admired, and he undertook a
rigorous set of supplementary subjects, even during the early
years of his legal career.

Such advice also proved immensely profitable when the
time came for him to choose a field of law, at the beginning of
his career. Many family members and friends had long been
involved in the legal and political life of London. Both his father
and his father-in-law were accomplished and respected men
who knew their city well. They were probably the ones who
advised young Thomas to take the job of undersheriff. Unglam-
orous as it was, this position eventually opened to him every
door of the city. It also gave him the widest possible exposure to
his fellow citizens and to the full body of law itself.

The position of undersheriff had the added advantage of
giving More a good excuse not to become entangled in the
intrigues of the royal court. As an officer of the city, he could
not have done any work for the king without creating a conflict of interest between city and crown. And during these
years, More definitely chose to be a private citizen, not a royal
servant.

One of the most famous cases of his law career occurred in
1517, the year before he finally did join the royal service. In this
case, More successfully defended the pope's rights to a ship
that had been claimed as forfeiture by the crown. He won not
only the case, but also an even greater renown among his fellow Londoners, largely because of the "upright and commendable behavior" he exhibited throughout.[24]

The extent and depth of the respect More commanded became particularly obvious during the riots that occurred in London on "Evil May Day" of that same year. Once again, his mastery of rhetoric and his thorough knowledge of both human nature and his own people put him in a position to do what no one else could have done.

The best historical account of the Evil May Day incident is given in Edward Hall's chronicles. There Hall explains that tensions between foreign and native merchants had become so great that a riot broke out, despite the efforts of the city fathers to prevent it. In the midst of this chaos, More almost brought one group of rioters "to a stay," but then another group "threw out stones and bats, . . . bricks and hot water," and undid the progress he had made towards establishing peace.[25]

The most artful account of this same event is given by Shakespeare in *Sir Thomas More*. (Although five writers collaborated in this play, Shakespeare was the one who dramatized the segment dealing with More's role in this memorable event.)

In this riot scene, the Lord Mayor and the earls of Surrey and Shrewsbury have all tried to speak to the crowd, but only More is given a hearing. Once he has the crowd's attention, he begins, as any masterful diplomat would, by finding out their major complaint. Only after they express their desire to get rid of the foreigners does More respond. At this point, he begins by helping his listeners to see these foreigners as real human beings. This he accomplishes by vividly appealing to their imaginations and to their sense of compassion:

> Imagine that you see the wretched strangers,
> Their babies at their backs, with their poor luggage
> Plodding to th' ports and coasts for transportation,
> And that you sit as kings in your desires,
> Authority quite silenced by your brawl. . . . (2.3.80–84)

By helping his fellow Londoners to imagine themselves as kings over these "wretched strangers," he shifts their focus from self-interest to a sense of conscience and of personal responsibility.

That much accomplished, he then challenges the rioters to take an honest look at the effects of their rebellious action. He

begins with a question designed once again to engage their consciences, and then immediately goes to the heart of the matter:

> What had you got? I'll tell you: you had taught
> How insolence and strong hand should prevail,
> How order should be quelled, and by this pattern
> Not one of you should live an aged man,
> For other ruffians, as their fancies wrought,
> With selfsame hand, self reasons, and self right
> Would shark on you, and men like ravenous fishes
> Would feed one on another. (2.3.86–93)

This vivid depiction of their sharklike behavior strikes even
the most impassioned of the rioters as quite accurate. "Before
God," cries one character, "that's as true as the Gospel!"
Another chimes in, "This is a sound fellow, I tell you. Let's
mark him."

Shakespeare's More then goes on to reveal gradually the
true nature of these rioters' activity: it constitutes rebellion
against the "majesty of law." Next he appeals to their common
humanity in an effort to correct their distorted view of themselves and of the foreigners:

> [If you yourselves were exiled from your homeland,]
> ... Would you be pleased
> To find a nation of such barbarous temper
> That breaking out in hideous violence
> Would not afford you an abode on earth,
> Whet their detested knives against your throats,
> Spurn you like dogs, and like as if that God
> [Owned] not nor made not you, nor that the elements
> Were not all appropriate to your comforts,
> But chartered unto them? What would you think
> To be thus used? This is the strangers' case,
> And this your [monstrous] inhumanity. (2.3.141–151)

This appeal to their common humanity is a resounding success, as evidenced by the response of "All": "Faith! He says true;
let's do as we may be done by." Finally, after asking More to
"stand our friend to procure our pardon," the citizens lay down
their weapons and submit to his rule.

Though in obvious ways this dramatization departs from historical fact, Shakespeare presents faithfully those qualities for which More was best known—his quick wit, his commitment to justice, his unquestioned integrity, his compassion for others, and his deep understanding of the human heart.

After such an event, what good king would fail to insist that these qualities be placed at the service of the kingdom as a whole? And yet, as we will see, Thomas More was reluctant to enter the royal service.

Chapter Eight

"Born for Friendship"

"WHOEVER DESIRES A PERFECT EXAMPLE of true friendship will seek it nowhere to better purpose than in More."[1] So wrote Erasmus about "the friend I love best."[2] To Erasmus, who had traveled all over Europe, this man stood out as one "born and made for friendship."[3]

In an attempt to explain More's particular charm, Erasmus focused especially upon his unusual generosity and open disposition to all. "No one," he wrote, "is more openhearted in making friends or more tenacious in keeping them, nor has he any fear of that multiplicity of friendships against which Hesiod warns us. The road to a secure place in his affections is open to anyone. In the choice of friends he is never difficult to please, in keeping up with them the most accommodating of men, and in retaining them the most unfailing."[4]

Although More was not afraid of having too many friends, and although he was open to all, he was not indifferent to matters of character. He sometimes found it necessary to end a friendship; but even this he did in a friendly way. Erasmus says, "If by any chance he has picked on someone whose faults he cannot mend, he waits for an opportunity to be quit of him, loosening the knot of friendship and not breaking it off."[5] As we will see, More applied this principle even to King Henry. When he loosened his bond with Henry by resigning from the chancellorship, he did not break off his good will towards him.

This is how Erasmus explains More's unusual personal appeal: "When he finds openhearted people naturally suited to

61

him, he enjoys their company and conversation so much that one would think he reckoned such things the chief pleasure in life. . . . In society he shows such rare courtesy and sweetness of disposition that there is no man so melancholy by nature that More does not enliven him, no disaster so great that he does not dissipate its unpleasantness."[6]

Erasmus marvels at how skillful More is in adapting "himself to the mood of anyone," although "nobody is less swayed by public opinion."[7] This skillful adaptability was one of the main elements of More's social and political success. He became a master at handling tense situations. Habitually, he turned aside offensive comments with a lighthearted remark;[8] he artfully but forcefully changed the topic of conversation whenever necessary;[9] he was moderate and courteous in arguing with others, especially when he was in the winning position.[10] Always, it seems, he prudently used his humor and wit to protect "his noble freedom and serenity of soul."[11]

Such diplomatic skill in the widest range of situations was what led his friends Erasmus and Robert Whittington to describe More as "a man for all seasons."[12] In using this phrase, Erasmus was alluding to St. Paul's statement "I became all things to all . . ." (1 Cor 9:22).[13] Another friend, Richard Pace, made the same point in a quite different way. More, he wrote, "is not so vulgarly witty and urbane that you would think politeness was his father and wit his mother. [Yet] every now and then, whenever the occasion demands, he imitates good cooks and pours sharp vinegar over everything."[14]

Of his many friendships, the one that More shared with Erasmus is particularly revealing. These intellectual giants held a great deal in common. They each understood the challenge and aspirations of their own age. They each spent five years acquiring the command of Greek they would need to make their respective contributions to the Renaissance and to world culture. Erasmus would use his Greek to bring about reform within the Church through the recovery of Scripture; More would use his Greek to bring about reform within the city through the recovery of classical political thought (but as reinterpreted in the light of biblical revelation).

As mentioned earlier, More and Erasmus translated Lucian together, and their publication soon became one of the most popular and influential translations of that period. Then, in imitation of Lucian, they wrote ironic literature satirizing the abuses of their own age. Eventually they would pursue different careers; More became a statesman, while Erasmus remained the scholar. Nonetheless, More continued to encourage Erasmus in his work.

From their first meeting in 1499, More and Erasmus were fast friends, and for good reason. They had similar intellectual gifts, they both saw clearly the need for reforming church and society, they agreed on the best means for such reformation, and they immensely enjoyed each other's wit and company.

The strength and self-confidence of young More was undoubtedly a strong support for the rather emotionally battered Erasmus.[15] The illegitimate son of a priest, Erasmus was never at home in the monastery. Once he left, he had little economic security and no permanent home.

In contrast, More lived the whole of his life in London, and he came from a prosperous and well-respected family. Although his mother died when he was young, and so did two of his three stepmothers, More was close to his father, whom he deeply loved and admired.

More brought out the best in Erasmus, and understood him with greater depth than perhaps anyone else did. Erasmus, often moody and melancholy, profited greatly from More's artful and merry friendship. "Yes," he once said, referring to More and himself, "he can make the camel dance!"[16]

The important project which More and Erasmus shared was the promotion of a "sound learning" that would provide the much-needed human foundation for "true religion."[17] Erasmus repeatedly said that all his efforts were "devoted to the promotion of honorable studies and to the advancement of the Christian religion."[18] More and Erasmus both referred to this period as a hopeful one for the "renaissance of good literature";[19] for a little while they even thought they were witnessing the "dawn of a golden age."[20] Their great ambition was to see nations ordered to virtue and the common good, not to conquest and war. To achieve this renaissance, they both returned to the wisdom of the ancient Greeks. There they found a vision of personal and political life that became the foundation of what is now known as "Christian humanism."

Erasmus and More helped each other in the struggle to remain faithful to their firmly held beliefs. When More lost his temper with the French humanist Brixius, Erasmus stepped in. He reminded More of the importance of international harmony among humanists, and he also wrote to Brixius to mediate their difference. Not long afterwards, More played a similar role when Erasmus became angry with the theologian Edward Lee.[21]

When Erasmus grew old, sick, disheartened, and weakened in will, More helped him in a special way. At this time, during the bitter feud between Luther and Rome, Erasmus was the center of European attention. In 1526, at the height of the controversy, More wrote to him, urging him on to complete his writings against Luther, out of "concern for all of Christendom."[22] Erasmus had diplomatically pointed out the inconsistency of Luther's denial of free will with the teachings of the Bible; now More encouraged him to complete "the brilliant works you have been writing to promote Christian piety." Referring to his refutation of Luther, More tells Erasmus: "You could have no other work in mind that would be more profitable for others, more satisfying to your friends, and more notable or more urgent for your own self. You would find it hard to believe the eagerness with which all good men are looking forward to that work."[23]

This project was "urgent" for Erasmus himself because many people all over Europe were still wondering if he was against Luther or for him. That More reminded him of this urgency is a sign of his concern for his friend and the pivotal role that Erasmus was playing.

Throughout the first part of the letter, More seems to assume that Erasmus' delay in responding to Luther is due to sickness or preoccupation with other projects. Then, however, he presents another reason that he fears may be the real cause. "But if," he says, "according to some reports, the delay is due to the fact that you have been terrorized, and have lost all interest in the work, and have no courage to go on with it, then I am thoroughly bewildered and unable to restrain my grief."

If Erasmus has indeed been intimidated, More is not about to let him stay that way. Putting the present moment in the perspective of Erasmus' whole life, More gives him a rousing call to courage: "You have endured, dearest Erasmus, many, many struggles and perils and Herculean labors; you have spent all the best years of your life on exhausting work, through sleepless nights, for the profit of all the world; and God forbid that now you should so unhappily become enamored of your declining years as to be willing to abandon the cause of God rather than lose a decision."

Having sympathized with Erasmus over his long and thankless years of toil, More then anticipates and immediately dismisses an objection Erasmus might have raised. "I am not afraid," he says, "that you will now throw up to me that quotation from the comic poet: 'When . . . healthy, everybody can easily give advice to a sick man, but if you were in my place, you might think differently.'"

What makes More so sure that Erasmus will not try to use such an excuse? "You have given," he says, "extraordinary proof of a heart that is valiant and trusting in God. It is impossible for me to doubt that you will continue bravely to exhibit such strength of spirit right up to your dying breath, even if there were a disastrous catastrophe. For you could never fail to trust that God in His merciful kindness would intervene to calm the disturbance."

Writing at length about why Erasmus has no reason to fear, he nonetheless assures him of his full support and his willingness to help. "If you notice," he says, "that your reply involves some danger which you cannot elude and which I cannot foresee, then please, do at least this much: write me a confidential note." This solicitous care for Erasmus in a time of special need is but one example of More's friendship in action.

More's closest friend seems to have been the Italian merchant and banker Antonio Bonvisi. Bonvisi was the one who cared for More in the Tower, despite the personal dangers involved. He sent More a warm camel gown and numerous

gifts of wine and food. One of the last letters More ever wrote
was to Bonvisi. Greeting him as "of all friends most friendliest,
and to me worthily dearliest beloved,"[24] More closes this
farewell letter with the unequivocal statement that Bonvisi is
"of all mortal men to me most dearest," the very "apple of
mine eye."[25]

More begins this moving letter by telling Bonvisi that he
wants him to know how much he has been "comforted with
the sweetness of your friendship, in this decay of my fortune."
Thinking back over their forty years of friendship, More recalls
how often he was made to feel he was not "a guest, but a continual nursling in Master Bonvisi's house." Now in prison, he
can hardly believe the ongoing loyalty and generosity of this
friend. Indeed, he declares, "few men so fawn upon their fortu-
nate friends, as you favor, love, foster, and honor me, now
overthrown, abjected, afflicted, and condemned to prison."
Such a "faithful and constant friendship in the storms of fortune" More considers a singular gift of a benevolent and merciful God. To have so great a friend helps "relieve a great part of
these troubles and griefs of mine."[26]

At the end of the letter, More prays that God "will bring us
from this wretched and stormy world into His rest, where we
shall need no letters, where no wall shall dissever us, where no
porter shall keep us from talking together, but that we may have
the fruition of eternal joy" in the company of the Holy Trinity.[27]

How did such an extraordinary friendship begin? And what
must Bonvisi have been like, to have captured the heart of a
Thomas More?

Bonvisi was a man of remarkable character, but not a great
deal is known about him. He was a wealthy banker and merchant in London who, like More, refused to compromise his religious convictions. Despite his economic importance to England,
he too would fall into permanent disfavor with Henry VIII,
partly because he was such a conspicuous character in his own
right, and partly, no doubt, because he was well known as having been a friend of More's. Bonvisi would pay dearly for his
loyalty to the Catholic Church. Elizabeth Rogers tells us that "he
fled from England in 1544. His house . . . was seized in 1550 and

he was specially excepted from the pardon of the Parliament of 1553."[28] But here we have gotten ahead of our story.

Long before 1515, More and Bonvisi became close friends. To get some idea of why, all we have to do is delve into one of several delightful anecdotes from More's early letters. More recounts with zest a most entertaining evening spent at what probably was Bonvisi's home. In any case, the story shows the many qualities that More admired in this deeply Christian man of the world.

One of the dinner guests was a theologian famous for disputing whatever anyone else said. More tells the story of what happened that evening: "As a joke, the merchant [Bonvisi] brought up the subject of mistresses. He began to defend the position that it was not so evil to have one woman at home as to run through a number away from home. Here again the theologian closed in and ferociously took him to task, not that he appeared to have any real grudge against mistresses but that he hated agreeing with anyone on anything, or perhaps the man just liked variety. Anyway, he asserted that it was the conclusion of a certain Most Translucent Doctor, who [had written] that most singular book entitled *A Directory for Men Who Keep Mistresses*, that a man who has one mistress at home is more sinful than a man who has ten whores away from home, not only because of the evil example it sets but also because there are more opportunities to sin with a woman at home."[29]

Bonvisi was already having fun arguing with the theologian, but then he noticed that this religious was not at all familiar with Scripture. So he then "started to play with the fellow and draw various arguments from authority. As he went along, he made up various brief texts which appeared to support his position, and even though he had arbitrarily contrived them all out of thin air, he would quote one as if from some epistle of St. Paul, another as if it were from an epistle of Peter, and still another as if it were straight from the Gospel. Indeed, he was so diligent in doing so that he always included a chapter citation for what he was quoting, except that if a book was divided into sixteen chapters, he would purposely quote from the twentieth."[30]

The theologian, of course, was not about to admit his ignorance. Instead, "even though he knew nothing at all about the contents of Sacred Scripture, and though he did not doubt that the words being quoted were actually there, and though he thought it wrong to oppose or defy the authority of Scripture but at the same time considered it shameful to give up the field in defeat, even when he was caught in such desperate straits, please observe with what cunning that Proteus slipped out of the net. As soon as some supposedly scriptural text was quoted against him right out of thin air, 'You quote well, sir,' he said, 'but I understand that text as follows.' And then he would interpret it, not without some bipartite distinction in which he would first say that one meaning supported his opponent and then he would evade it by finding another. But whenever the merchant closed in too intently and claimed that the theologian was not giving the true sense of the text, then the fellow would swear— so devoutly that anyone could have believed him—that Nicolas de Lyra interpreted that text the same way."[31]

If Bonvisi was as fun-loving and keen-witted as this story indicates, it is no wonder that he and More became such great friends.

Two other longtime friends of More's were Francis and Elizabeth Cranevelt.[32] He was a leading humanist of Europe; she, a woman of unusual refinement and charm. Since Francis was a lawyer and a councilman for Bruges, More came to know him well during an embassy there in 1521. Away from home for months, More enjoyed greatly the company of the Cranevelts and their eleven lively children.

What is quite revealing about the letters More wrote to Cranevelt is his playful joking with regard to Mrs. Cranevelt. At the end of one letter, for example, he signs off by saying, "Farewell to your wife—mine by day, yours by night."[33] In a later letter he writes, just as playfully, "As for my mistress your wife, or rather your mistress my wife, since I betrothed myself to her there long since. . . ."[34] More repents in a subsequent letter for having gone too far in his jesting, and he asks that Cranevelt "greet my lady your wife (for I dare not again change the order)."[35] But in yet another letter he asks Francis to "give my regards to our mistress and wife."[36]

These letters, however, are generally filled with ordinary business. More asks Cranevelt to help him find a house he can rent while in Bruges for the embassy. "Please give some thought to a house," he says, "and perhaps the one that I had before would not be the worst, but the price was the worst. Find out at what price it could be rented for two months from May 1 and thereafter by the week. And also what it would cost to rent eight or ten beds, together with the rest of the suitable furnishings. And at your leisure let me know about these things. . . . If the candlesticks have not yet been sent, do not send them but keep them there till I arrive."[37]

When complications arise over the renting of the house, Cranevelt suggests that More stay with him and his family. More does not wish to burden them by staying long, but does want to stay for a short time "in order to enjoy for a while the spontaneous kindness of you and my lady, your wife, until I have an opportunity to consider in person what house I could most conveniently move into."[38]

Another letter shows the deep character of their friendship, revealing (playfully, as usual) More's personal feelings as a married man. "I pray," he says, "that your spouse, a lady of the highest dignity, will have a happy journey, complete her business exactly as she wishes, and swiftly return, though I remember that you once wrote to me that the most pleasant sleep is in a bed without a wife, but these are the words of husbands on the first nights after their wives have been sent away, for on the remaining nights desire comes creeping back and, unless the wife has left a proxy, it makes sleep unpleasant. As for your wife, I think she is so prudent that she has taken away all her maidservants with her. Farewell, most delightful of all men."[39]

Such letters give us our most direct evidence of More's domestic character and charm, our most direct access to the man "born for friendship."

Chapter Nine

A Reluctant Career Change:
From Citizen to Subject

AT FORTY-ONE, Thomas More was a happy and accomplished man. His family had flourished so well under his cultured care that they would soon be famous throughout Christendom; they would also soon move to a large estate outside London so that the children's families could remain there merrily together. *Utopia* was widely acclaimed and had just been published in its third edition within two years. More's achievement in law was so great that he had become a wealthy man; he loved his work as a judge and had the satisfaction of helping many, especially the poor, in a tangible way. He was a governor of Lincoln's Inn, and a member of the prestigious and highly influential Doctors' Commons. He was also able to keep up with his fellow intellectuals in various parts of Europe.

At this pinnacle of his civic career, More was asked to join King Henry's service as a royal counselor. He was reluctant to accept, and with good reason. He knew precisely what would be involved in the all-consuming world of royal service. He had lived at Lord Chancellor Morton's palace; he had friends who were serving at the court; and he had recently participated in two royal embassies abroad. More knew the demands of this life as well as anyone.

If he had been interested in working for the King, he could have been doing so long since. After all, he had known the King since Henry was a child. In fact, he was on such familiar terms with him that, twenty years earlier, he had taken Erasmus to see Prince Henry—unannounced. Such familiarity was enjoyed by few of Henry's subjects.

As his closest friends knew, More did not want to take the "serious risks" which a life at court would present.[1] He had four concerns in particular. The first two show that his family's good was foremost in his mind from the very beginning of his professional life. The other two show how well he knew the demands that a life at court would bring.

To begin with, More realized from his own study of history and of human nature that even the best of kings could become a tyrant. As he boldly wrote in his poem celebrating Henry VIII's coronation, "Unlimited power has a tendency to weaken good minds—and that, even in the case of very gifted men."[2] What he was trying to warn Henry about is just what ended up happening to this monarch who started out so full of promise.

Secondly, More loved his family deeply and therefore knew the care they required. To be a good husband and father, he had ordered his law practice in such a way as to allow him sufficient time to spend with them. In becoming directly subject to the powerful will of another, More would have given up the independence he needed, at least in the early years of marriage. These were the crucial years for establishing family traditions and providing the stability his family would need in order to flourish. While he and Jane were working out the initial challenges of marriage, and while the children were very young and needed the most attention, he seems to have deliberately avoided court life. The wisdom of this decision must have become especially evident when Jane died in 1511, leaving him to care for their four children, all of whom were under six.

The third concern was personal. More loved to write, and he loved having the leisure to read and reflect. Even before entering the royal service, he found himself stealing time from sleep and meals to satisfy this hunger. Once he joined the King's service, however, his literary ambitions would be "lost forever," as Erasmus lamented.[3]

The fourth concern was also personal. More recognized the dangers of pride, and he knew that he was not immune. Before placing himself in a position of so much moral danger, he wanted time to prepare and test himself. Just as he had taken several years to discern his vocation and prepare for marriage, so he took years to prepare himself spiritually and professionally before taking on the challenges of court life. He saw clearly that high office was "full of toil and danger, void of all real and lasting honor." He also knew that its "empty splendor" could dazzle the eyes and bring about one's downfall.[4]

In addition to these concerns, More had reservations about Henry's character. From the first year of his reign, Henry had been carried away with a chivalric view of war. In 1512, while More and Erasmus were emphasizing the importance of peacefully working toward a united Christendom, Henry committed England to a war with France. In 1513, against the advice of his own counselors, he himself led an army into France—endangering his life, and thus the stability of his country, just for dreams of chivalric glory. Such reckless behavior indicated to More that Henry suffered from a deep-seated "lust for power."[5]

Why, then, did More ever agree to join Henry's council? Perhaps the decisive reason was an important change in Henry's foreign policy that occurred in 1517. In that year, Pope Leo X issued a bull imposing a five-year truce among all Christian nations. Chancellor Wolsey, aware of the way the political winds were blowing, devised his own Treaty of Universal Peace. In this new climate, More saw an opportunity to do immense good for England and for all of Christendom. Besides, he already had many humanist friends who served on King Henry's council. Pace, Linacre, and Tunstall, to name only a few, were men whom he greatly respected and who shared with him the ideal of a united and peaceful Christendom.

Nonetheless, More had a private conference with Henry before joining his service. We know that the topic of conversation was the exercise of conscience, because More wrote about this meeting seventeen years later, in the Tower. As he diplomatically reports, Henry told him he "should look first to God and after God to him." This was, More says, "the first lesson that his Grace gave me when I first came into his noble service. Never could a king give his counselor or any other servant a more indifferent command or a more gracious lesson."[6]

With this assurance that his conscience would be respected, More agreed to serve as Henry's counsel—but still reluctantly. He expressed this reluctance shortly afterwards, in a letter to his trusted friend Bishop John Fisher. "Much against my will," he says, "did I come to Court—as everyone knows, and as the King himself in jest sometimes likes to reproach me. So far I keep my place there as precariously as an unaccustomed rider in his saddle."[7]

More's sense of precariousness may have come from a realistic assessment of the capricious man whom he served. Nonetheless, Henry had a special affection for More. As we have seen, Henry enjoyed his company so much that he often sent for More just to talk—"sometimes about matters of astronomy, geometry, divinity, and such other faculties, and sometimes about his worldly affairs."[8]

Almost immediately, he began to serve as Henry's personal secretary.

More's good influence on Henry is perhaps best seen in the unusual government reform which Henry approved in May 1519. Although this reform cannot be traced to More alone, he was a member of the council that devised it, and it bears the mark of his good judgment.

One important element in this reform was the dismissal of four young and boisterous councilors in favor of "men of greater age and repute." As the Venetian ambassador put it, "the King, resolving to lead a new life, had removed these companions of his excesses."[9]

This reform was further specified in lists of "reminders" for the King. One was entitled "A Remembrance of Such Things as the King's Grace Will Have to Be Done." This list included limits on the King's budget, specific ways he should supervise royal income and expenditures, and procedures for his direct involvement in fostering the welfare and justice of his kingdom.[10] A second list dealt with issues that the King "intended in his own person to debate with his Council and to see reformation done therein." It also enumerated specific matters of defense, government, foreign affairs, and general public welfare.[11]

A third list, called "A Privy Remembrance," is reminiscent of a poem More had written about the lofty calling of a king.[12] In that poem, More had counseled that "he will be safe who so rules his people that they judge none other would promote their interests better." That lofty ideal is restated at the beginning of "A Privy Remembrance," where the King is reminded "to put himself in strength with his most trusty servants in every shire for the surety of his royal person and succession."[13]

Unfortunately, Henry never followed through on these good intentions, although More successfully appealed to his conscience for many years afterwards.

As time went on, More served as Henry's main secretary and came to have "a strategic part to play in the politics of the 1520s."[14] He was also active in judicial matters. From the very beginning of his royal service, he heard many of the cases that were brought before King Henry.

Despite his unusual favor with Henry, More was not spared the pressures and dangers of normal political life. For example, upon joining the King's service, he was appointed to the Privy Council, the head of which was Cardinal Wolsey. At one of the first meetings More attended, Wolsey proposed to acquire yet another lucrative and powerful office. When he "strongly urged" this proposal, it "was meekly followed by all the Dukes, Counts, and other nobles who formed the King's Council. No one dared to contradict or to suggest any objection until More's turn came to speak." More then gave so many powerful arguments against this proposal that the council eventually changed its mind—much to Wolsey's displeasure. Afterwards Wolsey angrily said to him, "Are you not ashamed, Master More, being the lowest of all in place and dignity, to dissent from so many noble and prudent men? You show yourself a stupid and foolish Councilor." More's response was courteous, but bold and unflinching: "Thanks be to God that the King's Majesty has but one fool in his Council."[15]

This early incident may well explain why Wolsey "rather feared [More] than loved him."[16]

In 1520, another early incident threatened More. In fact, it threatened him with the most extreme dangers that public office can bring: political downfall and death. Only two times in his whole adult life was More known to lose his temper, and this was undoubtedly one of them.[17]

He was forty-three at the time. He had been in the King's service for two years, and had just accompanied Henry to solemnize peace with France at the famous Field of Cloth of Gold. Shortly after this peace conference, the French courtier Germanus Brixius publicly attacked him, accusing him of disloyalty to the King. More responded with one of the strongest pieces he ever wrote; it was a counterattack written with all the forcefulness of urgent self-defense.

Actually, this outbreak of hostilities had been eight years in the making. In the war of 1512–1513 between England and France, the English warship *Regent* and the French *Cordelière* blew up and sank while attacking each other. Most members of both crews were killed, along with their captains. Brixius, who was not only a courtier of the French queen but also a fairly accomplished poet, turned this unfortunate event into an epic praising the French and ridiculing the English. To do so, he radically changed the facts.

As an act of patriotism in time of war, More wrote a few epigrams satirizing Brixius; six years later, Erasmus published these poems, along with the rest of More's epigrams. More was wary of having these satirical epigrams included. He suggested that Erasmus "give some thought to the propriety of printing my remarks about Brixius, as some of them are rather caustic—although it might well seem that I had provocation from his insulting comments about my country."[18]

Brixius did indeed take great offense. So great, in fact, that he wrote a retaliatory diatribe, entitled *Antimorus*, in the early part of 1520. This response was not at all motivated by patriotic concern. The war between France and England was now over, and these two countries had just solemnized their peace accord. Rather, Brixius attacked More personally and maliciously, with the intention of destroying his reputation and even his life. More's reply was swift, decisive, and highly effective. So strong was this response, in fact, that some have interpreted it as "unrestrained rhetorical fury" that was both savage and petty.[19]

As he explained, however, Brixius had attacked first, and with the intention of placing him in "dire peril."[20] Brixius not only had published lies, but had "taken secret steps to secure my undoing, so far as it was in his power."[21] More considered these slanders nothing short of "criminal," and he took seriously the advice he was getting from others, that he should protect himself against these calumnious attacks.[22] He explained to Erasmus that his "sole object" in responding to Brixius was self-defense; he was not about to let Brixius destroy him without a fight.[23]

In his "Letter to Brixius," More deploys the full force of his satirical wit. He even addresses Brixius by name—but only because Brixius chose to attack first and in public, with intent to destroy. Though in the end he agreed to withdraw this letter from circulation, More did not do so—good lawyer that he was—until he had a public document that could be used for his defense, if the need should arise again.

Despite such encounters with men like Brixius, or perhaps because of his prudence and effectiveness in dealing with them, More received even greater honors and positions of responsibility.

In 1521 he was knighted and made royal undertreasurer—additional indications of how much his services were valued. By 1522 he was serving as Henry's private secretary; it was in this capacity that he clearly, though discreetly, voiced his disagreement with Henry's plans to wage war against France.[24] In 1523 he was appointed Speaker of the House, and showed his characteristic initiative and courage when he immediately gained freedom of speech for Parliament—a significant "first" in the history of modern government.[25]

In 1524 the political climate changed decisively when England broke its own Treaty of Universal Peace by invading France. More recognized that Henry and Wolsey were wholly intent on war. (It was probably at this time that he gave his famous assessment of the friendship that existed between Henry and himself: "If my head could win [the King] a castle in France, . . . it would not fail to go."[26]) Perhaps because he was known to oppose any such war, he was given a change of duties. Did this happen at More's own request? We do not know. All we know is that in 1525 he was appointed chancellor of the Duchy of Lancaster, a position involving a vast range of work and requiring a vast range of talent. It was also a position that gave him, at last, the latitude to demonstrate his ability to govern.[27] Despite their differences on the question of war, Henry continued to trust More's judgment on practically everything else. This trust was confirmed in 1526, when More was appointed to the royal council's subcommittee of four.[28] These four shared responsibility for the major concerns of the realm, excluding matters of war. A further sign of trust was to come the next year, when the King consulted Sir Thomas for the first time about his intended divorce.

Throughout these years, More worked hard for peace throughout Europe. He was critical of those who placed provincial interests over the genuine common good of Christendom. He was also critical of those who supported nationalistic wars for their own aggrandizement while ignoring countries in need. He lamented, for example, the readiness of Christian peoples and princes to turn their backs on those suffering persecution from the Turks.[29]

More's peace efforts came to fruition in the summer of 1529, when he served as one of England's chief delegates in negotiating the Peace of Cambrai. This treaty, which ended years of war with France, More considered to be one of his greatest accomplishments in life. Some years later, when writing his epitaph, he would mention briefly his service as king's counselor and chancellor. Then he would express, at surprising length, what Cambrai still meant to him:

> He served as the King's ambassador at various times and in various places, last of all at Cambrai. . . . In that place he witnessed, in the capacity of ambassador, to his great joy, the renewal of a peace treaty between the supreme monarchs of Christendom, and the restoration of a long-desired peace to the world. May heaven confirm this peace and make it a lasting one.[30]

Shortly after this peace was confirmed at Cambrai, a peace that offered so much promise to Christendom, More was asked to be Lord Chancellor of England.

At no other time did Henry VIII need good counsel more urgently than he did now. At no other time did Christendom need Henry's leadership more urgently than it did now. Yet More's counsel was soon to be ignored, and Henry was soon to be the first major ruler to divide a Christendom that had been united for hundreds of years.

Chapter Ten

Daring Educator, Artful Parent

IN THE HISTORY OF EDUCATION, Sir Thomas More holds an important place—a distinction that was recognized even in his own day. The education he planned and supervised for his children was, in fact, so successful that his home and school became famous throughout Europe. Actually, his success is quite understandable, considering what he brought to the task.

First of all, he had the rare opportunity to read and reflect upon all that the classical and medieval authors of note had written on the subject—and not only the philosophers, but also the poets and historians and Church Fathers who criticized those philosophers. In this area, as in many others, More showed his genius and integrity by weighing every received opinion and not ascribing complete truth on all topics to any one thinker.

His second advantage was that some of his closest friends were among the most noted educators of Christendom. His spiritual advisor Fr. John Colet studied at Oxford, Florence, and Rome and afterwards dedicated his considerable fortune to building St. Paul's School for boys. Erasmus and Vives, also friends of More's, were classical scholars who wrote a great deal about the proper ways of educating.

From antiquity, More learned his favorite metaphor for education: cultivating the garden of the soul. In this garden must be planted good affections and principles, while "the nettles, briars, and other . . . barren weeds" of pride and deceptive pleasures are carefully and consistently rooted out.[1]

This process, which takes years, aims at fostering in the soul a strong and healthy love for virtue and for truth, not at reinforcing the natural tendency to sensual comfort, excitement, and pleasure. To achieve a strong spiritual love requires that one actively temper the senses while engendering, planting, and watering the spiritual affections "many a time and oft."[2] True virtue, in other words, is not simply a matter of habits, although habits are obviously needed. True virtue is essentially a freely chosen and fervently cultivated love for the highest and most enduring goods, not for the passing pleasures that are often mistaken for them.

More's educational philosophy is most simply and briefly set forth in his famous "Letter to Gonell." William Gonell was the children's teacher. In this letter, More explains that regardless of the subject, Gonell should "esteem most whatever may teach them piety towards God, charity to all, and modesty and Christian humility in themselves."[3] Only by achieving these "real and genuine fruits of learning" would his children come to possess "solid joy."[4]

More goes on to explain that "the whole fruit of their endeavors should consist in the testimony of God and a good conscience. Thus they will be inwardly calm and at peace and neither stirred by praise of flatterers nor stung by the follies of unlearned mockers of learning."[5]

Because the greatest danger to self-possession and clarity of conscience is pride, he warns Gonell not to debase his children's "generous character of mind" by appealing to what is "vain and low."[6] Well aware that the easiest way to motivate any person is by appealing to personal pride, since our fallen condition makes us so susceptible to it, he gives special directives on this point:

> Dear Gonell, the more do I see the difficulty of getting rid of this pest of pride, the more do I see the necessity of getting to work at it from childhood. For I find no other reason why this inescapable evil so clings to our hearts, than that almost as soon as we are born, it is sown in the tender minds of children by their nurses, it is cul-

tivated by their teachers, it is nourished and brought to maturity by their parents; while no one teaches anything, even the good, without bidding them always to expect praise as the recompense and prize of virtue. Thus long accustomed to magnify praise, they strive to please the greater number (that is, the worse) and end by being ashamed to be good. That this plague of vainglory may be banished far from my children, may you, my dear Gonell, and their mother and all their friends sing this song to them, and repeat it, and beat it into their heads, that vainglory is despicable and to be spit upon, and that there is nothing more sublime than the humble modesty so often praised by Christ; and this your prudent charity will so enforce as to teach virtue rather than reprove vice, and make them love good advice instead of hating it.[7]

If More did not appeal to pride to motivate his children, what did he appeal to? This is a difficult question, and nowhere does he offer a simple answer. But the greatest motivating factor he used appears to have been his deep friendship with each of his children. Even when away on business, he kept in close touch, sending letters and poems which encouraged them onward. He also expected letters in return—written first in English and then translated into Latin. The letters to his children are among the most touching of More's writings. In one letter, he writes to his daughters (who have been traveling):

I cannot adequately express, my delightful daughters, how greatly pleased I am by your charming letters and no less by the fact, as I notice, that though you are on the road moving from place to place, you yet abandon none of your habit either of dialectic exercises or of writing themes or composing verse. This fully convinces me that you love me as you ought, since I observe you feel so much concern in my absence that you practice zealously what you know gives me pleasure when I am with you. When I return I shall make you realize that this disposition towards me is as profitable to yourselves as I realize it is pleasurable to me. For believe me, truly there is nothing which refreshes me so much in the midst of this bothersome business as reading what comes from you.[8]

Here More appeals, not to pride, but to the bonds of love.

He also used a playful touch to make work seem like fun. Although he did not sing very well himself, he nonetheless took part in family singing. He made it a special point to see that dinner conversation was a palatable mixture of the serious and the entertaining. This congenial atmosphere made learning fun and virtue attractive. More himself drew attention to this aspect of his family life, as a blessing that ought never to be taken for granted, in a precaution he gave his children:

It is now no great achievement for you children to go to heaven, for everybody gives you good counsel, everybody gives you good example; you see virtue rewarded and vice punished, so that you are carried up to heaven even by the chins. But if you live to see the time when no one will give you good counsel or will give you good example, when you shall see virtue punished and vice rewarded, if you will then stand fast and firmly stick to God upon pain of your life, although you be but half good, God will allow you in as if you were all good.[9]

This precaution would prove all too necessary during the hard times to come.

More even punished in a way designed to engender reflection and good will, not to cause resentment or a will hardened by self-justification. Margaret Giggs, an adopted daughter, often told "how sometimes she would deliberately commit some fault that she might enjoy More's sweet and loving reproof."[10]

The recipient of one such reproof was More's daughter-in-law, Anne. As the story comes down to us, Anne

> often had requested her father-in-law, Sir Thomas, to buy her a necklace set with pearls. He had often put her off with many pretty slights, but at last, for her persistence, he provided her one. Instead of pearls, he had white peas used instead. So when he next came home, his daughter demanded her jewel. "Marry, daughter, I have not forgotten you." So out of his study he sent for a box, and solemnly delivered it to her. When she with great joy looked for her necklace, she found, far from her expectation, a necklace of peas, and so she almost wept for grief. But her father gave her such a good lesson that never after did she have any great desire to wear any new toy.[11]

The final part of this story is that Anne's portrait shows her wearing a pearl necklace, undoubtedly a gift from her wise and generous father-in-law.

More could also punish harshly when the situation called for it. We have only two examples. One involved a young servant who had been actively spreading heresy in More's own household; he had even taught a child there to disrespect the Eucharist. "For amendment of himself and example" to the others, the servant was whipped "like a child" before the whole household.[12]

The second incident involved a village vagrant who had a special love for pranks that embarrassed pious ladies at Mass. He would wait for the Consecration, when all was quiet and people were most absorbed in prayer. Then he would look for a woman bent in prayer, creep up behind her, and throw her dress up over her head. Needless to say, the village folk were not amused; but what was one to do with someone who was obviously a bit mad? More's solution was to have the town constables flog the man until he confessed his fault and "his remembrance was good." Years later, More remarked that he had heard "no harm of him" since.[13]

Another important element of More's influence as an educator was the example he embodied of the lessons he taught. His own behavior gave ready proof that what he proposed to others was indeed important. For example, he himself led the family's night prayers, showing through daily example that his life had a clear purpose and direction. His children also knew that their father prayed more than just at these brief moments before going to bed. They saw him spend long periods in the family chapel and in the "New Building," which he had constructed at some distance from the main house to facilitate his study and meditation. Because he struggled to live up to them himself, More could speak with uncommon authority about all the highest motives: love for family, duty to country, devotion to God.

Hundreds of other details showed his family the power and attractiveness of virtue. He saw to it that theirs was a bright and cheerful home, filled with music, stories, good conversation, a constant flow of friends, hard and meaningful work, care for each other, and care for the poor.

Though they were, by any standard, quite wealthy, the Mores were taught never to consider money their own. This lesson Sir Thomas taught his children by both word and deed. In a writing contest he set up between his daughter Meg and himself, he explained how to use riches properly:

> It is not a sin to have riches, but to love riches. "If riches come to you, set not your heart on them," says Holy Scripture. . . . He who forgets that his goods are the goods of God, and who reckons himself an owner rather than a disposer, takes himself to be rich. And because he reckons these riches to be his own, he casts his love on them and so much is his love set less upon God. For as Holy Scripture says, "Where your treasure is, there is your heart."[14]

This theoretical lesson was proved by More's own practice. For example, he rented a house for the poor and had his children care for it.[15] Then there was the year of famine when More fed a hundred people a day at his home.[16]

In all that he did, More sought to befriend his children and lead them to the divine Teacher within.[17] He befriended them to such an extent that they came to want to do good and to seek God, just to please the father they so greatly loved. In other words, More cultivated virtue in his children by treating them as he saw God treating him.

More's love for his children was evident in all that he did. Yet one of the most charming proofs of it is the poem he composed on horseback while "on a long journey, drenched by a soaking rain." He wrote this poem in Latin; what follows is an excerpt from the prose translation.

> I compose these verses for you in the hope that, although unpolished, they may give you pleasure. From these verses you may gather an indication of your father's feelings for you—how much more than his own eyes he loves you; for the mud, the miserably stormy weather, and the necessity for driving a diminutive horse through deep waters have not been able to distract his thoughts from you or to prevent his proving that, wherever he is, he thinks of you. For instance, when—and it is often—his horse stumbles and threatens to fall, your father is not interrupted in the composition of his verses. Poetry often springs from a heart which has no feeling; these verses a father's love provides—along with a father's natural anxiety. It is not so strange that I love you with my whole heart, for being a father is not a tie which can be ignored. Nature in her wisdom has attached the parent to the child and bound them spiritually together with a Herculean knot. This tie is the source of my consideration of your immature minds, a consideration which causes me to take you often into my arms. This tie is the reason why I regularly fed you cake and gave you ripe apples and fancy pears. This tie is the reason why I used

to dress you in silken garments and why I never could endure to hear you cry. You know, for example, how often I kissed you, how seldom I whipped you. My whip was invariably a peacock's tail. Even this I wielded hesitantly and gently so that sorry welts might not disfigure your tender seats. Brutal and unworthy to be called father is he who does not himself weep at the tears of his child. How other fathers act I do not know, but you know well how gentle and devoted is my manner toward you, for I have always profoundly loved my own children and I have always been an indulgent parent—as every father ought to be.[18]

This tender and lighthearted love poem to his children is indeed moving, but the ending of this opening section is rather unexpected and potentially disturbing. After all, what good parent, aware of the dangers that come with spoiling a child, would preach that every father ought to be indulgent? What about the old adage "Spare the rod, spoil the child"?

This first section must be considered in light of the equally surprising and thought-provoking one that follows. For in the next part, More somewhat downplays the natural love that he has presented so attractively. The second section of the poem presents another kind of bond, one so much more profound than the natural bond of fatherhood that "it seems to me I used not to love you at all." This increased love

is produced by your adult manners, adult despite your tender years; by your instincts, trained in noble principles which must be learned; by your pleasant way of speaking, fashioned for clarity; and by your very careful weighing of every word. These characteristics of yours so strangely tug at my heart, so closely bind me to you, my children, that my being your father (the only reason for many a father's love) is hardly a reason at all for my love of you.

What reason could there be for loving one's children, apart from their being one's own? Virtue. More loved his children with ever greater love as he saw their free growth in virtue. As he concludes his poem, he appeals to their mutual human love as a way of spurring them on to even greater heights of accomplishment:

> Therefore, most dearly beloved children all, continue to endear yourselves to your father, and by those same accomplishments which make me think that I had not loved you before, make me think hereafter (for you can do it) that I do not love you now.

"You can do it!" More tells his children. But "it" refers to the attainment of genuine virtue, a state of life that no overly indulgent parent can promote.

But how can one teach virtue? More had observed and studied many ways. He was familiar, for example, with the way of the Stoics, who stressed the importance of fighting passion until it no longer exerts its influence. This position was best articulated by Seneca and Cicero. Yet, although More borrowed freely from these authors and recommended their writings, he did not choose the Stoic way.

Why? Because he did not think virtue could be founded simply on habit. True, all virtues require habits; but for More, what was of greatest importance was what would motivate and direct those habits. He wanted his children to act from love. Thus, he saw the primary task of education as cultivating a good conscience and noble loves. And in that order of importance—conscience first—because one must constantly use good judgment to discern what is indeed noble and good.

Also necessary for proper education of the soul would be what More called "right imagination and remembrance,"[19] a state of mind born of careful instruction and good conversation.[20] The need for "right imagination" is especially evident when one considers the problem of "remembering" during a time of pressure or temptation. At such a time it can be virtually impossible to stay focused on what is right—unless one has been properly prepared beforehand. Without the help of an imagination previously shaped by deeply treasured conviction, images of pleasure or impulses of passion are almost sure to take over and block out the light of reason.

Good conversation was one of the most common and effective means which More used to cultivate right imagination and good remembrance in the souls of his children. He saw every conversation, no matter how trivial its subject, as an opportunity to cultivate the garden of that child's soul. Not only did these everyday conversations cultivate reflection and self-knowledge, but they also provided the best opportunities for planting and cultivating those precepts and principles which every person needs.

More's ability to speak and play with his children on their own level surprised many of his dignified friends. As one early biographer put it, "Although he was in high office and always busily engaged in affairs of State, yet he came down to the level of his children's studies, joking with them in neat and witty phrases."[21]

Playful irony was the dominant characteristic of More's clever way of engaging the minds and hearts of his children, who often wondered if their father was speaking seriously or in jest. This means of testing and developing judgment and character More learned especially from Socrates and Lucian. It was a means to develop that capacity most necessary for true virtue: a capacity for the type of reflection that eventually matures into contemplation. More understood clearly that all human beings are created to contemplate God. This one purpose of life ordered everything else in his work as a parent and educator.

Other means that he used to develop this capacity for reflection and right remembrance were daily prayer and instruction in the faith. Through these, he helped his children cultivate the habit of considering ordinary events from a supernatural point of view. Whenever, for example, they would complain of some suffering or discomfort, he would merrily remind them that people do not "go to heaven in featherbeds."[22] He also told stories that helped develop in each child a well-formed conscience. The most famous of these, "The Tale of Mother Maud," is a story about a wolf and an ass who go to confession to a fox.[23] It is but one delightful example of how More could explain complex and demanding ideas in an attractive and illuminating manner. The family also read and discussed a great deal together. Family readings often took place before or during dinner, since More made a special point of seeing to it that dinner conversations were a good mixture of the serious and the entertaining. Visitors like Erasmus marveled at how well the children could follow an argument and participate in sustained conversation; they also marveled at the cheerful atmosphere of this large and busy household.

These children never doubted their father's love. Even when away on business, he kept in close touch, sending letters and poems to encourage and amuse them. From these trips he brought gifts both pleasant and profitable. He brought unusual pets, such as the family monkey, or sweets that all could enjoy. He was fond of collecting old coins, both for display and for history lessons. And he brought many other things he knew his family would enjoy—things as diverse as songs they could play and sing together and exotic plants for their family garden. This was not a Stoic approach to cultivating virtue.

In the forming of virtuous dispositions, More also saw an important role for university studies. In disagreement with a young biblical scholar who claimed that the liberal arts are a waste of time, More argued that they are especially helpful in the strengthening and sharpening of one's powers of reason. "Just as the hand," he said, "is [made] the more nimble by the use of some feats; and the legs and feet more swift and sure by custom of going and running; and the whole body the more agile and lusty by some kind of exercise; so is it no doubt, but that reason is by study, labor, and the exercise of logic, philosophy, and other liberal arts corroborated and quickened."[24]

More considered the study of liberal arts to be of great importance. In fact, he attributed his success in law, politics, and international diplomacy to his sound education in the liberal arts. Erasmus agreed, arguing that this education was responsible for More's success in combining "so much real wisdom with such charm of character" that "it would be hard to find anyone who was more truly a man for all seasons."[25] Nonetheless, neither

More nor Erasmus confused learning and intellectual agility with virtue and character. As More put it, the liberal arts can "prepare the soul for virtue."[26] They can quicken the reason; they can form and perfect good judgment; they can clarify the highest principles which "both instruct and inspire the mind in the pursuit of virtue"; they can develop prudence in human affairs. By themselves, however, they cannot produce virtue or strong character.

That More did a great deal of thinking about these issues is particularly evident in the fact that he raised five brilliant daughters (including his adopted daughter and a ward) who would have been denied a liberal arts education by the custom of the times. More considered this education so important that he hired tutors from Oxford and personally supervised not only his son's but also his daughters' education in languages, mathematics, science, history, literature, and philosophy. In doing so, he was criticized by the European literati, Erasmus included, but he soon won them over to his novel educational practices.

More's fundamental principle in education was crystal-clear: "Put virtue in the first place . . . , learning in the second."[27] In this way, as we have seen, he was convinced that his children would grow to be "inwardly calm and at peace and neither stirred by praise of flatterers nor stung by the follies of unlearned mockers of learning."[28] In stating this principle, More was simply reaffirming the commonsense observations of Plato and Aristotle that a person needs stability of character to see the world with objectivity. Since passion and pride cloud the intellect, he realized, the point of a complete education is to help a person achieve the self-mastery needed for reason to reign.

The liberal arts, he said, can foster this self-mastery not only by developing reason, but also by helping people reach "the contemplation of celestial realities through the study of nature."[29] Such contemplation can bring about a profound grasp of first principles. When this depth of understanding is combined with the experience found especially in the study of history, law, and literature, students can "learn prudence in human affairs"[30]—and thus acquire the "one special thing without which all learning is half lame . . . : [a] good mother wit."[31]

More considered a well-trained wit to be one of the greatest helps available in this world. Nevertheless, he saw clearly that it cannot ensure the preservation of virtue. Lucifer, after all, became so enamored with the power and beauty of his brilliant wit that he failed to remain loyal to his first love. Similarly, Adam and Eve became so caught up in the attractive power of their own "fond fantasies" that they neglected to attend to the true demands of life. Such is the drama of freedom, More would say. And the best defense of that freedom is vigilance in virtue, aided by the best mother wit one can fashion.

Chapter Eleven

Spiritual Handbook II:
The Four Last Things

SHORTLY AFTER BECOMING A KNIGHT, a member of the Privy Council, and the King's private secretary, More challenged his oldest daughter to an unusual writing contest. Margaret had married just the year before and was expecting her first child—so what would be an appropriate subject for these two litterateurs at this promising stage of their lives? Surprisingly, Sir Thomas proposed that they each write a vivid account of the four last things: death, judgment, heaven, and hell.[1]

His reason for proposing this topic is suggested in the treatise itself and in the other letters he sent Margaret about this time. In these letters he encourages his daughter to complete her education before the growing duties of her new life as wife and mother make that more difficult.[2] That education was partly literary, partly practical (he urged her to learn medicine), and, as this contest shows, partly spiritual.

More states in the introduction to his own version of *The Four Last Things* that the consideration of this topic "contains more fruitful advice and counsel to the forming and framing of man's manners in virtue and avoiding of sin than many whole and great volumes of the best of old philosophers or any other that ever wrote in secular literature."[3] These four "herbs" make up a medicine of such strength that they could keep the soul from sickness throughout life.

The same themes that were contained in his first spiritual handbook are developed in this second one. However, *The Four Last Things* has greater rhetorical power and uses an imagery that is far more vivid—so vivid, in fact, that it seems explicitly designed to help one recall and focus on the most fundamental ideas.

As he did with his "Twelve Rules of Spiritual Battle," More begins by inviting the reader to consider the relative value of pleasure. Pleasure is his starting point, he says, because "I well perceive the world so set upon the seeking of pleasure that they set by pleasure much more than by profit."[4] Throughout the first part, he tries to show the truth of that Christian paradox whereby "abandoning and refusing carnal pleasure while pursuing labor, travail, penance, and bodily pain will bring with it to a Christian—not only in the world to come, but also in this present life—real sweetness, comfort, pleasure, and gladness."[5]

This paradox recalls a major theme of his first spiritual handbook: that the pleasure of fleshly delight is not a genuine or lasting pleasure; that it is "but a false, counterfeit image of pleasure."[6] To order one's life to such counterfeit images will cause a "grudge and grief of conscience that makes the stomach wamble . . . and vomit."[7] Whoever persists in pursuing such counterfeits will "by a mischievous custom of sin perceive no fault in his evil deed" and will thereby "lose the natural light of reason and the spiritual light of faith."[8]

For health and clear sight, one needs a well-cultivated soul that has come to love the "spiritual pleasure . . . of truth."[9] So long as the soul is "overgrown with the barren weeds of carnal pleasures," it will have "no place for the good corn of spiritual pleasure."[10]

To acquire a healthy soul, one relies on the great doctor, Christ.[11] By following both the example and the instructions of this physician, any soul can achieve a "mastering of outward, fleshly pain with inward, spiritual pleasure."[12]

The whole point is to "keep our minds occupied with good thoughts,"[13] for a "wandering mind" is never associated with "wisdom and good manners."[14] In this context, one can better understand More's claim that "the active study of the four last things, and the deep consideration of them, is the thing that will keep you from sin."[15] This "diligent remembrance" is well worth the effort it takes, for it is sure to flower in "not a false imagination, but a very true contemplation" of God and the world as they exist.[16]

Another point of similarity with the earlier spiritual handbook is the care taken to point out the centrality of pride, "the mischievous mother of all manner of vice."[17] Pride that has been allowed to develop "carries with it a blindness almost incurable."[18] The eyes of the conscience will be dulled unless the "right ointment" has been applied long before such blindness can set in.[19] One powerful ointment More suggests here is the "remembrance and consideration" of death and the peril of hell.[20]

To help in this fight against blinding pride, More offers three images of the human condition.

First he pictures a proud prince who glories in the grand station in life that has been granted to him. "How slight a thing [that] would seem," he says, "to anyone who would often and deeply remember the death that shall shortly take away all this royalty." This proud prince is forgetting that "he shall within a few years . . . have his dainty body turned into stinking carrion, be borne out of his princely palace, laid in the ground, and there left alone, where every lewd lad will be bold to tread on his head."[21] More points out that a "deep consideration of this sudden change, so surely to come and so shortly to come, would withdraw the wind that puffs us up in pride."

A second image compares the world to a stage on which each person is given a part to play. How foolish it would be for some worthless fellow to get puffed up with pride just because he happens to get the part of a lord dressed up in a golden gown. "Would you not laugh at his folly, considering that you are very sure that when the play is done he shall go walking as a knave in his old coat?"[22]

This image, however, More considers "too merry for this matter." "A more earnest image of our condition," one that he deems "a very true figure" of our state, compares life to a prison.[23] (More favored this image throughout his life; it appears in both his earlier and his later works.[24])

> As for escaping, no man can look for [any hope of
> that]. The prison is large and has many prisoners

in it, but the jailor can lose none. He is present in
every place that we can creep into. . . . There is no
remedy, therefore, but as condemned folk and
remediless in this prison of the earth we drag on
for a time, with some bound to a post, some wandering abroad, some in the dungeon, some in the
upper ward, some building themselves bowers
and making palaces in the prison, some weeping,
some laughing, some laboring, some playing,
some singing, some chiding, some fighting. No
man, almost, remembers in what case he stands
until, suddenly, with nothing such looked for,
young, old, poor and rich, merry and sad, prince,
page, pope, and poor-soul priest[25]—now one, now
another, sometimes a great rabble at once, without
order, without respect of age or of estate—all,
stripped naked and shifted out in a sheet, are put
to death in different ways in some corner of the
same prison, are thrown there in a hole, and are
eaten either by worms under the ground or by
crows above. Now come forth, you proud prisoner, for I know . . . all your pride is because you
forget that [this world] is a prison.[26]

Besides these, More uses many other vivid images to reveal
what cannot easily be seen and to dissuade his readers from giving in to the various deceptions spawned from the "cankered
root of pride."[27]

The whole problem in the acquiring of virtue is that the
"mind is more kindled in the feigned figure of its own device"
than in reality itself.[28] Yet how could something so irrational be
true of a rational being? The answer is that, as rational beings,
we are genuinely free—free enough to choose a "false imagination" of our own fabrication over "a very true contemplation" of
what actually exists. To contemplate reality as it is, we must first
have trained ourselves to flee the "vain pleasures of the flesh
that keep out the very pleasures of the soul."[29]

Compared to the first, this second spiritual handbook is
more sensational and negative. While *The Life of John Picus*

emphasizes the love of God, *The Four Last Things* concentrates upon the remembrance of death. Yet to phrase it this way is misleading, because More never finished his treatise on the four last things. He did not finish even the first of its four parts. Had this treatise been finished, More's treatment of heaven would, no doubt, have reiterated the themes of his youth—themes that were developed again toward the end of his life. For even in this unfinished work, More states clearly that the whole purpose of meditating on the four last things is to enhance "the love of God and hope of heaven, and inward liking . . . of good and virtuous business."[30]

Chapter Twelve

Reformation over Revolution:
Covering the Nakedness of Noah

THOMAS MORE AND ERASMUS were reformers long before Luther came on the scene. For many years they actively promoted the "renaissance of good letters," a program of reform founded upon the rebirth of the ancient ideal of virtue. As they saw it, education in virtue—moral, civic, religious, and intellectual—was the best means for achieving genuine reform while maintaining peace and international unity.

Fundamental to this renaissance was the understanding that only when virtue reigns can reason reign, and that only when reason reigns can some measure of justice and peace be realized. When, therefore, Luther emphasized the corruption of reason, denied the possibility of achieving virtue, rejected free will, and taught that his elect had a nonrational access to truth, More and Erasmus strongly opposed these revolutionary views as both untrue and destructive. These revolutionary dogmas, they were convinced, could only lead to war and bloodshed.

From their positions as leading intellectuals of their day, More and Erasmus came to see Luther's program as nothing less than a clarion call to arms. Luther denounced and dehumanized his opponents by calling them "papists," monsters, murderers, and the vilest of dregs.[1] At the same time, he praised those who were "utterly destroying the abominations and scandals of the Roman pestilence."[2] Such fighting words could hardly be interpreted as a dispassionate attempt to heal a church that sorely needed pastoral attention. Erasmus complained that Luther had "shattered almost the whole world" with his angry attacks.[3] More agreed, saying to the Lutheran leaders of war, "You hurled a burning torch on all of Germany. You lit the wildfire that is now consuming the world."[4]

As More explained, this burning torch often took the form of wanton slander.[5] He was well aware of the need for reform in the Catholic Church, but he strongly opposed the idea that it was totally corrupt and should therefore be destroyed. For well over a thousand years, the Catholic Church had been recognized as a legitimate institution, enjoying full protection of the law. To attack it as viciously as Luther did was therefore a civil offense and a direct danger to peace and international unity.

Behind these incendiary attacks was Luther's angry rejection of all previously established authority, in favor of his own.[6] To defend his position, Luther had to assume that all the early Church Fathers and all the other believers of the previous fifteen hundred years had never received the true faith.[7] In all that time, was Luther the first to gain access to it? What, More asked, had become of Christ's promise that the gates of hell would not prevail against his church?[8] Why should anyone accept Luther's private faith over the consensus that had been maintained throughout a unified international church since the time of Christ, a period of some fifteen hundred years? In challenging Luther's exalted claims, More pointed out that when Christ came, he performed many miracles to establish his claims. What miracles had Luther performed to prove his authority?[9] If he could point to no proof, why should any reasonable person believe him?

Along with Erasmus, More warned against the effects of Luther's "abolishing completely the authority of public agreement."[10] Luther's defense of his own private fancy "against the judgment of all the holy Fathers [and] against the universal judgment of the whole Church" could only serve to "drag into doubt the meaning of the sacred writings." Such a disregard for authority could not fail "to stir up a tumult from the heedless disagreement of private individuals."[11]

One source of public agreement which came under particular attack was law, both ecclesiastical and civil. Luther was convinced that the Roman Church had set up its own laws in opposition to the spirit and teaching of the gospels.[12] In his fervor, he made extravagant claims that he would later have to modify. He insisted, for example, that "neither pope, nor bishop, nor any individual has the right to impose a single syllable on a Christian person, unless this is done by the latter's consent."[13] Any such imposition would constitute tyranny.

The lawyer in More was quick to draw out the absurdity of this position. "Happy, therefore," he retorted, "are thieves and murderers, who will never be so insane as to agree to a law according to which they will pay penalties. Indeed, this farsighted father does not see that according to this reasoning, should everyone unanimously agree, yet the law can have force only until a new citizen is born or someone else is enrolled as a citizen."[14]

More went on to show the extreme political danger of Luther's position. Without the guidance of good law, he pointed out, a country "would rush forth into every kind of crime."[15] Indeed, if Luther's teaching about law were to be widely accepted, it would result in "the utter and inescapable destruction of all peoples."[16]

Closely associated with this complete disregard for law was Luther's position that the believing Christian "cannot lose his salvation by any sins, however great."[17] As More saw it, this teaching served to "invite the whole world to security in sinning."[18] It would "add spurs to those who rush toward all the worst actions" by "promising them impunity through faith alone . . . for the worst crimes."[19] It would also "destroy the possibility of all human endeavor and all attempts at virtue."[20] By "raging against good works," Luther would only "lure people to vice and unteach virtue."[21]

All the major leaders of Christendom shared More's concern about the effects of such ideas within their countries. In England, Henry VIII personally challenged Luther's fighting words by taking the unprecedented step of writing his own book in response. Few monarchs in history have written books on any subject, let alone one that deals with particular points of theology. But in July 1521, with some help from More, Henry VIII published *On the Seven Sacraments* in response to Luther's *The Babylonian Captivity of the Church*. In this reply, Henry argued that Luther should have acted like Noah's good sons, who respectfully cared for their drunken father. Instead, he acted like the son who pointed out his father's faults publicly and scorned the old man in his nakedness. Whether this comparison was Henry's idea or More's, we do not know. But More did use this analogy several times in his own writings.[22]

The story of Noah and his sons is recorded in Genesis. There we read that during the first harvest after the flood, Noah became drunk on the new wine, presumably because of its unusual and unexpected strength. As Noah lay naked in his tent, Ham called in his brothers to see their father's pitiful state. Out of love and respect for their father, however, Shem and Japheth "took a robe and, laying it upon their shoulders, went backward and covered their father's nakedness" (Gn 9:23). When Noah awoke, he blessed Shem and Japheth and their descendants, but cursed Ham's descendants with being the "meanest of slaves."

Applying this story to Luther, Henry wrote:

> If Luther had been an honest man and a zealous Christian, he would not have preferred his own private glory before the public good of all others. Nor would he have desired to have the credit of a scorner among the wicked, laughing at the nakedness of his sleeping father, uncovering and pointing with his finger. Instead, he would have covered his father's nakedness and would have privately advised him, following the example of St. Paul, who commands us not to deride or reproach our superiors, but to exhort them. If Luther had done this, I have no doubt that the holy Pope (well known to all men for his goodness), being awakened, would have blessed his son and given him thanks for his piety, and would not have cursed him in his anger.[23]

Luther did not respond kindly to such criticism. In fact, his reply (*Against Henry*) was so vulgar and strident that it was entirely inappropriate for a king to give it any kind of response. King Henry did, nevertheless, command the best writer of his court to compose an answer, and to use the full force of his wit in doing so.

By using the techniques of classical comedy, especially Juvenalian satire, More sought to ridicule Luther's presumptuous claims and to reveal their absurdity. In a manner consistent with the renaissance of good letters which he promoted, More chose to counter Luther first and foremost by relying on the power of the pen instead of the weapons of war. He was, however, well aware that Luther himself was intent on war and posed the gravest of dangers to church and state and to the very existence of Christendom itself. Not since the time of Cicero had a government official of such preeminence used so extensively his own pen as the principal means of protecting justice. Like Cicero, More was a lawyer and rhetorician, gifted with genius and deep patriotism, who wrote extensively in defense of what he held most dear. Before he finished, More would write nearly a million words in opposition to those who were attempting to destroy the traditions and institutions which supported a united Christendom.

More's first response to these violent attacks on his church and his king was published in 1523. His *Response to Luther* was a satirical tour de force which Erasmus compared to Juvenal because it succeeded so admirably in "[giving] Luther the finger."[24] The "imperial" More was not one to speak timidly.[25]

The original title of More's *Response to Luther* gives a good indication of his overall intent in writing this book. It runs as follows:

The choice, learned, witty, pious work of
the most learned William Ross
in which he very admirably exposes and refutes
the frantic calumnies
with which the most foul buffoon, Luther,
attacks the invincible king of England and France,
Henry, the eighth of that name,
the defender of the faith,
renowned no less for his learning
than for his royal power.[26]

The persona who speaks throughout the book is this "William Ross," an English lawyer. Ross is blunt, earthy, and thoroughly indignant at Luther's irresponsible attacks upon his king and his church. As a lawyer, he is also keenly aware that arguments alone will not persuade a jury. Therefore, right from the beginning, he lets everyone know that he intends to make full use of his learned wit to expose and refute the "most foul" buffoonery of Luther's "frantic calumnies."

It is an undisputed fact that Luther did use extremely foul language in denouncing his opponents. This must be kept in mind by anyone who reads this book, which is the most shockingly vulgar of More's writings.

One sample of Luther's self-righteous and contemptuous rhetoric against King Henry suffices to show what More faced. Luther wrote:

> [King Henry] would have to be forgiven if humanly he erred. Now, since he knowingly and consciously fabricates lies against the majesty of my king in heaven, this damnable rottenness and worm, I will have the right, on behalf of my king, to bespatter his English majesty with muck and shit and to trample underfoot that crown of his which blasphemes against Christ.[27]

In response to such disrespect for his king, Ross gradually unleashes the full power of his wit in loyal defense. He begins calmly enough, using an ironic address imitating the Roman comedian and satirist Terence: "Come, do not rage so violently, good father." But politeness soon gives way to strong rebuke, and strong rebuke to the same kind of vulgarity Luther himself employed.[28] As More explained, since he had been ordered to "clean out the dungy writings of Luther like the Augean stable," he could not afford to be afraid to throw around what the animals had left.[29] Besides, since so many people were finding their "sole pleasure" in Luther's abusive language,[30] More judged that his persona could respond effectively only by answering in kind.[31]

Throughout, Ross does what the title of this work indicates: he tries to expose Luther as a buffoon unworthy of serious consideration. He repeatedly expresses his amazement that Luther could possibly have expected clear-sighted Englishmen to take the word of "a single buffoon" over "so many holy Fathers, the custom of so many centuries, and the public faith of the whole Church."[32]

Ross points to Luther's refusal to argue, charging him with being "quick to rail and mock"[33]—even to the point of "mad brawling."[34] He considers this hotheadedness so characteristic of Luther that he calls him Tosspot,[35] and also Cerberus (with reference to Virgil's three-headed dog from hell, which barks furiously at anyone it sees entering its domain).[36]

Responding to such an opponent posed enormous rhetorical and ethical difficulties to More. How, for example, could one argue effectively against a person who refused to face issues on the "level field" of reason?[37] Luther's popular appeal arose from his talent in stirring up passions (especially anger), not from the strength of his scholarship.

Although More refrained from using what he considered unethical means of rhetoric, he wrote with all the legitimate wit and force that he judged necessary to protect the simple and the innocent against being deceived. As he later wrote to Erasmus, all his efforts were "directed toward the protection of those who do not deliberately desert the truth, but are seduced by the enticements of clever fellows."[38]

Not wishing to respond to Luther's incendiary rhetoric with more of the same, he chose ridicule and satire instead—classic techniques of comedy designed to stir the mind, not the passions. As a man of law and literature, More understood the destructive character of anger. He quite agreed with Homer's observation that anger can cloud the reason and become intoxicating with its honeyed taste.[39]

More did not rely solely on ridicule and satire, however; he also made a direct appeal to the common sense of his hearty fellow Englishmen. As the title of his book indicates, his intent was not simply to ridicule Luther's absurd and presumptuous railings; it was more basically to confront and refute Luther's accusations. For this express purpose, More designed a certain style of refutation, one which has received more criticism for the

tedious length of its argumentation than for the biting and occasionally vulgar nature of its satire.

Yet to call the arguments of a highly successful lawyer
"tedious" is either naive or disingenuous. In all of his polemics,
More wrote with the mind of a well-trained lawyer, and he consciously sought to wage the battles of reform on the "level
plain" of reason.[40] Only in this way, he was convinced, could a
satisfactory and lasting solution be achieved. Unless reason pre-
vailed before the public tribunal, "the mad rabble of troublemakers" would triumph in times of unrest, even though there
was a "greater number of good and peace-loving citizens."[41]

Because such troublemakers were sure to respond to
Luther's call for "liberty and license"—an invitation supposedly
coming from Scripture itself[42]—More predicted that widespread
violence was sure to follow.[43] This prediction came true very
shortly afterwards. First came the Peasants' Revolt in Germany
in 1525, which ended in the slaughter of some seventy thousand
peasants, common folk who had taken Luther's revolutionary
ideas to heart. Then came the shameful sack of Rome in 1527,
when Lutheran soldiers were finally able to seek savage revenge
upon those "monsters" and "vile dregs," the "papists."

Chapter Thirteen

Wearing the Chain of Office

IN HOLBEIN'S FAMOUS PORTRAIT, Sir Thomas More is wearing the striking chain of office commonly referred to as the SS collar.[1] In time, this collar became part of the standard dress of England's chief justices. In More's day, however, it was an insignia of public service reserved for knights and nobility.[2] This collar of gold may well have been given to More when King Henry knighted him in 1521.

We know that More valued this badge of service. Even when he was taken to the Tower in 1534, he continued "wearing, as he commonly did, [this] chain of gold about his neck." The knight who was his escort "advised him to send home his chain to his wife, or to some of his children," but More refused. "Nay, sir," he said, "that I will not, for if I were taken in the field by my enemies, I would they should somewhat fare the better by me."[3] What he actually meant by this statement would be hard to determine exactly, given his notorious use of irony and understatement. Nevertheless, his clear reference to battle shows his determination not to proceed without all of the means and props of authority that were at his disposal.

What did the S's of this chain signify for More?[4] Though there is no clear answer, the best clue appears in *Utopia*. In book one of that work, the major debate revolves upon the value of *servitus*. Raphael scorns public service because he sees it as a form of servitude; in striking contrast, the character Morus argues that *servitus* is the duty of every good person.

Throughout his life, More felt the weight of his public duties. Just as he wore a hair shirt to remind himself of Christ's sufferings, so he may have worn a chain heavier and more splendid than most to remind himself of the service he should give in that position of public trust.

More showed most fully his capacity for service in public office when he was chancellor of the Duchy of Lancaster, from 1525 to 1529. During this time he wore the chain depicted in Holbein's portrait of 1527. He would continue to wear it both during and after his time as Lord Chancellor of England.

As chancellor of the Duchy of Lancaster, he assumed all the duties of a political ruler. Since Lancaster was one of the largest and most important of the King's extensive property holdings, this position gave More an opportunity to exercise a full range of administrative and judicial duties. He "assumed full responsibility for the Duchy lands and finances." In addition, he was given "a heavy workload as an equity judge in the Duchy court at Westminster."[5]

While at Westminster, More also continued to serve as part of the King's inner circle of four, at least two of whom were to be in "continual attendance" to King Henry each day.[6] Apart from these burdensome counseling duties, governing the Duchy of Lancaster was a demanding job in and of itself. Among other things, More supervised the interests of some forty thousand people, nominated judges and sheriffs, and appointed individuals to lesser offices. The records that exist make it clear that he took an active role in the wide-ranging business of Lancaster. From these records, Margaret Hastings sketches a good picture of a typical day in his life at this time:

> "Master More," for example, receives bond from sureties for a defendant's future appearance. More becomes impatient with the farmer of a mill for not making repairs which he had undertaken to make, and calls "hastily for the bond," presumably to collect the penalty due the king for non-fulfillment. The sergeant-at-arms appears in the court to answer an executor demanding the arrearages of the king's rent. He writes hasty

marginal notes on the memorandum for a decree
in an enclosure case. "Master Chancellor himself"
examines witnesses in an important case. He
delivers "by his own hands into this court in the
Duchy Chamber at Westminster three books of
patents sealed with the Duchy seal belonging to
my Lord Marques concerning the honor of
Leicester. . . ."[7]

Although business and administrative matters must have
taken up a considerable amount of his time, the records that
survive indicate that the greatest part of More's work was
judicial. We have records of over three hundred cases from
his court, covering an immense variety of actions. Hastings
tells us:

> Of these, ninety-seven have to do with right in
> land or attached to land. . . . Sixty-five have to do
> with violence in the country-side. . . . Twenty-two
> complaints are of interruption of rights of com-
> mon. Twenty-one are presented by royal officers or
> farmers that defendants have refused to pay
> monies due or have rescued animals taken in dis-
> traint. Seventeen are . . . complaints against royal
> bailiffs and other officers for monies levied or
> beasts taken illegally. Fifteen have to do with the
> killing of the king's deer or poaching in waters
> held by the king's farmers. Three especially inter-
> esting cases have to do with mining rights. . . . Two
> are prosecutions of jurors for perjury; one involves
> treasure-trove, and so on.[8]

As in his city court in London, More's reputation as an honest and hard-working judge in Lancaster made him well loved
by those he served. Although no one knows exactly when or
where it originated, this popular rhyme is a testimony to Judge
More's reputation for conscientious public service:

> When More sometime had Chancellor been,
> No more suits did remain.
> The like will never more be seen
> Till More be there again.[9]

All in all, people agreed that More was "a hardworking administrator, a peacemaker more concerned to get at the sources of violence in the countryside than to inflict harsh penalties, a protector of the weak against the strong, and an astute lawyer who could cut through the mass of detail to the heart of the matter in hand."[10]

Chapter Fourteen

Chelsea: A Home of International Fame

MORE'S FAMILY AND HOME are well known, in part because of the noted painter Hans Holbein. By Christmas 1526, this German master was in England, thanks to the generosity of his patron, Sir Thomas More. Holbein stayed with More's family on and off until the beginning of 1528, and so he came to know them quite well. Under Sir Thomas's direction, he composed a family sketch that has become quite noteworthy in the history of art. This intriguing picture merits study and long reflection because in it More wished to capture what he considered most essential in the life of his family.

Revolutionary in its informal character,[1] this family sketch is the "first example of an intimate group [setting]" of a nonceremonial kind in northern Europe.[2] It shows the family in action. Books are scattered on the floor. The family monkey is crawling up Lady Alice's dress. Some family members are talking at ease; others are looking off in the distance at objects we cannot see. The family home is large and well suited for entertainment. The fine woodwork and wall hangings in the background, a lattice window at the right, and freshly cut flowers on ornate cupboards indicate the good taste of this lordly manor. The ready availability of pewter trays and pitchers suggests that hospitality is frequently offered, and in a refined manner. The clock in the middle is a new invention of the Renaissance. To its right is a musical instrument, ready at hand for use in this household that so loved music.

For a Renaissance sketch, this one is highly unusual in that no definite focal point emerges. Perhaps this was meant to reflect the initial appearance of most busy families. Yet this apparent lack of focus serves a directly positive function as well: it engages the viewer's curiosity and active participation. Anyone who seriously studies this sketch must ask, What is it that unifies this work of art? What precise moment of the family's life has Holbein captured?

Our attention goes first to the many people in the foreground. But what unifies this diverse group? All are dressed in beautiful formal attire. Towards the middle is Sir Thomas, wearing his gold chain of office. The candle on the right tells us that it is evening, and it leads us to ask why the whole family is so well dressed at such a late hour. And why, in conjunction with all this formal attire, do we see books strewn on the floor and a monkey crawling up Lady Alice's elegant dress? This mixture of formal and informal elements is enchanting, but puzzling.

Also puzzling is the activity of this family. Sir Thomas and daughter Cecily are looking in the same direction, toward the right, at something outside the picture. What has attracted their attention? Cecily is holding a rosary, and Lady Alice is kneeling, with eyes focused on an open book, so it would appear that they are about to begin their evening prayers. But what are the others doing, and what has just occurred? Margaret is staring off in the distance, apparently lost in thought. Elizabeth, with a book under one arm, also seems lost in thought. Although she is now standing at the far left, she has apparently been sitting with her two sisters, and most of the books are to the right of her empty bench. Margaret Giggs, the adopted daughter we mentioned earlier, is hovering over old Sir John and pointing out something in a book, though he is showing no interest. Anne, a ward entrusted to More, is in the background, looking somewhat timidly at the older ones in front. Young John seems ready for the family prayers—unless the book he is reading has to do with the discussion that has just taken place. Standing next to him is Henry Patenson, the family fool. His presence makes it clear that bookish activities have not comprised the whole of the evening. Sir Thomas is the picture of serenity in the midst of this busy scene, as is Lady Alice. Positioned separately, these two appear as the strong pillars of their home.

The picture's main puzzle still remains: what has been going on that would call for the entire household to be dressed in their finest and for More to be wearing his chain of office at this late hour? It was surely more than one of their regular family discussions and readings. It also had to be more than an ordinary visit with friends. Could it have been a philosophic disputation held by More's daughters for benefit of the King?[3] We know that at least one such discussion took place about this time.[4] We also know that Henry enjoyed visiting More, often unexpectedly, at his home.

Whatever the answer, however, the sketch succeeds in drawing us into the happy, serene, engaging atmosphere of the More family at Chelsea. More worked hard to create this attractive atmosphere in his home. He carefully supervised his children's education;[5] he passed on his own love for music;[6] he collected interesting animals and artifacts on his many trips.[7] He knew how to make learning fun and virtue attractive.

Indeed, More made the move to Chelsea for the sake of protecting and fostering his family's life. Why else would a city boy move to a farm? He moved there in 1524, when his court duties became more demanding and his children began to have their own families. By 1532 he already had eleven grandchildren, and he wanted them all to be together.

He also sought to promote in his family "the desire of heavenly things."[8] Besides his well-known reminder that one cannot expect to get to heaven in a featherbed, he used many other memorable examples from everyday life. In teaching them how to resist the devil, for instance, he compared Satan's tactics to those of the family monkey! Just as the monkey, he said, "will be busy and bold to do shrewd turns" when no one is looking, and yet will jump back when caught, so the devil acts. When the devil finds someone "idle, slothful, and without resistance ready to receive his temptations," he will try anything to achieve his purpose. But if the devil finds a person diligently resisting his temptations, he soon jumps away. More also advised his children to mock the devil. This tactic, he pointed out, is effective because the devil, being full of pride, "cannot abide to be mocked."[9]

Later, in his final days at Chelsea, More devised ingenious ways to prepare his family for the great suffering that his imprisonment and execution would cause them. As he used to say, "troubles foreseen hurt less."[10] One of his early biographers explains how More went about this:

> Sometime before his trouble, More would talk with his wife and children of the joys of heaven and the pains of hell, of the lives of the holy martyrs, of their grievous martyrdoms, of their marvelous patience, of their passions and deaths that they suffered rather than offend God; and what a happy and blessed thing it was for the love of God to suffer loss of goods, imprisonment, loss of lands and life also. He would further say to them that, upon his faith, if he might perceive his wife and children encourage him to die in a good cause, it would so comfort him that, for very joy, it would make him merrily run to death.[11] He showed them beforehand what trouble might befall him.[12]

One of the first of these lessons occurred shortly after More's resignation. To prepare the family for the hard times ahead, he called them all together and, looking back over the whole of his life, said to them:

> I have been brought up at Oxford, at an inn of chancery, at Lincoln's Inn, and also in the King's Court . . . from the lowest degree to the highest. Yet I have now little more than one hundred pounds a year. So now, if we are to continue together, we must be content to become contributaries together. But by my counsel it shall not be best for us to fall to the lowest fare first.

By advising that they descend gradually to the level of mere subsistence, More showed his usual prudence in dealing with human nature. Yet he went on to prepare them for even worse possibilities, to show them that they could still be happy and at peace. What, he asked, would they do if—despite the best of their collective efforts—they were unable to sustain themselves even at the level of mere subsistence? His answer reflected his usual good cheer. "Then," he said, "we may yet, with bags and wallets, go abegging together, and hoping that for pity some good folk will give us of their charity . . . and so [we can] still keep company and be merry together."[13] (An easy way out of this poverty was offered to More, but he refused to consider it. In recognition of his prodigious efforts to defend the Church, the English bishops collected for him the enormous sum of four to five thousand pounds. More thanked them graciously, but refused to accept any of this money.[14])

In his determination to prepare his family for the worst, More played what some have criticized as a cruel trick. As Stapleton learned from the family, More "hired one of the King's officers to come to his house when all the family was at table, to knock suddenly at the door, to come in, and to cite him in the King's name to appear next day before the royal commissioners." The result was not surprising. "All," says Stapleton, "were thrown into confusion by the unexpected message, but while some wept and lamented, others showed a brave resignation." After this little drama was over, More praised those who had demonstrated bravery, and encouraged the others to accept adversity better.[15] Such lessons proved so successful that when the time of arrest actually came, everyone was prepared.[16] These lessons also permanently changed the children's attitude towards adversity.[17]

Chelsea was the kind of manor that any royal dignitary needed for entertaining friends and foreign visitors properly. The location for this family home was well chosen. It was close enough to London, yet not too close. As Heywood tells us, "On one side stood the noble city of London; on the other, the beautiful Thames with green gardens and wooded hills all around."[18] It was also very close to Westminster, the place where More carried on most of his judicial duties. Because both London and Westminster were easily accessible by boat, he was able to work en route, as his eight official watermen rowed him to his various destinations. This arrangement undoubtedly gave him more privacy and more time with the family than he had when living in London.

The house itself was spacious rather than magnificent. One can tell from its floor plans alone that it was large enough to accommodate the families of his four children, and friends as well.

Despite the spaciousness of the house, however, More soon found it necessary to construct the "New Building," in a corner of his property that was fairly distant from his busy home. This quiet retreat housed his private chapel, library, and gallery. There he retired to study and pray and write—sometimes for the whole day.[19]

In 1528 he retired to the New Building to pray with special fervor for the recovery of his oldest daughter. The "sweating sickness" had become epidemic; Margaret had fallen deathly ill with it, and the doctors had given up hope. More went to his New Building and "there in his chapel, upon his knees, with tears most devoutly" begged God in his goodness and power to grant her health "if it [was] His blessed will." As he prayed, it "came into his mind that an enema should be the only way to help her." When he suggested this to the physicians, they marveled that they had not thought of it themselves. After they administered it, Margaret began to improve and, "contrary to all expectation," was eventually restored to perfect health.[20]

More also prayed with special fervor when his son-in-law became "a marvelous zealous Protestant";[21] zealous enough, in fact, to have developed a special hatred for his devout father-in-law.[22] After long discussions with young Roper, More "privately talked in his garden with his daughter Margaret." He said, "Meg, I have borne a long time with your husband; I have reasoned and argued with him in those points of religion, and still given to him my poor fatherly counsel, but I perceive that none of this is able to call him home. Therefore, Meg, I will no longer argue and dispute with him, but will clean give him over, and get me for a while to God and pray for him."[23]

Shortly afterwards, Roper returned to the Catholic faith, never to abandon it again.

More quickly made himself at home in the village of Chelsea and its surrounding area. Never one to put on airs, he "very often . . . invited his poorer neighbors to his table."[24] Before becoming Lord Chancellor, he often personally visited the poor, "helping them not with small gifts, but . . . as their need required." When his position made this impossible to continue, he sent "some of his household who would dispense his gifts faithfully to needy families, and especially to the sick and the aged." Eventually, as we have seen, he rented a building to care for these villagers, "providing for them at his own expense" and entrusting their care to his own children.[25]

More also sang in the parish choir. We know this from Roper, who tells us that the Duke of Norfolk visited one Sunday and was astonished that the Lord Chancellor would stoop to act like a mere parish clerk.[26] Little did he realize that More participated in other lowly activities as well. Besides serving Mass, he took part in long and tiring parish processions like anyone else—on foot. Even as Lord Chancellor, he refused to ride his horse in these processions. "I will not," he explained, "follow my Lord on horseback, Who goes on foot."[27]

More's most famous guest at Chelsea was King Henry. Because he loved More's company, the King would "suddenly sometimes come home to his house at Chelsea to be merry with him." On one of these unexpected visits, Henry had dinner with the family and then afterwards, in one of More's "fair gardens," "walked with him for the space of an hour, holding his arm around his neck." This incident prompted Roper to congratulate his father-in-law on the extraordinary favor he enjoyed with the King. Roper had never seen Henry treat anyone this way, not even Cardinal Wolsey. More then gave his son-in-law a lesson in realism and humility that has become famous. "Son Roper," he said, "I may tell you that I have no cause to be proud because of this; for if my head could win him a castle in France, . . . it should not fail to go."[28]

During these golden days at Chelsea, Sir Thomas never let himself forget the dark realities of history. Another memorable conversation, again between him and his son-in-law, reveals the depths of his perception. This conversation also took place in those golden days before Henry became obsessed with his divorce. It began with Roper's praising "the happy state of this realm," blessed with "so Catholic a prince that no heretic dare show his face"; blessed also with "so virtuous and learned a clergy, so grave and sound a nobility, and so loving and obedient subjects, all in one faith agreeing together."[29]

Presented with this gilded vision, More surprised Roper by

not joining in with his triumphal condemnation of heretics. He responded, instead, with a sobering prophecy. "Son Roper," he said, "I pray God that some of us—as high as we seem to sit upon the mountains, treading heretics under our feet like ants—do not live to see the day when we would gladly wish to be in league with them, letting them have their churches quietly to themselves so that they would be content to let us have ours quietly to ourselves."[30]

Roper gave Sir Thomas many arguments "why he had no cause" to take such a dark view of the future. Offering no explanation, More simply replied, "Well, I pray to God, son Roper, that some of us do not live till that day." Angrily, Roper shot back that such a view was "very desperately spoken." Roper never forgot More's response. Ever the thought-provoking diplomat, More merrily said: "Well, well, son Roper, it shall not be so, it shall not be so [because I say so]."[31]

More's greatest help in running Chelsea was the capable executor of this thirty-four-acre farm, Lady Alice. How much he trusted her judgment and skill in management is well illustrated by an event that occurred near the beginning of September 1529.

The harvest that year was the first good one in quite some time. In fact, such a famine had developed that More had fed one hundred people a day, at his home, during the winter of 1528.[32] Food had become so scarce and, therefore, theft so prevalent that the government had resorted to punishment by hanging.

Just as this most welcome harvest was completed and all of More's barns were full, a fire broke out, caused "by the negligence of one of his neighbors' carts."[33] The result was the destruction of all of More's barns, part of his house, and several of the neighbors' barns as well.

Lady Alice immediately sent son-in-law Giles Heron to inform her husband. Sir Thomas was at court, attending the King. While Giles stood by, More wrote a quick response. Given the spontaneous, unpremeditated character of its composition, this letter is of special value. Written just seven weeks before he would become Lord Chancellor of England, it reveals More's true mind and character. Few could have written such a letter, having just suffered such crippling losses. More begins the letter by sympathizing with Alice. But then he points out that, God having allowed this to happen, "we must and are bound not only to be content but also to be glad [of His will]." After all, it was God who "sent us all that we have lost and since He has by such a chance taken it away again, His pleasure be fulfilled."[34] What comes next in the letter must have been quite difficult for the practical-minded Alice to accept. "Let us," he says, "heartily thank [God] as well for adversity as for prosperity, and perhaps we have more cause to thank Him for our loss than for our gain, for His wisdom sees better what is good for us than we do ourselves."

Proceeding along this line of reasoning, he then makes a request: "Therefore I pray you be of good cheer and take all the household with you to church and there thank God both for what He has given us and for what He has taken from us and for what He has left us—which, if it pleases Him, He can increase when He will; and if it pleases Him to leave us yet less, so let it be at His pleasure."[35]

More next asks that Alice find out what their neighbors lost and assure them that he will compensate them for it. If it meant that any "poor neighbor of mine" would bear a loss because of something that "happened in my house," he writes, "I would not leave myself a spoon."

As for the many practical details following upon this loss, More leaves those to his capable and trusted wife. He asks that she work out, for example, the best course of action to get the corn they will need for consumption in the winter and for seeding in the spring. Since the loss is so great, he realizes, they may not be able to keep the land at all. He asks Alice, in the event that they have to sell it, not to discharge any of their workers without giving them proper provisions or without finding another place for them to go.[36]

Assuring Alice that he will come home as soon as he can, Sir Thomas finishes his letter by sending his good wishes to the children and signing off, "Your loving husband."

Chapter Fifteen

The Power of Artful Conversation I:
A Dialogue of Sir Thomas More, Knight

BY 1528, INTEREST IN LUTHER was spreading rapidly in London. To counter his influence, the bishop of London asked Thomas More to use his wit and wisdom to defend the Catholic Church—in English. At that time, most scholars and literary notables were still writing in Latin. Except for Chaucer's work, there were as yet few masterpieces in the English tongue.

As we noted earlier, More had worked extensively to develop his fluency in both Latin and English. Most of what he wrote, however, was in Latin. Granted, some of his early poems were in English, and he had written an English version of *The History of King Richard III*, but that is basically all the English that we have from his pen up to 1529. Now, however, at the request of a friend, More undertook the enormous labor of writing ten major English works. He wrote them all within five years—three of those years being already the busiest of his life. The effort was so enormous that it eventually broke his health, though never his spirit.[1] His days already filled with the pressures of his professional life, he would work on this in the early hours of the morning, bent over a dimly lit writing table.

In 1529, More published his first English defense. For it he chose the genre that appeals most directly to reason, the Socratic dialogue. Although he entitled it *A Dialogue of Sir Thomas More, Knight*, it is now, unfortunately, most commonly known as *A Dialogue Concerning Heresies*.[2] But More himself did not use the word "heresy," even in the long version of his title:

Sir Thomas More's Coat of Arms
(Argent a Chevron engrailed between
three Moorcocks Sable).

Thomas More by Hans Holbein. © The Frick Collection, New York.

Sir Thomas More in 1527, at age 50, while chancellor of the
Duchy of Lancaster.

Tho: Moor L'Chancelour

Holbein took unusual care in composing this nearly life-size study for the family portrait. It is the only known instance in which Holbein pricked a drawing for transfer (these markings are especially noticeable around the face and neck).

◄ *Thomas More at the Opening of Parliament, 1523.*
Ready to give his plea for freedom of speech, Thomas More is standing among the Commons, at the bottom of this engraving. He faces Henry VIII, who is enthroned in regal magnificence. To Henry's right are seated Archbishops Wolsey and Warham; Bishop Tunstall is standing behind them, delivering his oration. In front of the King stand three earls holding cap of maintenance, baton, and sword. To the left of the King are two counselors and the Garter King of Arms, who stands in front of a group of the peers' eldest sons. The lords are seated on benches along the side, to the King's left; opposite them are the bishops and abbots. The judges (including Sir John More) are seated in the center, on woolsacks, and two clerks are busy at work behind them.

More sent this preliminary sketch to Erasmus after the family portrait was completed. That oil portrait (approximately 100 x 140 in.) was subsequently lost.

Based on Holbein's family sketch, this oil portrait was commissioned, through the courtesy of the Thomas More Society of Dallas, to commemorate the 460th anniversary of More's death. See Appendix 5 for the identification of each person.

In 1984, copies of this bronze bust were cast for members and friends of the Thomas More Society of America in Washington, D.C.

At the right is a page from More's prayer book. It has the following annotation (in More's hand) at the top:
    "To think my most enemies my best friends."
It continues at the bottom:
    "for the brethren of Joseph could never have done
    him so much good with their love and favor as
        they did him with their malice &
            hatred."
(Other examples of such annotated pages can be found in Appendix 6.)

Ad ſextam de cruce.

Oꝛa ſexta ie
ſus eſt cruci cō
clauatus. Atꝗ cum
latronibus pendens
deputatus. Pꝛe toꝛ
mentis ſitiens felle
ſaturatus. Agn⁹ crī
men diluit ſic ludifi
catus. H⁹ Adoꝛam⁹
te chꝛiſte: et benedici
mus tibi. R̄ꝫ. Quia
per ſanctam crucem
tuam redemiſti mū
dum. Oꝛemus. Oꝛatio.

Omine ieſu chꝛiſte fili dei viui: pone
paſſionē crucē et moꝛtē tuā inter iu
diciū tuū ꝗ aias noſtras nunc ꝗ in hoꝛa moꝛ
tis noſtre: et largiri digneris viuis miſericoꝛ
diā et gratiā / defunctis requiē et veniā / ec
cleſie tue pacē et concoꝛdiā / et nobis pctoꝛi
bus vitā ꝗ gloꝛiā ſempiternā. Qui cū patre
et ſpū ſancto viuis et regnas deus. Per oīa
ſecula ſeculoꝛ. Amē. Gloꝛioſa paſſio dn̄i no
ſtri ieſu xp̄i eruat nos a doloꝛe triſti / ꝗ pdu
cat nos ad gaudia paradiſi. Amē. Pater no
ſter. Aue maria gratia.

This larger-than-life bronze statue in Chelsea, London, was unveiled in July 1969 by the Speaker of the House of Commons. Also presiding were the Archbishop of Canterbury, the Archbishop of Westminster, and the Moderator of the Free Church Federal Council.

A dialogue of Sir Thomas
More, knight: one of the
counsel of our sovereign lord the king and
chancellor of his Duchy of Lancaster. Wherein is
treated divers matters as of the veneration
and worship of images and relics
praying to saints and going on
pilgrimage. With many other
things touching the pestilent sect of Luther and
Tyndale by the one
begun in Germany
and by the other
labored to
be brought into England.

This long title (long titles were common in the early days of printing) concentrates on issues and on More's responsible position as knight, counselor, and chancellor—not on emotionally charged judgments about heresy. Making good use of his sterling reputation, More tackled the many "divers matters" that had begun to concern his compatriots. With the restraint and judiciousness one would expect from a respected judge, he showed that he was interested in reasoning, not in stirring up passions.

According to C. S. Lewis, this book is "perhaps the best specimen of [the Platonic dialogue] ever produced in English."[3] It certainly shows More's art of conversation at its best.

Masterfully conceived, the *Dialogue* is a series of six conversations, taking place on four days, between Sir Thomas and a college student who has been influenced by all the new ideas of the age. In the course of these lively exchanges, More discovers the roots of the youth's confusion by asking probing questions and by artfully addressing his concerns. These conversations take place in the study and in the garden of More's home in Chelsea. More's hospitality is so great that he entertains his young guest at lunch or dinner four times, in addition to conducting these engaging conversations. Their serious discussions do not, of course, take place at the family meals; More understood well the wisdom of respecting the full range of human needs. Indeed, such sensitivity was an integral element of his artful conversation.

One basis for C. S. Lewis's high praise of this book is surely the subtlety of its characterization. The young man, for example, is no stock character; he is unusually bright, witty, and articulate, and has highly complex motives. Throughout the *Dialogue* he is called "the Messenger," because he has been sent by a friend of More's to seek counsel regarding the many confused ideas of the time. Despite the press of business, More makes time for this young man and cares for him as he would for the longtime friend who sent him.

More's art of conversation in exploring and answering the Messenger's many difficult questions is highly instructive.

The book opens with the Messenger's arrival at Chelsea. More welcomes him and reads carefully his letter of introduction. He then listens for a long time as the Messenger presents his many complaints and questions about the state of the Catholic Church. The young man is concerned about the nature of such devotional practices as making pilgrimages and praying to saints, but he is particularly disturbed by the harsh way heretics are treated. It seems to him "that the clergy, for malice and envy, do untruly defame" many good people whom they call heretics.[4] By relying upon law and public burnings, they act "contrary to the mildness and merciful mind of [Christ] their master and against the example of all the old holy Fathers." The Messenger is also convinced that all studies except Latin and Scripture are a waste of time.

Faced with these many involved issues, More does not want to give an immediate, "unadvised answer." So he simply gives the young man a hearty welcome and, "pretending lack of leisure," asks him to return the next morning. More then reflects on the young man's difficulties and works out a four-step plan to address the issues raised.

The next day, More devotes the entire morning and most of the afternoon to the young Messenger. Their discussion begins just before 7:00 in More's study. Although it appears to follow the rambling course of any lively and spontaneous conversation, More actually focuses the whole morning's discussion upon the most basic question the youth raised the night before: How do we know what is true? Sir Thomas helps the Messenger develop a more thoughtful appreciation of the complexities of the world, including the complexities of how we know. To deny the very possibility of miracles, for example, is to oversimplify the concepts of nature and of God. Or to subscribe to the principle of *sola scriptura* is to overlook the difficulties involved in reading and interpreting any text, be it sacred or secular.

After several hours of discussion, More asks the Messenger if he thinks a person should "better trust his eyes than his wit." The youth is surprised at the question, having always assumed that his eyes are perfectly reliable. More then gives this earthy and vivid rejoinder to counter the Messenger's naivete: "The eyes may be deceived and think they see when they see not, if reason gives over its hold—unless you think the juggler . . . cuts your girdle before your face in twenty pieces and makes it whole again, and puts a knife into his eye and sees never the worse. And turns a plum into a dog's turd in a boy's mouth."[5] At this point the servant comes in and asks if he should get dinner ready! More and the youth have another good laugh (they have had many a good laugh already) while the bewildered servant is told to prepare a better meal than the one the juggler proposed!

This combination of realism and humor characterizes much of Sir Thomas's conversation with the youth. Some of More's best merry tales are in these pages. They are composed and arranged to encourage people to take a less simplistic view of life—and to take their own theories less seriously.

Just as we learn from experience that our eyes do not perceive everything accurately, so, says More, we eventually must come to realize that one cannot accurately read and interpret everything by wit alone. For the youth to argue, therefore, that all one must know is Scripture and Latin (Latin was, at that time, necessary for reading Scripture) is absurd. Besides a particular language, many other things are needed—especially a well-trained reason and access to the vast collective learning of the Church—if one is to read Scripture according to the mind of its Author.

The youth, again surprised, concludes that the Scriptures

must not have been written very well if they cannot be easily understood.[6] Arguing that the complexities of Scripture are actually part of God's high wisdom, More once again opens to this youth whole new horizons.

So engaging is their conversation that they are reluctant to break for lunch. However, since they do not want Lady Alice to get angry, they do leave More's study, talking and laughing as they go.

After lunch they go for a walk in More's garden and find a pleasant place to sit, under an arbor. Starting right where they had left off, More tactfully directs their afternoon discussion to a second important issue, one closely related to the first: the nature and necessity of the Catholic Church. Only when this is clarified does he return to the unresolved questions about pilgrimages and the veneration of images, relics, and saints. By midafternoon, we are told, the Messenger "felt himself so fully answered and contented that he thought himself able to content and satisfy any one that he should happen to meet who held the contrary."[7]

More bids him farewell, but he prudently sets up another time to discuss the issues he has not yet answered. Sure enough, in two weeks' time the Messenger's euphoria has worn off, and he returns with many more questions that are bothering him. These perplexities have increased, at least in part, because of talks he has been having with his university friends.

Somewhat reticent before the authority and intelligence of Chancellor More, the Messenger at first says that he and his friends at the university have only one question about all that More said before. Actually, he and his friends have many questions. But there is only one that they present directly, and it has to do with the status of Scripture in the Church. This leads into a long discussion about William Tyndale's translation of Scripture, which had been banned from England. The Messenger and his friends have rashly assumed that the clergy simply want to keep the laity under their control; More, however, shows that the problem is with Tyndale's Lutheran interpretations. Sir Thomas strongly defends the importance of Scripture, and he too favors an English translation—as long as the translation is faithful to the text and approved by the Church.[8] The Messenger agrees with More's balanced and sensible arguments and says he is fully content and satisfied.

At this point in the argument, they again break for lunch. Afterwards, they proceed into the garden to tackle the difficult issues which Sir Thomas has deliberately kept for last. But More does not even have to bring them up. Now that the Messenger is more relaxed, he speaks freely about the concerns that bother him the most. Over the last three discussions, the Messenger has come to see that Luther's and Tyndale's views are indeed heretical—that is, that they set up a sect representing a "side way" taken from the common belief of the whole Church.[9] But why treat them so harshly? It seems to the Messenger that the clergy have maliciously outlawed the Reformers' writings just so that the laity will not read about the many clerical abuses.

More does not deny that much reform is needed, but he does argue that the Church, as Christ's bride on earth, deserves due respect. An important part of giving that respect is to use legitimate means to bring about her reform—not to recklessly champion revolutionary ideas that reject "the whole consent and agreement of all Christian people this fifteen hundred years confirmed."[10]

More also leads the Messenger to realize how little he actually knows about the teachings of Luther and Tyndale. The Messenger is attracted by their call for reform in the Church and for the popular use of Scripture. More agrees with these aims, but shows that what Luther and Tyndale propose goes far, far beyond these two objectives. To demonstrate the revolutionary quality of their actual proposals, he asks the youth to take a look at what these men have actually written.

Not only do Luther and Tyndale deny the Church's authority and the validity of most of the sacraments, not only do they consider "all the world wild geese" except themselves, they also deny free will and thus ascribe responsibility for evil to God, not to his creatures. At the same time, the "one special thing" they use to spice everything else is a doctrine of liberty which teaches that "having faith, they need nothing else." By claiming a personal freedom that is independent of "all governors and all laws, spiritual or temporal, except the Gospel," these revolutionaries were, as More saw it, paving a sure path to war.

In fact, war had already erupted. As More reports, during the summer of 1525, seventy thousand Lutherans were slain in Germany before order was restored—an order that resulted in "a right miserable servitude."[11] Then in 1527, angry Germans sacked Rome and tortured the "unsaved papists" who lived there.

More recounts to the Messenger what diplomats reported about that sacking of Rome. These examples of cruel behavior are, he maintains, the practical consequences of Luther's and Tyndale's theories:

> Like very beasts [the German soldiers] did violate the wives in the sight of their husbands, slew the children in the sight of the fathers, and, to extort the discovering of more money, when men had brought out all that ever they had to save themselves from death or further pain, and were at pacts and promises of rest without further business, then the wretched tyrants and cruel tormentors, as though all that stood for nothing, ceased not to put them afterwards to intolerable torments. . . . Too piteous and too abominable were it to rehearse the villainous pain and torments that they devised on the pitiable women, whom afterwards they beastly abused—wives in the sight of their husbands, and maidens in the sight of their fathers.[12]

Even children did not escape the cruel inventiveness of these "abominable beasts":

> Some failed not to take the child and bind it to a spit and lay it to the fire to roast, the father and mother looking on. And then begin to bargain a price for sparing the child—after first a hundred ducats, then fifty, then forty, then twenty, then ten, then five, then two—when the pitiable father had not one left since these tyrants had all before. Then would they let the child roast to death. And yet in derision, as though they pitied the child, they

would say to the father and to the mother, "Ah, fie,
fie for shame, what a marvel is it that God send a
vengeance among you. What unnatural people you
must be that can find it in your hearts to see your
own child roasted before your face, rather than part
with one ducat to deliver it from death."[13]

More reports these examples in all their horrifying detail to
remind the young Messenger what happens when people are
not encouraged to respect law and virtue—and when an elect
group dehumanizes whole classes of people such as "the
papists."

The young Messenger objects that such cruelty cannot be
blamed on Luther and his followers in particular, since all wars
engender cruel behavior. More says (as Erasmus had said earlier)
that Luther's denial of free will "plainly sets forth all the world to
wretched living."[14] After all, if the way we act is not within our
control, what incentive is there to struggle against one's passions
and temptations? Furthermore, if our actions make no difference
to God, why should they make any difference to us? More considers Luther's denial of free will to be "the very worst and most
mischievous heresy that ever was thought upon, and also the
most mad."[15] "Surely," he says, "it is so far against all Holy Scripture well understood, so far against all natural reason, so utterly
subverting all virtue and good order in the world, so highly blaspheming the goodness and majesty of almighty God in heaven,
that it is more than wonder how any earthly person that has
either one spark of wit in his head, or toward God or man one
drop of good will in his heart, should not abhor to hear it."[16]

Yet, objects the Messenger, even if one agrees that such
teaching is madness, why treat the mad teachers so cruelly?
Why not just help reasonable people come to see how foolish the
teaching is?

More tries to help the Messenger realize that getting someone
(even oneself) to be reasonable is no easy matter, especially when
strong passion is involved. By appealing to strong passion, Luther
has stirred thousands to angry violence against individuals and
institutions protected by law. In such a situation, the law has the
duty to step in and treat such offenders, not cruelly, but with the

force necessary to safeguard peace and justice. Historically, More points out, the heretics themselves have always been the first to use violence. Only after this has occurred have good princes been driven to use force for the "preservation not only of the faith but also of the peace among their people."[17] More has no doubt that reason will prevail if force is not used,[18] but his reading of history shows that social revolutionaries do not hesitate to use violent and unlawful means to get their way.

To substantiate this reading of history, More goes back a thousand years and recalls the problems Augustine had with the Donatists. For most of his long life, St. Augustine "had with great patience borne and suffered their malice, only writing and preaching in reproof of their errors, and had not only done them no temporal harm, but also had prevented and resisted others who would have done it." Finally, however, "for the peace of good people," Augustine found it necessary to exhort "Count Boniface and others to repress them with force and threaten them with bodily punishment."[19]

Augustine's experience was confirmed by "holy Saint Jerome and other virtuous Fathers." Yet none of these Church Fathers allowed the Church itself to use physical force against heretics; this was a matter for the civil government, a means sometimes needed in the effort to avoid "common sedition, insurrection, and open war"—all of which could "in the beginning be right easily avoided, by punishment of those few that were the first."[20]

Such punishment, More explains, can be a civil and moral obligation, since "nature, reason, and God's behest bind first the prince to safeguard his people" and then also "bind every man to help and defend his good and harmless neighbor against the malice and cruelty of the wrongdoer."[21]

What makes heresy such a difficult social disorder, says More, is the hardened pride which is inevitably involved. Since "pride is the very mother of all heresies," heretics can come to a point where only the frantic pleasure of their own will can satisfy and content them.[22] These proud fantasies arise among the learned "because they want to be singular among the people"; they arise among the not-so-learned because they "long to seem far better learned than they are."[23] In either case, the reward for their labor is the "delight of beholding what pleasure the people have in their preaching."[24]

This involved discussion comes to a halt when supper is announced; but before going, More gives the Messenger several passages to read and compare by the time they meet again the next morning. One of these, from the *Decretum* (the official book of Church law, the one recognized throughout Christendom), demonstrates that current procedures regarding heretics are no different from those that were in force at the time of the "old Fathers and holy doctors and saints." Other passages are from "certain works of Saint Cyprian, Saint Augustine, and some other holy doctors"; finally, there are some from Luther's and Tyndale's books.

When they meet again the next day, the Messenger announces that he is convinced. He says that Luther and Tyndale are "so plainly confuted by the old holy Fathers that, if I had seen so much before, it would probably have shortened much of our long communication."[25] In fact, the youth wonders how so many Germans can follow Luther and so many Englishmen can follow Tyndale.

More responds by pointing out that the appeal of these men is not to reason, but to "fond affection."[26] By conjuring up "false enchantments" about impossible liberties, they have understandably gained many followers. The number of these followers could increase, More warns, while the number of true Christians could be reduced to a small sect—but this sect will nevertheless be a church that will always "remain and be well known" by the profession of a faith that can be traced back to Christ. Regardless of what might happen in any one hour of darkness, Christ's church will, without fail, grow large again.[27]

With these challenging and yet comforting words, More sits down to lunch with the young Messenger for the last time. But first he prays that all might be one flock again, so filled "with charity in the way of good works in this wretched world that we may be partners of the heavenly bliss which the blood of God's own Son has bought us."[28]

Chapter Sixteen

Royal Passion vs. Law and Tradition

THE DANGER THAT MORE SAW in Luther's revolt was soon over-shadowed by a far greater danger, one coming from a friend. This friend had recently been declared Defender of the Faith for his highly visible opposition to Luther and his followers. Yet within a few years, this same man was recruiting staunch Lutherans to support his own will.

The story of King Henry VIII's transformation from golden prince to unyielding tyrant, along with More's response to it, is one of the most instructive features of More's life and political career.

The two had known each other since Henry's childhood. As we have seen, young More was so familiar with the Prince that he could stop by just to introduce a friend. More knew well that Henry had vast ambitions as well as strong beliefs and substantial piety. Within Henry he saw basically the same great spiritual combat going on that he experienced in himself and that he had reflected upon so deeply while writing *The Life of John Picus* and *The History of King Richard III*. For this reason, nothing that unfolded came as a surprise to him.

Henry's strongest battle between passion and principle began in 1525, when he became infatuated with Anne Boleyn. This love affair was qualitatively different from any of the many others that he had had or would have—for Anne was an expert in the game of love.

Anne had learned from the misfortune of an older sister who had had an affair with Henry and who had eventually been discarded, although decently compensated. Anne had the advantage of having been educated at the French court, where she had compiled a sophisticated array of amorous weaponry. Her ability to charm Henry was so great that people at court wondered if she was an enchantress; later, Henry himself accused her of sorcery. The only witchcraft actually involved, however, was Aphrodite's power over the unwary.

In any case, Henry was under Anne's spell for ten years. For the first seven of those years, they never had sexual relations, because Anne would not settle for anything short of marriage. Under such pressure, Henry began his long search for a way to divorce Catherine.

The official reason Henry gave for wanting a divorce was his belief that he had been living in sin with Catherine. Catherine had been married to Henry's brother Arthur, and according to Leviticus 20:21, "if a man shall take his brother's wife, it is an impurity; he has uncovered his brother's nakedness; they shall be childless." For his violation of this command, Henry claimed, God had punished him by giving him no male heir to the throne. Of course, this injunction was directly contradicted by another command in Deuteronomy.[1] Besides, Henry and Catherine had not been childless—their daughter Mary was a healthy and intelligent girl of eleven when Henry was pressing for his divorce. The heart of this matter is revealed in Shakespeare's last play, Henry VIII, when one of the characters explains that Henry's "conscience" had "crept too near another lady"[2]—a lady whose conscience was "soft" and "cheveril" (flexible, stretchy).[3]

The most dramatic part of Henry VIII is the trial scene, where Catherine and Henry are before the court that is to judge the validity of their marriage. In this scene and in the play as a whole, Catherine emerges as the noblest of characters—a view that reflects the esteem and admiration which the English had for their beloved queen.

In this scene the court has been solemnly assembled. King Henry has just been called, and he has officially answered. When Queen Catherine is called, she rises without answering, walks past the court officials, and unexpectedly kneels at the King's feet, saying:

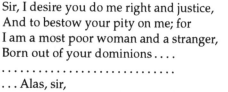

> Sir, I desire you do me right and justice,
> And to bestow your pity on me; for
> I am a most poor woman and a stranger,
> Born out of your dominions....
> ....
> ... Alas, sir,
> In what have I offended you? What cause
> Hath my behavior given to your displeasure
> That thus you should proceed to put me off
> And take your good grace from me? Heaven
>   witness,
> I have been to you a true and humble wife,
> ....
> ... Upward of twenty years, and have been blest
> With many children by you.[4]

After developing this moving petition and after seeing that Henry will not respond, she rises and walks out of the court, disregarding the calls for her return.[5] This action shows her profound understanding of her husband; it also shows the strength and shrewdness of character imparted to her by her mother, Isabel of Spain. For the rest of her life she would continue to do what she had always done: appeal to the King's conscience and to the noblest aspects of his character, but without ever wavering about the truth of the matter.

To the very end, Catherine insisted that she was Henry's lawful wife and therefore England's rightful queen. As she testified under oath, she and Arthur had never consummated their marriage, because of Arthur's ill health; Henry himself admitted, on various occasions, that he accepted this as fact.[6]

Throughout the seven years that Henry worked for his divorce,[7] Catherine resisted with such patience and serenity that he found her peace of mind unsettling to his own. In fact, Catherine (like many others) expected that Henry's infatuation would be fleeting, as had been the case so often before. She also expected that political pressures from such powerful allies as her nephew Emperor Charles V, the pope, and the bishops would move Henry to reconsider. Unfortunately, however, few if any of these men (except for Bishop Fisher) had Catherine's

courage. Thomas More did; and he faulted those who aban-
doned their positions of leadership in the time of greatest need.
Henry was a man who understood the importance of law
and tradition. He had been raised in a country richly blessed
with both, and to the end of his days he loudly insisted that he
had remained faithful to them. Although he later became hardened in the fond fantasies of his own mind, he remained unde-
cided for a long period of time. For ten years, from 1525 to 1534,
Henry carried on a war within himself, a raging war over the
course of action he should follow.

As noted earlier, Henry had long been given over to chivalric dreams of conquest and empire. Despite his education in
classical and religious subjects, he was enamored with the honor
of battle and moved by lust for power. This he showed not only
in his reckless wars against France but also in his imprudent
attempts to become Holy Roman Emperor.[8] As we have seen,
More revealed the heart of Henry's character when he wrote:
"Among many kings there will be scarcely one, if there is really
one, who is satisfied to have one kingdom. And yet among
many kings there will be scarcely one, if there is really one, who
rules a single kingdom well."[9]

In 1528 Anne exacerbated Henry's lust for imperial power
by giving him a book that justified everything he would ever
want to do. That book was William Tyndale's *The Obedience of a
Christian Man*. More called this "a book of disobedience" and
diplomatically cautioned Henry about its content.[10] Henry was
already highly cautious about the author; he had, in fact, banned
Tyndale from England for advocating Luther's revolutionary
ideas. Nonetheless, he was soon seduced by the claims of Tyndale's new book.

This book is famous in the history of political thought
because it gives the first justification in the English language for
the divine right of kings. Up to this point, Henry had always
conceived of his right to rule as coming from the pope. This is an
important fact that explains why he had so strongly insisted to
More in 1521 that the pope's power could not be exaggerated.[11]

More had a quite different understanding about the source of
political power. Since human beings are free by nature, he said,

power to rule comes from essentially self-governing people. As he put it, "The consent of the people both bestows and withdraws sovereignty."[12]

This understanding of legitimate authority was a far cry from that of Henry. For him, using Parliament was a matter of political necessity, and he did not hesitate to manipulate Parliaments to suit his own purposes. It is therefore not surprising that Henry found Tyndale's *The Obedience of a Christian Man* most attractive. Tyndale made the astonishing claim that the king received his power not from the people, and not from the pope, but directly from God himself. Before long, the ambitious Henry wholeheartedly embraced this new theory.

Simon Fish's *Supplication for the Beggars* was another highly influential work that Anne Boleyn supplied for Henry. This emotionally charged pamphlet, addressed to King Henry himself, pleaded for him to come to the aid of the beggars, whose number and desperation had increased enormously of late. And what was the sole reason for the dire plight of these beggars? The clergy.

In fact, Fish claimed, the clergy were responsible for all the great ills England was suffering at that time. Not only had they extorted most of the best lands in England, but they were constantly going around begging for more and more of the country's wealth. As a result, nothing was left for the other, really poor, beggars. In addition, the clergy acted like a state within a state and had deliberately set out to thwart the king's power and influence.

This thoroughly anticlerical pamphlet came out in February 1529, and already by September, More's response was circulating. That More responded at all to this seventeen-page pamphlet is an indication of the strong interest Henry showed in it.

In More's artful *Supplication of Souls*, cries and pleas come forth from purgatory, warning the good people on earth against those "seditious persons" who are working both "to destroy [the clergy,] by whom we are much helped," and to spread the pestilent and poisonous opinion that purgatory does not exist.[13] Crying out in their pain and suffering, these poor souls in purgatory urgently appeal to their friends and relatives for help. They also ridicule Fish's malicious exaggerations and point out that his whole purpose is "to bring [the clergy] in displeasure of the King and hatred of the people."[14]

Throughout, the souls in purgatory warn that Fish's real intent is "to inflame the King's Highness against the Church."[15] In fact, if Fish succeeds in turning his beggars against "bishops, abbots, priors, prelates, and priests," he will then turn these same beggars against the laity, "against merchants, gentlemen, kings, lords, and princes, and complain that they have all, and say that they do nothing for it but live idle, and that they are commanded in Genesis to live by the labor of their hands and the sweat of their faces, as he says about the clergy now."[16]

As to who will lead such revolutions, "there can never lack some needy, ravenous landed men who will be ready to be captains in all such rebellions."[17] What has already occurred in Germany may happen in England as well.[18] Like Luther in Germany, Fish is working to get widespread political support from those who have "gaped and gasped" after the Church's land and wealth. In so doing, these so-called reformers have made it clear that their aim is to destroy the Church, not to reform it.

These supposed reformers, says More, are only operating "under the pretext of reformation." Actually, they are intent on making a "new division of every man's land and substance, never ceasing (if you allow them) until they make all beggars as they themselves are, and at last bring all the realm to ruin, and this not without butchery and foul bloody hands."[19]

The alternative to such bloody revolution, More suggests, is to "devise some good wholesome laws to help in all these matters."[20] These wholesome laws would respect the wisdom of tradition and would recognize the necessary imperfection of any human justice. Henry too believed in such wholesome laws—until he found that they stood in the way of his own passionate desire to obtain a divorce.

Why, under such dangerous circumstances, did More agree to serve as Henry's Lord Chancellor? What could he possibly hope to accomplish?

Chapter Seventeen

Lord Chancellor of England

MORE WROTE TO ERASMUS that he had, on October 25, 1529, assumed England's highest appointed office, for "the interests of Christendom."[1] Indeed, during his two and a half years as Lord Chancellor of England, More constantly battled those who were urging Henry to break with a Christendom that had been united for hundreds of years. These counselors, of "God knows what kind,"[2] encouraged Henry to act like a Roman emperor and assume control of both church and state—and, therefore, control of his own divorce.

Until May 1532, the interests of Christendom appeared to be prevailing. On May 15, however, in an unexpected turn of events, the battle was lost. More resigned his office the very next day. But all along, he had seen this momentous struggle as a battle for Henry's mind and heart. How that battle was fought and lost is the most dramatic story of More's tenure as Lord Chancellor.

Henry appointed Sir Thomas More as Lord Chancellor in large part because he wanted a layman, not a cleric, in that position. True, More was the ablest of lawyers, an experienced judge, and a longtime friend. But first and foremost, Henry wanted to send a strong message to Rome. Though he did not yet know how he would proceed to achieve his divorce, he knew that one way of showing he meant business was to intimidate the pope, or at least try.

So he did just that. Early in October, he stripped Cardinal Wolsey, England's leading prelate, of his office as Lord Chancellor, charging him with *praemunire*.[3] This was a serious crime,

usually classified as a form of treason, punishable by confisca-
tion of property, imprisonment, and even execution. It was a
charge that Henry would use many times in future years to
intimidate uncooperative clergy. Pressured by his own desires
and by his advisors, he was becoming increasingly despotic
and more and more determined not to let any cleric limit the
exercise of his will. It was, in fact, for this very reason that the
Reverend Thomas Cranmer rose so quickly. This unknown
priest proved quite malleable to Henry's will, and so he
became (in 1533) Archbishop of Canterbury. But he would not
become Lord Chancellor; never again would Henry appoint a
cleric to that post.

This change greatly restricted the office of Lord Chancellor,
a position that had grown immensely under Wolsey. Nonetheless, as chancellor of the entire realm, More still had extensive
judicial and political responsibilities. His greatest responsibility
was to serve as the chief justice of England. Legal historian John
Guy tells us that in this office, More handled an average of 912
cases per year (as compared to the 535 cases handled by the
industrious Wolsey).[4] Almost half of these dealt with property
disputes, about fifteen percent were business-related, and the
rest were of a wide assortment "ranging from forgery and fraud
to false imprisonment, defamation, extortion, tithes disputes,
and testamentary squabbles."[5]

More's tenure came at a time when a great deal was required of judges, if they were to apply England's ancient common
law system to the growing complexities of a fast-developing
nation. John Guy, who recently reviewed the archival records of
the 2,356 suits which came before the chancery during More's
thirty-one months in office, summarizes his findings in this way.
More cultivated, he says, "a distinctive policy of self-involve-
ment, scrupulousness, and discretion. In the last resort, his great
contribution was exactly this: to rejuvenate the ancient theory
that judges had a personal duty in conscience to see right done
by all whose business was entertained in the courts they
directed."[6]

Few judges in More's time shared the belief that they had
"a personal duty in conscience to see right done" in their

courts. But as "keeper of the king's conscience," Chancellor More took his role with the utmost seriousness.[7] For this reason, he issued injunctions rather frequently—so frequently that many of the common law judges began complaining.

Well, what does a chief justice do when his fellow judges are becoming disgruntled? More invited them all to dinner. But ahead of time he prepared briefs of every injunction he had given. Once everyone had enjoyed a fine meal, More reviewed each of his injunctions, explaining the grounds on which it had been awarded and convincing his guests that, in his place, they would have reached a similar decision on the evidence before them. After showing the reasonableness of his actions, he argued that his injunctions would not be necessary if they would take care of such matters themselves.

The evening as a whole was a triumph for More, but not a complete triumph.[8] The judges agreed with him in theory, but in practice most would still go on refusing to exercise personal responsibility. Later, More explained to Will Roper why so many judges would not judge. "I understand, son," he said, "why they do not like to do so—it is because they see that they can, by the verdict of the jury, cast off all quarrels from themselves to the jury, which they can then use as their chief defense."[9]

Though his major responsibilities were judicial, Chancellor More also devoted considerable attention to the issue of peace within the realm. He agreed with established English law, and with the lessons taught by the thousand-year experience of Christendom, that in order for peace to reign, heresy must be controlled. At that time, heresies were identified as seditious attempts to undermine existing authority. As we have seen in chapter 12, More heard Luther's call to destroy the heart of Christendom, the Catholic Church, as a call to war. He therefore followed traditional procedures to insure the safety of this legitimate and time-honored institution.

He also continued wielding his pen to defend the Church from unjust attack. He recognized that the Church, like any other lawful institution, needs defense against slander. But in the course of applying the law, he also saw the law's limitations. And so he energetically used his rhetorical abilities to supplement the legal remedies.

More's greatest challenge as Chancellor, however, was the rapidly changing political situation. Within a few days of his appointment, he addressed what was to be known as the most revolutionary parliament in England's history. By the time it was dismissed, this parliament would separate England from Rome, and thus destroy a united Christendom; it would ratify Henry's imperial and caesaropapist pretensions, and unite church and state under Henry's control.

The story of this revolution is instructive for any age, especially in light of More's conviction that it could have been averted had there been a few more statesmen in England.[10] The story is also highly dramatic. Curiously enough, More had already written about a similar incident. Years earlier, in his history of England, he had pointed out how tyranny comes about through the negligence, greed, and cowardice of respectable people in respectable positions.[11] This drama was now being enacted for the second time during More's own life. In the case of Richard III, civil lawyers and judges had been most at fault. In this second case, however, as More respectfully pointed out, the bishops were the ones most at fault; they failed to be statesmen in the time of Christendom's greatest need.

To understand the political revolution that was about to take place, one needs to be aware of the roles played by three major factions which emerged during More's chancellorship. Each of these factions sought to control royal policy.[12]

When More agreed to accept the chancellorship, those supporting Catherine of Aragon had the leading hand in Henry's council and in Parliament. Catherine was much loved among the people, and the nobles were afraid that her powerful nephew Emperor Charles V would wage war against England if Henry mistreated her.

A second group, led by Cromwell, Cranmer, the Boleyn family, and the legal scholar Christopher St. German, advocated the destruction of the Church's independent status. Cromwell and St. German worked to get the Church regulated by Parliament, while Cranmer and the Boleyns fostered Henry's imperial ambitions. Although this group had the least support, they would eventually be the victors.

The third of these political groups was composed of the old blue bloods whose interest lay in advancing the King's will. This faction would be led by the Dukes of Norfolk and Suffolk. They were united in wanting their old enemy Wolsey punished, preferably destroyed. Otherwise they favored the status quo. They were not, therefore, sympathetic to Cromwell's radical proposals, at least not for the first two years or so of More's chancellorship.[13]

These three groups were in evidence, though not in a distinct way, at the opening session of the famous Reformation Parliament. This parliament met in November 1529, only a few days after More became Lord Chancellor. In this new capacity More addressed the first session and called for reform.[14] How he envisioned this reform we do not know, since most of his personal papers were seized after his imprisonment. But he certainly did not envision a reform that would authorize the breakdown of Christendom, the end of the Church's independence, and his own execution.

The first session of this parliament dealt with nothing more serious than the King's request for his debts to be pardoned, and the usual grievances against the clergy. The next session was delayed for an entire year because Henry still did not have a plan for getting his divorce. Cranmer had come up with one, but in 1529 Henry was still opposed to it as being too radical. In time, however, the King began to see things differently. Cranmer was made Archbishop of Canterbury precisely so that he could put his plan into effect. The plan was quite simple: Henry should use his royal supremacy as "emperor"—that is, as head of church and state—to obtain his divorce, thus bypassing Rome.

The idea was simple, but its execution required several difficult steps. First, Henry had to build a case for his divorce that would appear respectable. Since at that time it was generally considered both theoretically and legally impossible, Cranmer suggested that they collect (and, if necessary, buy) the endorsements of universities and private scholars.[15] This work took up most of 1530, but was complete by the time Parliament reconvened in January 1531.

To build this case, Cranmer worked throughout 1530 on a theological defense of King Henry's caesaropapist power.[16] This defense was basically the position set forth by Tyndale, but elaborated—and made to appear respectable by omission of any mention of Tyndale's tarnished name.[17]

This theoretical defense, the *Collectanea Satis Copiosa*, was essentially done by September 1530. Henry read it with uncommon care. In the one copy that still exists, his handwriting can be seen in forty marginal notes, most of them expressing his enthusiastic agreement with, and also his surprise at, the findings of Cranmer's research.[18]

Later that same month, Henry explained to the papal nuncio his new imperial rights, and he used his royal prerogative to forbid the exercise of "foreign" (i.e., papal) authority in England.[19] During this time, More "had a narrow escape of being dismissed" for his opposition.[20] But that is getting ahead of our story.

Although the theoretical groundwork was set forth in the *Collectanea*, such theories would mean nothing unless they could be translated into law and policy. And this could not happen without support from the Convocation of Clergy and from Parliament.

To test the feasibility of getting this support, Henry called together a number of well-disposed lawyers and members of the clergy in the second week of October.[21] He asked them if "Parliament could and would enact that . . . the divorce be decided by the Archbishop of Canterbury."[22] After studying and discussing the matter, these advisors "deliberatively answered that it could not be done."[23] This answer angered Henry, and he delayed the opening of Parliament for several months, "in the hope . . . that in the meanwhile he [might] hit upon some means of bringing over to his opinion the said lawyers, as well as some members of his Parliament."[24]

One highly influential lawyer, Christopher St. German, soon came to his aid and began drafting reform legislation for the upcoming parliament. This legislation authorized Parliament to reform the clergy and to take away the Church's independence. St. German also gave scholarly support to Henry's plan in the second dialogue of his highly influential *Doctor and Student*. There he argued that English common law should have precedence over canon law.[25] In effect, this would mean turning Christianity into a civil religion.

By the time Parliament met, the nobles knew which way the royal winds were blowing, and they had taken up the defense of Henry's declared imperial status. Eustace Chapuys, ambassador of Charles V, reported his surprise at being lectured by the Duke of Norfolk on this topic.[26]

Henry was well prepared for the second session of Parliament, which opened on January 16, 1531. As was customary, the Convocation of Clergy met at the same time. In an effort to intimidate the clergy into submission, Henry charged all of them with *praemunire*, claiming that they had committed a crime by having had recourse to ecclesiastical courts.[27] At the same time he also demanded that they recognize his caesaropapist status by declaring him to be the Supreme Head of the Church in England. The *praemunire* charge was nothing but another of his heavy-handed tactics to get this recognition— and one that was patently absurd. For hundreds of years, England had supported these ecclesiastical courts; even Henry had consistently done so.

In February, Bishop John Fisher devised a brilliant maneuver whereby the Convocation would recognize Henry as Supreme Head of the Church, but only "as far as Christ's law allows."[28] The Convocation also agreed to pay the enormous fine of one hundred thousand pounds for their "offenses," in exchange for Henry's permission to allow their ecclesiastical courts to operate as usual. Having considered the alternative— that the Church would be driven underground if it could not count on the state's protection—the bishops were quite willing to pay this exorbitant ransom.

Now that Henry had obtained his nominal supremacy, he took the next step towards obtaining his divorce. In March, More was given the highly unpleasant task of presenting both houses of Parliament with the report of the universities' approval of Henry's divorce. Parliament's response to this report was not enthusiastic. Asked what he himself thought of it, More discreetly but tellingly replied that he had "many times already declared [his opinion] to the king."[29]

These adverse reactions from both Parliament and the Convocation left Henry uncertain about his next move, for the rest of that year. But Thomas Cromwell came up with a plan so shrewd that it soon succeeded in manipulating England's fledgling democratic process to obtain the King's will.

More was aware of Cromwell's tactics, and he strongly disapproved. He would later say to him: "Master Cromwell, you are now entered into the service of a most noble, wise, and liberal Prince. If you will follow my poor advice, you shall, in the counsel you give to His Grace, ever tell him what he ought to do, but never what he is able to do. So shall you show yourself a true faithful servant and a right worthy Councillor. For if a lion knew his own strength, it would be hard for any man to rule him."[30] Unfortunately, Cromwell and others (especially Cranmer) did not tell Henry what he ought to do. Instead, they helped him achieve what he wanted to do.

Many months before the next session of Parliament convened, Cromwell set to work mobilizing discontent against the clergy. This he accomplished through a well-organized propaganda campaign for which he had solicited such noted writers as William Tyndale and Christopher St. German. When the Parliament of 1532 convened, two well-prepared bills were introduced. The first, which Cromwell himself had prepared and promoted, was the Commons' Supplication against the Ordinaries. Initially of little importance to Henry, this bill of grievances would eventually become the cudgel used to achieve his desires. About this, we will see more later.

The second bill, also promoted by Cromwell, was the Restraint of Annates Act. "Annates" were annual taxes the clergy sent to Rome, taxes that were highly unpopular with the laity. Under the pretext of ending this unpopular drain on the country's resources, Cromwell set the stage for a political and legal revolution.

As was to be expected, this bill met strong opposition in both houses. The debate became progressively more confrontational until it finally exploded in an open clash between Henry and the Archbishop of Canterbury, William Warham.[31] Because the clergy in the House of Lords remained unanimously opposed, Henry took the unusual step of personally visiting the Parliament chambers, on three different occasions, in order to intimidate enough of the nonclergy to force its narrow passage. With all the pressure he applied, however, he still could not get the bill passed until it was changed to the *Conditional* Restraint of Annates Act.

And then, even with this qualification, the bill was rejected by the House of Commons. To secure passage, Henry had to take the virtually unprecedented step of calling for a division of the House—a blatant violation of its traditional liberty. As Chapuys reported, Henry "caused the House to divide, and some passed to his side for fear of his indignation, so that the article was agreed to, but rather more moderately than it was proposed."[32]

This was by no means a legislative victory for Henry, but it did gain him some ground, and some experience in a strategy he would continue to use. It also provided Cromwell with a list of potential supporters for the lobbying efforts he would make in the weeks preceding his and Henry's more radical move—a move that would eventually bring about the most revolutionary change in centuries.

The first step towards this revolutionary change was a rather innocent-looking bill, one that had significant popular support: the Commons' Supplication against the Ordinaries, a list of complaints against the bishops. Submitted and debated in February of 1532, this bill did not receive much attention until April. More, however, understood clearly the maneuvers behind this bill. Already in January he had published three books in defense of the Church, and of the clergy in particular. In these works, now known collectively as *Confutation of Tyndale's Answer*, he vigorously defended the Church's independence—in direct opposition to the propaganda campaign Cromwell was waging on Henry's behalf.

More's opposition, artful and indirect as it was, did not offend or anger Henry. Other critics would be less tactful, with disastrous consequences.

On March 28, 1532, Parliament adjourned for Easter, without giving much attention to this bill of complaints against the clergy. Henry also gave little importance to it; he simply sent it on to be answered by the leaders of the Convocation of Clergy. At that time, he was not set on any particular course of action. But by the time Parliament reconvened, on April 10, he was a changed man. He was preoccupied, even obsessed, with becoming England's emperor—a ruler capable of wielding despotic authority over both church and state. This change seems to have arisen from anger, an anger heightened by offended pride.[33]

One sharp offense to Henry's pride came from Queen Catherine's chaplain, Friar Peto, who preached at the Mass Henry attended on Easter Sunday, March 31. On that solemn occasion Friar Peto publicly denounced Henry and his advisors for proceeding with the divorce. On the next Sunday the insult was intensified when the King's chaplain responded and was heckled by one of Peto's supporters. Not surprisingly, the King became so angry that he had this supporter, and Peto himself, arrested.[34]

Shortly after Parliament reconvened, King Henry suffered another intense embarrassment when two members of Parliament boldly spoke out against his divorce, citing both economic and security reasons.[35] Then yet another blow came, from Bishop Stephen Gardiner. This was a man who generally knew how to appease Henry. In answering the Commons' Supplication, however, he failed significantly by undiplomatically denying the very basis of Henry's imperial power.[36]

All these humiliations help to explain why on April 30 Henry reacted with rage when he received the bishops' answer to the Commons' complaints. On that day he shouted that the bishops' answer was "very slender!"[37] Then he decided to bypass Parliament altogether and simply exercise the raw force of kingly power. As one historian put it, the Commons' Supplication was suddenly "replaced by a royal ultimatum."[38]

On May 10, Henry demanded the clergy's submission to his spiritual authority. This he did by sending, both to Parliament and to the Convocation, bills declaring that all future legislation passed by the clergy must receive the king's approval, and that all former legislation must be examined by a royal commission and be approved by the king. Parliament, with More in the lead, refused to authorize these demands. However, hard to believe as it is, the clergy's Convocation did authorize them. And in so doing, they wrote their own destruction into law.

In Parliament, More's opposition had been (as usual) subtle, indirect, and highly effective. At the height of the controversy over the submission of the clergy, for example, he had encouraged one of the leaders opposing Henry's plan, but in a remarkably tactful way. That young and daring leader, Sir George Throckmorton, spoke of this incident several years later. "Sir Thomas More," he recalled, "then being Chancellor, sent [word] for me to come speak with him in the Parliament chamber. And when I came to him, he was in a little chamber within the Parliament chamber. . . . And I think the bishop of Bath was talking with him at the time. And then he said this to me, 'I am very glad to hear the good report that goes around about you and that you are so good a Catholic man as you are. If you continue in the same way that you began and are not afraid to say your conscience, you shall deserve great reward from God and thanks of the King's Grace in time, and much [honor] to yourself.'"[39]

But even such tactful efforts were in vain. Once Henry realized that Parliament would not support him, he ordered that its members be dismissed as of May 14. By so doing, he could mute the effects of their opposition and prevent them from supporting the clergy in theirs. He and Cromwell could now concentrate on intimidating the Convocation of Clergy. Cromwell's well-orchestrated campaign against the clergy was now about to reap great benefits for his king.

When, on May 10, Henry first ordered the Convocation to submit, the clergy's initial reaction was "close to panic."[40] Nonetheless, they did show determination to resist; they sent representatives to Rochester to confer with Bishop Fisher, who had been unable to attend because of illness.

On May 11, Henry increased the pressure by using Cromwell's already familiar words[41] to denounce the clergy as "but half our subjects; yea, and scarce our subjects."[42] Thus threatened with charges of treason, the Convocation wavered and, on May 13, sought the King's clemency. At this point the bishops may yet have been directed by prudence. After all, they were well aware that the Church's independence was at stake, and that these battles between king and clergy had a long history in England. And they knew that before this time—at least until he had read Tyndale's *The Obedience of a Christian Man* and Cranmer's *Collectanea Satis Copiosa*—Henry himself had been respectful of the independent authority of the Church. So who could know what the future might hold?

By now, however, Henry was fully determined to get his divorce and to be recognized as an emperor, with vast authority over both temporal and spiritual matters. To force the hand of the Convocation of Clergy, to exact an immediate answer, Henry ordered that they be dismissed as of May 15. He also sent six leading nobles to show them how serious he was about getting the answer he wanted.

What occurred next might be interpreted and justified by some as prudence. But in the opinion of many, including Bishop Fisher, the Church was betrayed precisely by those most responsible for defending it.

Archbishop Warham, now in his eighties, was presiding over this Convocation. A seasoned man of political affairs, he had served as Lord Chancellor under both Henry VII and Henry VIII. He had also been leading the opposition to Henry's tactics since the fall of Wolsey, and with increased strength since the beginning of the year. So bold and outspoken was his criticism that Henry had, two months before, angrily rebuked him in the House of Lords. Henry had, indeed, spoken "foul language to him, saying that were it not for his age, he would have made him repent for having said what he did against His Majesty."[43]

Henry had also struck back at the archbishop by trumping up against him a particularly absurd charge of *praemunire*.

Supposedly Warham had, fourteen years earlier, ordained someone a bishop without first presenting him to Henry for approval. But whatever Henry's charges were, Warham was prepared to fight, in March and April, with everything he had. He made this clear in a daring speech he prepared for his defense.[44] In that speech he made clear his readiness to repeat what was perhaps the most effective action ever taken to defend the independence of the English Church: i.e., that taken by England's most famous martyr, Thomas Becket. He referred to this saint—this eminent predecessor of his—over thirty times, emphasizing his own willingness to die rather than compromise the Church's legitimate independence. If Henry and Cromwell wished to violate legal and historical precedent, then Warham would challenge them to do so—not under the dark subterfuge of night, but in the open light of day.[45] And, literally, over his dead body. Warham understood well that the blood of the martyrs is always the clearest, most unmistakable witness to justice in times when tyranny tries to hide under the artful intrigues of night.

Brilliant as his plan may have been, however, Warham never became a martyr. He never even delivered that powerful speech. The indignation he had expressed so courageously in the privacy of his study was never expressed in a public stand—at least not on May 15, 1532.

The old and honorable Archbishop, having weathered many a storm of royal passion, finally decided upon a tactic calculated to gain time for Henry's anger to subside. In order not to further enrage the King with open opposition, and not to enrage the clergy by relaying the King's unreasonable demands, Warham decided not to pose those demands to the full Convocation. On that fateful day of May 15, he allowed the lower house of clergy to disband without ever considering the new request. Possibly as few as three members of the upper house actually "authorized" the approval of the King's demands.

In any case, this "rump convocation" did not have the authority to speak for the whole, and therefore their resolution was not legally binding—which Warham knew.[46] What he could not know was that his hour was now past and that he would have no future opportunity for either compromise or confrontation. Perhaps he meant to deliver that extraordinary speech at the beginning of the next session of Parliament. But five months before that session of Parliament would convene, Warham died.

With Warham dead, and Bishop Fisher seriously ill, there remained no member of the clergy who was both willing and able to stand up to Henry. Both Fisher and More lamented this cowardice. As Fisher put it, "The fort is betrayed even by those who should have defended it."[47] More said, "If a bishop . . . neglects to do what the duty of his office requires for the salvation of his flock, [then he is] like a cowardly ship's captain who is so disheartened by the furious din of a storm that he deserts the helm, hides away cowering in some cranny, and abandons the ship to the waves. If a bishop does this, I would certainly not hesitate to juxtapose and compare his sadness with the sadness that leads, as St. Paul says, to hell. Indeed, I would consider it far worse, since such sadness in religious matters seems to spring from a mind which despairs of God's help."[48]

Had even one or two of the able English bishops been statesmen, the Church in England would not have had to fall. What these ecclesiastical leaders should have done, a civil leader like More could not do. Although he came to their defense in the Parliament, they alone could have defended themselves in their own Convocation.

The day after Henry's intimidation tactics proved successful, More resigned. As one author puts it, "At 3 P.M. in the garden of York Place, Westminster, More came into the royal presence and, watched by the Duke of Norfolk, handed back the white leather bag containing the great seal to Henry VIII. . . . The ironical inflection of More's voice, the piercing gaze of his eyes, and the nobility of his composure all gave the lie to his excuse that he was 'not equal to the work.' . . . Cromwell's victory of 15 May was 'narrow, blundering and legally suspect.' More's gaze in the garden told Henry so, and the king averted his eye."[49]

Yet Henry's turn from that steady gaze indicated that his conscience was still operative. From this moment until the

moment he died, More would not cease appealing to that conscience in every prudent way he could devise. In his courageous
persistence in giving good counsel, he proved himself to be the
loyal Kent to this headstrong Lear.

Chapter Eighteen

"Wise as Serpents, Innocent as Doves": After More's Resignation

W HEN MORE RESIGNED on May 16, 1532, he still maintained Henry's strong friendship. He left his office in Henry's good graces and was praised for the work he had done. A year later he was subjected to an intense scrutiny, but he could still publicly call Henry his friend. By early 1534, however, Henry was set upon his death. On February 21 of that year, Henry requested his indictment.

This dramatic change was not due simply to More's keeping of silence, though this was a silence that could be heard around the world. No, Thomas More was a statesman of rare ability and perception, and he was fully aware of the potential consequences of Henry's caesaropapist designs. He knew that the revolutionary move Henry was making was sure to destroy the unity of Christendom. It could and would end, for centuries to come, the legitimacy of the Roman Catholic Church in England. It could and would set back the development of parliamentary self-rule by a hundred years. Indeed, not until the seventeenth century would England begin to throw off the despotic effects of such unchecked monarchy—and then only at the cost of enormous civil upheaval and war.[1]

More was not one to sit back quietly while such dangerous conditions developed. As we will see, he devised a courageous and highly effective plan of opposition to Henry's despotic designs. One recent biographer has characterized More's actions as "so subtle and devious as to set not only Machiavelli, but also Richard III and Iago to school."[2] That More's actions were subtle is obvious to anyone who has studied his strategy; to characterize that strategy as devious or Machiavellian, however, is to mistake prudence for vice and wit for deception. Even a cursory look at More's writings makes this clear. In his very last work, for example, he reminds his fellow Christians that Christ "wished His followers to be brave and prudent soldiers, not senseless and foolish."[3] And at the end of this work, as in other writings, he admonishes them to "follow Christ's advice and become wise as serpents."[4]

To appreciate the subtlety of More's strategy requires some reflection on his assessment of the political situation. In the opening speech he made (as Lord Chancellor) to the Parliament of 1529, More said clearly what he had been saying for at least two decades—that both the church and the state were in great need of reform. Bringing about that reform, More believed, would require peace and the progressive development of law, within England and all of Christendom.[5]

More's speech to the Parliament of 1529 helps us not only to understand his objectives, but also to appreciate his diplomacy. In speaking before the King and Parliament, More tactfully calls attention to ideals and duties that Henry has been taking lightly for almost sixteen years. "The King," he says, "as a noble prince and shepherd of his people, has for many years spared neither pains nor expense to achieve a general European peace, now obtained at Cambrai."[6]

More does not mention all the years that Henry spent pursuing war. Nor does he mention that he himself joined the King's service only when Henry gave up that pursuit. Nor does he bring up the fact that he himself played a major role at the Peace of Cambrai and considered this peace to be the greatest achievement of his political career.[7]

In some ways, as indicated earlier, this achievement of peace throughout Christendom was the culmination of his eleven years of diplomatic effort. He had, in 1518, joined the royal court only after Wolsey and Henry had decided to work for peace throughout Christendom. This new peace policy, coming after nine years of frivolous foreign wars, was motivated largely by their costliness, futility, and unpopularity. These wars, undertaken by a youthful king still bent upon exploits of honor and chivalry, had been, in More's view, motivated by a dangerous lust for power—and he had discreetly said so.[8]

Both Wolsey and Henry had long known what More thought about these needless foreign wars. In 1522, when Henry had begun yearning for war once again, More had cautioned against it.[9] But though he had wished that his king would act as the noble shepherd of his people and would spare "neither pains nor expense to achieve a general European peace," he had been well aware of the many forces working against that wish. Especially powerful had been Henry's insatiable desires for honor and money, as well as his fear of losing prominence in the international struggle for power.

In his speech before Parliament and the King in 1529, More went on to explain the significance of the newly achieved peace at Cambrai. "This treaty," he said, "has guaranteed the unity and quiet of Christendom, has eliminated the risk of invasion from abroad, and has restored the prosperity of English trade, the benefits to trade being the result of unyielding royal endeavor."[10] If only the King's endeavors had been unyielding, the unity and quiet of Christendom could have been strengthened and preserved throughout Henry's reign and afterwards. Instead, Henry was never committed to such a program, with the possible exception of 1524–1529, when More exerted his greatest influence. When, therefore, More later complained "in a very piteous tone of the blindness of those princes" who put personal interests over the defense of Christendom, he surely had Henry in mind.[11]

In the same speech, More pointed out that one of the consequences of the previous concentration on war was "Wolsey's neglect" in attending to the necessary "reform in church and state." Henry, too, was guilty of neglect in this regard, even more so than Wolsey, but it would have been most imprudent to say so. Nonetheless, More did explicitly state that Henry had been "distracted by war."[12]

He then went on to explain that "many existing laws have become outdated . . . [and] Parliament has thus been summoned to reform the realm, and will be asked to enact reformist legislation in appropriate areas."[13] Unfortunately, his plans for reform have not come down to us. But as this speech indicates, he had made an accurate assessment of what England needed most: a peaceful and lawful reform that would look to the nation's common good and not to the king's passionate desires.

Counseling King Henry in ruling his passions was More's greatest challenge, and one of his greatest responsibilities. It was not only his personal responsibility as Henry's friend; it was also his professional responsibility as royal counselor. More officially held this office from 1518 until March of 1534, when his services as counselor were abruptly ended.[14]

Up to that point and even up to his death, More never stopped playing Seneca to this Nero. Already in 1516, he had revealed his acute awareness of the extraordinary difficulty involved in trying to give good advice to such a tyrant. He even invoked a Senecan play which shows the grave difficulties, but also the great goods, derived from giving good counsel to an unruly king.[15] In dealing with a person of such passion, he cautioned, "you must not abandon the ship in a storm because you cannot control the winds";[16] rather, you must seek to make things "as little bad as you can."[17]

In other words, More had known quite well what he was getting himself into when he joined Henry's court in 1518. Like Seneca, More was able for many years to help moderate his king's tyrannical passions. In 1519, for example, he helped formulate substantial reforms that Henry was willing to accept. He did everything possible to keep Henry focused on domestic issues and to steer him towards peace rather than the chivalric exploits of war.

What seems to have undermined these efforts was something pointed out by Erasmus and by More himself: the flattery of bad counselors.

In 1513, and again in 1517, Erasmus dedicated the translation of his favorite Plutarchan essay, "How to Tell a Flatterer from a Friend," to King Henry.[18] His prefatory letter begins: "Although this world contains no more agreeable society than that of a true and genuinely candid friend and there is nothing a man needs more in the conduct of his affairs, at the same time nothing is harder to find than such a friend."[19]

Because a king must "see to the well-being of thousands," wrote Erasmus, "[he] more than any other requires both many friends and right loyal ones too."[20] After citing many other counselors who served their kings well, Erasmus commented upon the service Nero received from Seneca, noting that "if Nero had obeyed his advice, he would have reigned longer and might have earned a place among the good emperors as well."[21] He then pointed out that a king's "exalted station, which attracts a multitude of friends, is the very circumstance that makes it difficult to distinguish true friends from false." And so he recommended Plutarch's "most useful treatise" to Henry.[22]

More often expressed his agreement with Plutarch and Erasmus on this point. Flatterers, he said, advance "inestimable harm"; in extreme cases they allow a person to take himself "for a god here upon earth and [to] think to win himself to be the lord of all the earth."[23] In his typically subtle way, he intimated in one of his last public statements that this was Henry's problem; as his trial concluded, he expressed his desire for "Almighty God to preserve and defend the King's Majesty and to send him good counsel."[24] Earlier he had said to his daughter Meg, "It is a great pity that any Christian prince should easily follow his passions because of a flexible council, or should be so shamefully abused by a clergy lacking the grace to stand constantly by their learning."[25]

More also agreed with Plutarch and Erasmus about the dangers and difficulties that can be involved in telling the truth. He had learned this lesson articulated so well by Erasmus: "Since the art of admonishing friends, like the art of medicine, requires not merely devotion but tact as well, in case we undermine friendship itself even while we clumsily try to cure our friend's faults, [Plutarch] has added a final section in which he makes it clear how gently one ought to admonish a friend if there is any good reason for it."[26] He was well aware that telling a "lion" what he ought to do could be dangerous business, even when this was done with exceptional prudence and tact.[27]

More's prudence and tact most often took the form of "reminding" Henry of his duties and commitments. This was the strategy he used not only in the poetry he wrote for Henry's coronation, but also in the court reforms he helped devise in 1519. Those reforms, entitled "Remembrances to the King," constituted a marked improvement in government procedures.[28]

In 1523, when he served as Speaker of the House, More used this diplomatic technique to obtain Henry's allowance of free speech in Parliament. He "reminded" Henry that effective deliberation required that "every one of your Commons be utterly discharged of all doubt and fear" over the way they might happen to express themselves in the heat of discussion.[29]

More found many applications for such reminders. In 1527, when Henry first asked him for counsel concerning his divorce, More reminded his sovereign that he was not a good person to ask about such an issue. First of all, he was no theologian. Secondly, he was, like the other court counselors, so bound to the King by the "manifold benefits daily bestowed" upon him that he would be tempted to please the King rather than counsel him.[30]

More also used this tactic in his polemical writings. Time and again, he would remind Henry of something that Henry himself had written or otherwise acknowledged. We have already seen, for example, how More in his *Dialogue Concerning Heresies* subtly called to mind Henry's own often-declared belief that Tyndale was a heretic and not trustworthy. Apparently this was something Henry had forgotten in his enthusiasm over Tyndale's defense of caesaropapism in *The Obedience of a Christian Man*.

In all his later polemical books, More gave Henry tactful reminders of his stated beliefs and then just as tactfully pointed to discrepancies between his actions and those beliefs.[31] The only books that More wrote as Lord Chancellor, the three parts of his *Confutation of Tyndale's Answer*, offer a preeminent example of how he carried out his most dangerous and important responsibility: reminding Henry of his role as a Christian king in defending the independence of the Church. Throughout, these books are indirect attacks on the very foundations of Henry's caesaropapist designs.

Why, during the busiest years of his life, did More find it necessary to write this long work? Because the fate of England

and of all Christendom was at stake. At considerable cost to his health and safety, he completed them in time for publication in early 1532, just as the most decisive session of Parliament was about to begin. He did this with full knowledge that Cromwell had been busy recruiting propagandists for his own revolutionary policies.

Comparing the approaches of these two men can help us understand what was happening during these crucial months.

In his *Confutation of Tyndale's Answer*, More called attention to the active and effective role Henry had taken in times past against those who attacked the Church. In fact, he said, he himself was only imitating the King in fulfilling this same duty—a duty made incumbent on them both by their oaths of office and by law. Throughout the three volumes of this work, More repeatedly (as the title implies) counterattacked Tyndale, the one most responsible for the theory of supreme sovereignty that Henry had by now espoused. Nevertheless, he kept reminding Henry of Henry's own stated convictions, and of what would happen to the country if he went against them. In this way, More persistently appealed to the conscience of the King, and of the English nation.

Cromwell's strategy, meanwhile, was something far different. His aim was to use the Commons' call for clerical reform to attack the clergy and to force them into complete submission. This attack was given the aura of legitimacy by England's greatest legal scholar of that time, the seventy-year-old Christopher St. German. This man's most famous book, *Doctor and Student*, which would be used as a primary textbook in English law schools from the 1530s until the end of the 1800s, argued that state law should always have precedence over church law. In later works, St. German even argued that the state should have the last word in disputes over Scripture, and in disputes within one's own conscience.[32]

Cromwell and St. German, both lawyers, must have caused More to reflect once again on the English history he had written before entering the King's service. In that history he had shown how Richard III had come to power "through law, not war"— thanks to the help provided by the great lawyers of his day.[33]

It may have been his eventual confrontation with St. German that cost More his life. By his successful demolishing[34] of Henry's and Cromwell's most experienced and persuasive spokesman, he was effectively undercutting all that Henry and the radicals at court were attempting to do. Such success could not continue. More would have to go.[35]

Chapter Nineteen

Imprisonment,
Despite the Thickets of the Law

ACCOMPLISHED LAWYER THAT HE WAS, More used every legitimate trick in the book to stay free while actively striving to defend those institutions that protected the freedom of all English citizens.

More was in grave danger, and he realized it, especially after May 23, 1533, the day Archbishop Cranmer "annulled" Henry's marriage to Catherine. His knowing response was recorded by his son-in-law. He said to Roper: "God give grace, son, that these matters within a while be not confirmed with oaths."[1] Yet that is precisely what would happen after the next session of Parliament.

His silence and his reputation for integrity were the strongest safeguards that More had. His reliance upon silence is famous, but few have considered how much he also relied upon his reputation for integrity. In his early poetry he had written that a reputation based on virtue provides, always and everywhere, the best protection.[2]

In June 1533, he wrote a letter to Erasmus stating that he considered it his "duty" to protect the integrity of his reputation so that he could continue to advance his efforts to maintain justice and peace in England. This letter includes his account of how his reputation stood at this point, one full year after he had resigned the chancellorship:

> After resigning my office, I waited until the opening of the new term, and so far no one has advanced a complaint against my integrity. Either my life has been so spotless or, at any rate, I have been

so circumspect that if my rivals oppose my boasting of the one, they are forced to let me boast of the other. As a matter of fact, the King himself has pronounced on this situation at various times—frequently in private, and twice in public. It is embarrassing for me to relate, but on the occasion of the installation of my most distinguished successor, the King used as his mouthpiece the most illustrious Duke—I mean the Duke of Norfolk, who is the Lord High Treasurer of England, and he respectfully ordered the Duke to proclaim publicly that he had unwillingly yielded to my request for resignation. The King, however, was not satisfied even with that extraordinary manifestation of good will toward me; at a much later date, he had the same pronouncement repeated, in his presence, at a solemn session of the Lords and Commons, this time using my successor as his mouthpiece, on the formal occasion of his opening address to that assembly which, as you know, we call Parliament.[3]

More wrote this letter with the explicit understanding that Erasmus would have it published as evidence of his good standing with the King. This good standing, however, would not last much longer, not when it became clear that More would hold fast in his opposition to Henry's designs.

Along with this letter, More sent Erasmus a copy of an inscription he had composed for his own tombstone—another ingenious tactic in his public self-defense. Besides having this text chiseled in marble, he was sending a copy of it to the most famous and best-connected figure in Europe. Among other things, More wrote of himself: "He so conducted himself all through this series of high offices or honors that his Excellent Sovereign found no fault with his service, neither did he make himself odious to the nobles nor unpleasant to the populace."[4]

In going to such lengths to clear his name from any suspicion of wrongdoing, More showed his prudence in a remarkable way: he used the full power of virtue to counter the unvirtuous devices of his opposition.

Meanwhile, the tension between Henry and More increased. In April 1533 More published *The Apology of Sir Thomas More,* a clever and courageous response to St. German's arguments for Henry's caesaropapism.[5] In June he refused to attend Anne's coronation ceremony. In July Pope Clement VII condemned Henry's divorce, and shortly afterwards an anonymous pamphlet supporting the Pope was printed by William Rastell—a nephew of More's, and his personal printer. More was, not surprisingly, under such strong suspicion that he found it necessary to send a written defense and disclaimer to Cromwell. In October 1533 he published another effective book against St. German, *The Debellation of Salem and Bizance.* Two months later he published, in response to further attacks, yet another lengthy defense of the Church.[6]

By the opening months of 1534, Henry was asking the House of Lords to indict More for treason, on what proved to be trumped-up charges.[7] Three times he asked them, and three times they refused. Throughout, More defended himself vigorously. Not only did he write to both Cromwell and Henry, but he even petitioned to have his case brought before the House of Lords.[8] Henry did not grant More's request. Instead, he set up a special commission, one consisting of Cromwell, Cranmer, Norfolk, and the new Lord Chancellor, Thomas Audley.

More met with this commission in the first days of March 1534.[9] It was a meeting that he himself recognized as a decisive turning point in his life. Before it took place, he had already seen clearly that Henry intended to destroy him; but once it was over, he rejoiced that now he "could never go back again."[10]

That encounter, one of the most dramatic events of More's life, left a strong impression on more than one person. Young Roper, in particular, would remember it vividly. Just before this meeting, he had "earnestly advised" his father-in-law to seek the commissioners' help in getting his name struck from the Parliament bill that listed him among those accused of treason.[11] So afterwards, when More returned in high spirits, Roper immediately asked him, "Are you, then, put out of the Parliament bill?" As Roper tells the rest of the story, we can imagine his astonishment at More's answer.

"By my troth, son Roper," said he, "I never remembered it."

"Never remembered it, Sir," said I, "a case that touches yourself so near and us all for your sake! I am sorry to hear it, for I verily trusted, when I saw you so merry, that all had been well."

Then he said, "Do you wish to know, son Roper, why I was so merry?"

"That would I gladly, Sir," said I.

"In good faith, I rejoiced, son," said he, "that I had given the devil a foul fall, and that with those lords I had gone so far, as without great shame I could never go back again."[12]

After such an opening in their conversation, it is no wonder that Roper was so attentive to what Sir Thomas said about the rest of the interrogation that he could, years later, give a detailed account of it.

More told him, says Roper, that when he arrived for his meeting with the royal commission, Lords Audley, Norfolk, Cromwell, and Cranmer "entertained him very friendly, asking him to sit down with them." But he declined their invitation, making it clear that he had come to take his stand.[13]

Lord Chancellor Audley, the first to speak, reminded More of the many great benefits he had received from the King, and then assured him that he "could ask for no worldly honor or profit from His Highness's hands that were likely to be denied"—if only he would join with "the Parliament, the bishops, and the universities."[14]

More's answer was "mildly made," but extraordinarily firm. Although he recognized gratefully the many benefits he had received from the King, he had hoped never to "have heard of this matter more," since he had "from time to time, always from the beginning, so plainly and truly declared [his] mind to His Grace," and since the King had said he would accept More's position and not bother him about it anymore.[15]

When it became clear that More was not going to give in, his interrogators moved from reason to threats.

> Then began they more terribly to touch [More],
> telling him that the King's Highness had given
> them in commandment, if they could by no gentle-
> ness win him, in his name with his great ingratitude
> to charge him, that never was there servant to his
> sovereign so villainous, nor subject to his Prince so
> traitorous as he.

More's response to this crude attempt at intimidation has become one of his most famous. "My lords," he said, "these terrors
are arguments for children, and not for me."[16] After other fruit-
less attempts, they finally gave up and "displeasantly departed," while he himself left "very merry."[17]

Although this interrogation established nothing against
More, Henry still kept his name in the Parliament bill for suspicion of treason. When the bill came before the House of Lords
again on March 6, the lords took the unusual step of asking King
Henry to allow them to hear More's case. Henry was so set
against More that he wanted this trial to be held—with himself
in attendance. By now he knew full well how much force his
mere presence could exert in getting the judgment he wanted.
However, Henry's counselors convinced him that under the circumstances, such a plan would utterly fail.[18]

Shortly afterwards, the Duke of Norfolk took More aside "in
familiar talk" and warned him that "it is perilous to strive with
princes," since "the wrath of the king is death." (This saying had
become a favorite of venerable old men, like Archbishop Warham,
who had learned all too well the power of royal wrath.) More
replied simply and calmly: "Is that all, my lord? Then in good
faith is there no more difference between Your Grace and me, but
that I shall die today and you tomorrow."[19] This response went so
starkly against conventional wisdom that it must have echoed in
Norfolk's ear many a time afterwards, especially when Norfolk
himself was condemned to death by this same angry prince.

Henry did not have his will that day, but he was still determined to find a way to bring about More's death. In the meantime, he found a way to inflict immediate injury: he abruptly cut
off More's major source of income, the salary he earned as king's
counselor.[20]

Just before Parliament was to be dismissed, Cromwell fashioned for Henry the pretext by which More would eventually be condemned to death. Cromwell's suggestion was to have any "word, writing, or deed attacking the King's new marriage and succession be made treason." But Parliament found this wording too broad. Eventually they came to an agreement: malicious deeds and writings could be considered acts of treason, but malicious *spoken* words would constitute the lesser offense known as misprision.[21]

On April 13, 1534, More was interrogated at Lambeth Palace and was asked to take an oath supporting the change of succession that would come with the King's new marriage. More was willing to accept this change of succession as formulated by Parliament; however, he was not willing to take this particular oath, the preamble of which had been formulated by Cromwell, not Parliament—an oath that went far beyond what Parliament's Act of Succession authorized. For refusing to take this oath, More was sent to prison. In a letter to his daughter, More pointed out the illegality of this decision. "I may tell thee, Meg," he said, "they who have committed me here for refusing this oath, that is not agreeable to the statute, are not by their own law able to justify my imprisonment."[22]

This obvious travesty of justice raised considerable difficulties for Audley and Cromwell, since both were lawyers. They therefore arranged as soon as possible "to find the means that another statute should be made for the confirmation of the oath so amplified with their additions."[23] This would be accomplished in November, at the next session of Parliament, but only with great difficulty.[24]

From the time of this imprisonment, More took pains to make a public record of all that transpired. This public record took the form of a series of handwritten letters to his daughter Margaret.

In the first of these letters, More gives a detailed account of all that took place on April 13.[25] Upon his arrival at Lambeth Palace, he was ushered in at once, even though others had arrived before him. When asked by the august commissioners if he would take the oath, he asked to see the actual text. After reading it carefully, More says, "then desired I the sight of the Act of the Succession, which was delivered me in a printed roll. After which [I] read [it] secretly by myself, and the oath [I] considered with the act."

After carefully studying both, he said that he was willing to swear to the succession as set forth by the Act of Parliament, but that he could not in conscience sign the oath. He made it clear, however, that he did not intend "to put any fault either in the act or any man that made it, or in the oath or any man that [might] swear it, nor to condemn the conscience of any other man."[26] He was simply refusing to sign the oath, without giving any explanation.

The Lord Chancellor then gravely warned More about the King's "great suspicion" and "great indignation"; he also showed him an impressive list of "the names of the lords and the commons who had sworn."[27] More was then "commanded to go into the garden," where other dignitaries were waiting to sign the oath. Declining to "go down because of the heat," he chose instead to wait in a room that looked down into the garden. From the window of that room, More saw what he describes, in his letter to Meg, as a pageant.[28]

First he saw the priest, doctor, and Lutheran sympathizer Hugh Latimer "come into the garden, and there walked he with divers other doctors and chaplains of my Lord of Canterbury, and very merry I saw him, for he laughed, and he took one or two about the neck so handsomely that if they had been women, I would have thought he had become wanton."[29]

Latimer's cheerful accommodation to Henry's will contrasted sharply with the stance of the next participant in this pageant. "After that," More says, "came Master Doctor Wilson forth from the lords and was with two gentlemen brought by me, and gentlemanly sent straight unto the Tower." Wilson, like More, had refused the oath.

The last of these pageant players was the Master Vicar of Croydon. This vicar was, like More, one of those select few who "were sent for, were sworn, and . . . had such favor at the council's hand that they were not delayed." Unlike More, the Vicar of Croydon sped through and signed the oath. Then, More writes, "either for gladness or for dryness or else that it might be seen (*quod ille notus erat pontifici*), [the Vicar] went to my Lord [Cranmer]'s buttery bar and called for a drink, and drank (*valde familiariter*)."[30]

This sentence is worth careful reflection; in the subtle wording of it, one can discover what More saw as the fundamental lesson of this whole pageant. To begin with, his list of possible reasons for the Vicar's going to the bar is revealing. Clearly he does not consider the middle one ("for dryness") very likely, given the more provocative nature of the motives suggested before and after. Then, to indicate which of these two motives he considers more likely, he gives hints in two Latin phrases. The first, an allusion to St. John's account of Peter's denial of Christ, suggests a parallel between the pageant More sees in Cranmer's courtyard and the drama of Peter's denial in the high priest's courtyard.[31] The other Latin phrase clearly throws weight upon the third motive, showing its spiritual significance. The Vicar seems to have welcomed the chance to show off his familiarity with Cranmer, the high priest of Henry's new religion.

Be that as it may, once the Vicar and the others "had played their pageant and were gone out of the place," More was again called before the royal commission. The commissioners began by showing him "what a number had sworn" that day, "gladly, without any sticking." More "laid no blame on any man" for doing so, but answered just as he had done before.[32]

The commissioners then rebuked him for obstinacy and insisted that he tell them why he would not take the oath. But all More would say was that "if I may not declare the causes without peril, then to leave them undeclared is no obstinacy."[33]

At this point Cranmer tried a clever tactic. As More relates it, "My Lord of Canterbury, taking hold upon what I [had] said, that I condemned not the conscience of them that swore, said to me that it appeared well that I did not take it for a very sure and certain thing that I might not lawfully swear it, but rather as a thing uncertain and doubtful." From there Cranmer went on to say, "'You know for a certainty and a thing without doubt that you be bounden to obey your sovereign lord your King.'" And then came the conclusion: "'Therefore are you bound to leave off the doubt of your unsure conscience in refusing the oath, and take the sure way in obeying your prince, and swear.'"[34]

More was surprised by this subtle argument coming from a person of such authority. All he would say in response was that "in my conscience this was one of the cases in which I was bounden that I should not obey my prince. . . . I had not informed my conscience either suddenly or lightly, but by long leisure and diligent search for the matter."[35]

The Abbot of Westminster then tried a similar argument. Surely More would admit, the Abbot reasoned, that any individual can err. So surely he must also admit that he could be mistaken in this matter, especially since the whole of Parliament held the contrary position. More's response to this argument was again respectful but firm. "I answered that if there were no more than myself upon my side and the whole Parliament upon the other, I would be sore afraid to lean to mine own mind only against so many. But on the other side, if it so be that in some things for which I refuse the oath, I have (as I think I have) upon my side as great a council and a greater too, I am not then bound to change my conscience and conform it to the council of one realm, against the general council of Christendom."[36]

This argument More would use many a time afterwards—the last, at his trial.

After such weak arguments failed to move him, Cromwell then turned to a mixture of flattery and intimidation. More describes what happened: "After this, Master Secretary (as one who tenderly favored me) said and swore a great oath that he had rather that his own only son (who is of truth a goodly young gentleman, and shall I trust come to much honor) had lost his head than that I should thus have refused the oath. For surely the King's Highness would now conceive a great suspicion against me, and think that the matter of the nun of Canterbury was all devised by my direction." More's response was, he tells us, simply that "the contrary was true and well known, and [that] whatsoever misfortune should happen to me, it did not lie in my power to help it without peril of my soul."[37]

Not knowing what to do next, the royal commissioners decided to leave More in the custody of the Abbot of Westminster until they could work out a new strategy. He was there until April 17; during that four-day interval, Henry consulted with his council, and finally decided to imprison More in the Tower of London.[38]

There being no legal grounds for his arrest, More was technically just being "held," in the hope that he would change his mind about the oath. Imprisonment would require a court conviction; in More's case, this would mean imprisonment for life and loss of his property.[39] In November, a new treason law was passed,[40] and Henry arranged that Parliament pass an attainder against More as a substitute for the usual court procedure.[41] By this fiat More's imprisonment was made perpetual, and his family reduced to poverty.[42] This law, as More pointed out, was itself unlawful. If he should die because of it, then his death would be a clear case "in which a man may lose his head and yet have no harm, but instead of harm, inestimable good at the hand of God."[43]

Meanwhile, Henry and Cromwell were continuing to work towards More's execution. Imprisonment was no longer a sufficient punishment for such a public and effective sign of opposition. Yet execution would prove difficult, since More had committed no violation that called for the death penalty. Attempts at intimidation, therefore, remained their principal strategy for trying to break his opposition.

On May 4, 1535, for example, they allowed Meg to visit More in prison—at the same time that three Carthusian monks and two other priests were being led past his window on their way to being hanged, drawn, and quartered for opposing the Supremacy Act. Far from unsettling him, however, this incident only edified More and strengthened him in his resolve. As they stood by the window, watching the monks march to their death, he said to his daughter:

> "Do you not see, Meg, that these blessed fathers are now as cheerfully going to their deaths as bridegrooms to their marriage? . . . God, considering their long-continued life in most sore and grievous penance, will no longer suffer them to remain here in this vale of misery and iniquity, but

speedily hence taketh them to the fruition of His
everlasting deity, whereas your silly father, Meg,
who like a most wicked caitiff has passed forth the
whole course of his miserable life most sinfully,
God, thinking him not worthy so soon to come to
that eternal felicity, leaveth him here yet still in the
world, further to be plunged and turmoiled with
misery."[44]

Yet More's misery on earth was not to last much longer.

On May 7 he was interrogated again, this time in the Tower
of London.[45] Cromwell presided, with four other officials in attendance, including the newly appointed solicitor general,
Richard Rich. As in his previous interrogation, More was invited
to sit, but he firmly refused. Cromwell then insisted that he state
explicitly his opinion about the King's new title, "Supreme Head
of the Church in England." He refused, fully aware that his protection from the Act of Treasons lay in silence. No urgings or
threats could move him. All he would declare explicitly was that
he was determined not "to study or meddle with any matter of
this world, but that my whole study should be upon the Passion
of Christ and mine own passage out of this world."[46]

When it became evident that Cromwell was getting nowhere with this approach, he sent More from the room and conferred with his fellow examiners. After deciding upon a new
strategy, he called him back.

Reminding him of the "obedience and allegiance" he had always shown "unto the King's Highness," Cromwell asked if he
believed "that the King's Grace might exact" of him "such things
as are contained in the statutes and upon the same punish-
ments as he might of other men." More answered simply, "I
would not say the contrary." Cromwell then revealed, in the
course of making threats, why they were trying so hard to
break More's obstinate silence: this resistance of his was caus-
ing others to resist as well.[47]

More must have been heartened to know that his firm stand
was an encouragement to others. He gave a spirited defense
against Cromwell. "I answered," he says, "that I give no man occasion to hold any point one way or another, nor ever gave any

man advice or counsel therein one way or the other. And for conclusion I could no further go, whatsoever pain should come thereof. I am, quoth I, the King's true faithful subject and daily bedesman[48] and pray for His Highness and all his and all the realm. I do nobody harm, I say none harm, I think none harm, but wish everybody good. And if this be not enough to keep a man alive, in good faith I long not to live."[49]

With this reasonable plea for justice, he managed to stay safe for a short time. Later that month, however, reason gave way to unbridled rage when Henry learned that Pope Clement had made Bishop Fisher a cardinal. The "anger of princes" now meant certain death for both Fisher and More.

On June 3 More refused to sit and was interrogated yet again, but this time by the highest-ranking members of Henry's council: Archbishop Cranmer, Lord Chancellor Audley, Master Secretary Cromwell, Lord Wiltshire (Anne Boleyn's father), and Lord Suffolk (Henry's brother-in-law). More was told again that the King "was not at all content or satisfied" with his answer. In addition, Cromwell reported that the King thought that More "had been the occasion of much grudge and harm in the realm" and had shown "an obstinate and evil mind" towards him. The King was therefore now commanding More upon his allegiance "to make a plain and terminate answer" whether it was "lawful that His Highness should be Supreme Head of the Church of England." If in his opinion it was not, then he should "utter plainly [his] malignity."[50]

More began his response with a strong denial: "I have no malignity and therefore I [can] utter none." Then he said, "Very heavy I [am] that the King's Highness should have any such opinion of me. . . . [Yet] have I no remedy to help it, but [can] only comfort myself with this consideration, that I know very well that the time will come when God shall declare my truth toward His Grace before him and all the world." He tells Meg, "And while it might perhaps seem to be small cause for comfort because I might take harm here first in the meanwhile, I thanked God that my case was such in this matter through the clearness of my own conscience that though I might have pain I could not have harm, for a man may in such case lose his head and have no harm."

More then went on to remind the King about "the most virtuous lesson that a prince ever taught his servant." That lesson, More said, King Henry "taught me at my first coming to his noble service." The lesson, simple but with profound implications, was this: to look "first upon God and next upon the King."[51]

All that More said, however, was ignored by his interrogators. Audley and Cromwell both insisted that the "King might by his laws compel [More] to make a plain answer, either one way or the other," about this statute. More simply replied that such a measure seemed "somewhat hard," although he would not dispute the King's authority. Had he not refrained from saying anything for or against this statute, even though it went against his conscience? Therefore, he said, it would be "a very hard thing to compel me to say either precisely with it against my conscience to the loss of my soul, or precisely against it to the destruction of my body."[52]

More stated unequivocally that he would not declare his mind on this statute and that he would not take any oaths. He also made it clear that he was just as willing "to be out of the world as in it." Yet if he was not afraid of death, his examiners asked, then why be so unwilling to speak out plainly against the statute? "Whereto I answered," More says, "as the truth is, that I have not been a man of such holy living as I might be bold to offer myself to death, lest God for my presumption might suffer me to fall, and therefore I put not myself forward, but draw back. Howbeit if God draw me to it Himself, then trust I in His great mercy, that He shall not fail to give me grace and strength."[53] This was undoubtedly not only a truthful answer, but a prudent one as well. What he refrained from telling them directly was that he understood their game perfectly. Under the law he was protected; but only for as long as law, not passionate will, reigned supreme.

Since this session also failed to bring results, the psychological warfare increased. On June 12, all of More's writing materials and books were removed. (This was done by Richard Rich. It was on this occasion that the famous conversation between them took place—or rather, did not take place, as we shall later see.) Yet nothing could vanquish More's sense of humor. As soon as his books were gone, he closed the shutters of his cell and quipped to his jailer, "When all the wares are gone, the shop windows are to be shut up."[54]

Two days later he was interrogated again, this time about his communications with Cardinal Fisher. Having gathered sufficient evidence to convict Fisher of treason (as newly defined), More's inquisitors now sought to identify him as Fisher's co-conspirator. Ultimately, this line of questioning also failed, but every possible angle was explored to ensnare More, despite his manifest protection by the law.[55] Although this inquisition brought forth no conclusive evidence, More's trial was scheduled for July 1; five days later, he was dead.

Chapter Twenty

Between Father and Daughter:
A Memorable Conversation

THROUGHOUT THE TIME OF HIS IMPRISONMENT, More's greatest sufferings did not come from his poverty or his poor health or his weak-willed friends. They came from his own family. Having taken such great care to educate his children, More now found that none of them supported him in his decision of conscience. Nor did his wife.

He was, indeed, a man alone. He did have the moral support of his elderly friend Cardinal Fisher, and that of the Carthusians, but he was not allowed to see any of them. Nor could he see his good friend Antonio Bonvisi, though Bonvisi did send him food, wine, and a warm coat. The only loved ones he could see—his wife and his children—provided food and paid for a servant to care for him, but they could not give him moral support. No one in the family could understand his "scruple of conscience."[1] They had all taken the oath, making whatever qualification they found necessary—"as far as the law of God allows," perhaps.

Lady Alice was especially opposed. Son-in-law Roper tells us that when she was finally able to see her husband for the first time, she "bluntly" greeted him thus: "'Master More, I marvel that you, who have always been taken for such a wise man, should now play such a fool as to lie here in this tiny, filthy prison and be content to be shut up with rats and mice when you could be about and at your liberty. . . .'" After quietly listening to her long reproof, More "with a cheerful expression said to her, 'I pray you, good Mistress Alice, tell me one thing.'" Roper continues:

"What is that?" she said.

"Is not this house as close to heaven as my own?"

To which she, after her accustomed fashion, not
  liking such talk, answered, "Tilly-vally, tilly-
  vally!"

"But what do you say, Mistress Alice?" he asked.
  "Is it not so?"

"Good God, good God, man, will you never stop
  repeating the same things?" she said.

"But, Mistress Alice, if they are true, it is very well
  [that I say them]."[2]

At this point Lady Alice "kept on pleading and harping on a
long life," so Thomas finally interrupted her.

"How long, my Alice, shall I be able to enjoy this
  life?"

"A full twenty years, if God so wills."

"Do you wish me, then, to exchange eternity for
  twenty years? Here, good wife, you do not
  bargain very skillfully."[3]

Despite such arguments, Lady Alice remained adamantly
opposed to her husband's "scruple of conscience." Because of
her strong opposition, More was probably unable to say to her
what he did say to his daughter Margaret: that he considered
his imprisonment a sign of God's special care for him;[4] that he
saw it as an opportunity to prepare for his death,[5] and viewed
his present pains as "profitable exercises in patience."[6]

The strength of the family opposition to More's stance is
well documented in a moving letter that might be called his
"Dialogue on Conscience."[7] In this letter, Meg records a
lengthy conversation she had with her father about his "scruple of conscience." The letter reports how she visited him in
prison and tried to persuade him to come home, for his own
good and that of the family. The response he gave to this invitation sets the tone for the entire conversation. Warmly and
humorously, but also pointedly, More called his daughter "mistress Eve, . . . come to tempt [her] father again."

What occasioned this visit and discussion was a letter that Meg had received from her stepsister, Alice Alington. On August 17, 1534, Alice had written to relay a conversation she had just had with Lord Chancellor Audley. The Lord Chancellor had come to hunt on the Alington estate with the explicit purpose, it seems, of warning Alice about the dangers threatening her obstinate father. Audley had taken risks to protect More from Henry's wrath during the Nun of Kent controversy.[8] He had also, as we have seen, been on various commissions set up to persuade More to relent in his opposition. Now Audley wanted Alice and the rest of the family to know that "I would not have your father so scrupulous of his conscience."[9]

Shortly after receiving this letter, Meg brought it to her father. But she did not show it to him right away. First she asked about his several illnesses: the chest ailment that had been afflicting him for several years now, the kidney stones, and the severe cramps in his legs.[10] Then she said with him their customary prayers and told him about everyone in the family. Only after all that, and after pleading that he find a way to please the King, did she hand him Alice Alington's letter. As she did so, she said what was only natural for a loving daughter to say: "If you do not change your mind, you are likely to lose all those friends that are able to do you any good."[11]

More responded first with a smile and a rather jovial question: "What, mistress Eve (as I called you when you came first), has my daughter Alington played the serpent with you, and with a letter set you at work to come to tempt your father again, and for the favor that you bear him labor to make him swear against his conscience, and so send him to the devil?"[12]

That smile then turned to an earnest revelation of his true mind. "Daughter Margaret," he said, "we two have talked of this thing more often than two or three times; and that same tale, in effect, that you tell me now—and the same fear too—you have told me twice before. And I have twice answered you too, that if it were possible in this matter for me to do the thing that might content the King's Grace without God being offended, there is no man who has already taken this oath more gladly than I would do, as one who reckons himself more deeply bound unto the

King's Highness for his most singular bounty, many ways showed and declared, than any of them all beside. But since, standing by my conscience, I can in no wise do it, and that for the instruction of my conscience in the matter I have not slightly looked, but by many years studied and advisedly considered, and never could yet see or hear that thing, and I think I never shall, that could induce my own mind to think otherwise than I do, I have no manner of remedy, but God has given me to the straight, that either I must deadly displease Him, or abide any worldly harm that He shall for my other sins, under name of this thing, suffer to fall upon me. Whereof (as I before this have told you too) I have, before I came here, not left unbethought or unconsidered the very worst and the uttermost that can by possibility fall. And although I know my own frailty full well and the natural faintness of my own heart, yet if I had not trusted that God should give me strength rather to endure all things than offend Him by swearing ungodly against my own conscience, you may be very sure I would not have come here. And since I look in this matter only unto God, it makes me little matter, though men call it as it pleases them and say it is no conscience but a foolish scruple."[13]

Meg said in response that she could not mistrust her father's good mind or learning, and yet she proceeded to do just that. She urged him to consider seriously this message from "your tender friend and very good lord," who, together with "all the nobles of this realm and almost all other men too," had taken a contrary position. In so advising him to consider the weighty opinion of others, Meg was undoubtedly invoking a principle of prudent counsel which More himself had taught her.

And he did read the letter carefully—three times, "in no manner hastily," but considering each word. He then expressed his gratitude to Audley for his kind concern.

He could not, however, agree with the suggestions of the letter.

Audley's advice took the form of two "Aesop" fables. Only the first of these was actually from Aesop; and, as More pointed out, it was one that Cardinal Wolsey had often used with great success to persuade "the King and the realm to spend many a fair penny" on war.[14]

As Audley told it, the fable went like this. Once there was a country inhabited mostly by fools. The few wise individuals knew that a great rain was coming, a peculiar kind of storm that would make anyone foolish who remained in it. They therefore made caves for themselves and stayed in them until the rain passed. Then these wise ones "came forth thinking to make the fools do what they pleased, and to rule them as they would. But the fools would have none of that, but would have the rule themselves for all their craft. And when the wise ones saw they could not obtain their purpose, they wished that they had been in the rain."[15]

More's first reaction to this story was one of surprise. What wise person, he asked, would ever desire to rule the foolish? After all, none are "so unruly as they that lack wit and are fools." Indeed, those "wise" ones who hid in the caves must have been stark-raving fools themselves.[16]

And what did this fable have to do with his own situation? He had never longed to be a ruler; he knew himself to be *Morus*.[17] Without further comment, he simply offered this prayer:

> [May] our Lord make us all so wise that we may each wisely rule ourselves in this time of tears, this vale of misery, this simple wretched world—a world in which, as Boethius says, a man who is proud that he bears rule over other men is much like one mouse being proud to bear rule over other mice in a barn. God, I say, give us the grace so wisely to rule ourselves here that when we shall go in haste to meet the great Spouse, we may not be taken as sleepers who, for lack of light in our lamps, are shut out of heaven among the five foolish virgins.[18]

These references to Boethius and the Bible work to establish a radically different context to the fable than what Audley and Wolsey had in mind.

More then proceeded to challenge—also discreetly, of course—the context and applicability of Audley's second fable. This story involved a lion and an ass going to confession, with results as different as the confessions themselves. In abbreviated form, this is how the story went: "The lion confessed that he had devoured all the beasts that he could come by. His confessor absolved him because [being a lion,] he was a king, and . . . it was his nature to [devour beasts]. Then came the poor ass and said that he took but one straw out of his master's shoe for hunger, by which action he thought that his master caught cold. His confessor could not absolve this great trespass, but by and by sent him to the bishop."[19] Lest the point of the tale be missed, Audley explicitly stated in conclusion: "I would not have your father so scrupulous of his conscience."

More's first comment on the tale was his rather understated observation that it "seems not to be Aesop's," since it is about confession and Aesop lived "in Greece before Christ's days." He then feigned ignorance of the moral of this perfectly obvious story. "It is somewhat too subtle for me," he said. "For whom his lordship understands by the lion and the . . . bishop, of all these things can I nothing tell. But by the foolish, scrupulous ass, . . . my lord's other words of my scruple declare that his lordship merrily meant that for me."[20]

Shrewdly, More bypassed completely the issue of the lion's identity, but he cleverly and directly took up the charge that he himself was being a foolish ass by making himself overly dependent upon the judgment of Bishop Fisher. Despite his great respect for Fisher, he said, "I was not led by him in this matter." In fact, he explained, "I never intend, God being my good Lord, to pin my soul to another man's back, not even the best man that I know this day living: for I know not where he may happen to carry it. There is no man living of whom, while he lives, I may make myself sure. Some may act for favor and some may act for fear—and so might they carry my soul a wrong way. And some-one might happen to frame himself a conscience and think that, while he did it for fear, God would forgive him. And some might think that they will repent and be absolved and so God will forgive them. And some may perhaps be of that mind that, if they say one thing and at the same time think the contrary, God more regards their heart than their tongue. . . . But in good faith, Margaret, I can use no such ways in so great a matter."[21]

To emphasize and illustrate this point, More told a fable of his own, a merry tale about "a poor, honest man of the country who was called Company." This man was serving on a jury, and he was the only one on the panel who was not from the same northern locality as the defendant. After listening to all the evidence, the other eleven jurors came to a quick decision in favor of their fellow Northerner. Company, "this honest man of another quarter," did not concur. But because he "sat still and said nothing," they paid no attention to him. They said, "'We are agreed now; come, let us go give our verdict.'"[22]

At this point, however, Company did intervene, declaring that "his mind did not go the way theirs did (if their minds went the way that they said)," and that they therefore should, perhaps, "tarry and talk about the matter and tell him such reasons that he might think as they did." But until they could convince him otherwise, "he must say as he thought," since "he had a soul of his own to keep as they had."[23]

The response to this reasonable request was not one based on reason. "'What, good fellow, is the matter with you?'" they asked. "'Are not we eleven here and you but one alone, and all we are agreed? Why should you stick? . . . Company, now by thy true name, good fellow, play then the good companion and come with us . . . for good company.'"[24] To help them put this issue in proper perspective, honest Company then asked this long question: "'When we shall go from here and come before God and He shall send you to heaven for doing according to your conscience, and me to the devil for doing against mine, [what will you say then if I say this to you]: "I went once for good company with you, which is the cause that I go now to hell; play you the good fellows now again with me. As I went then for good company with you, so some of you go now for good company with me." Would you go?'" No one, of course, would agree to that. And so Company would not go along with them either, "'for the passage of my poor soul passes all good company.'"[25]

Then, passing from story form to personal address, More said to Meg: "I pray you now, good Margaret, tell me this. Would you wish your poor father—being at least somewhat learned—to regard the peril of his soul less than this honest unlearned man? I meddle not, you know well, with the conscience of any man that has sworn, nor do I take it upon myself to be their judge. But now, if they do well and their consciences grudge them not, and if I with my conscience to the contrary should for good company go with them and swear as they do, when our souls hereafter shall pass out of this world and stand in judgment at the bar before the High Judge, if He judges them to heaven and me to the devil because I did as they did, not thinking as they thought, if I should then say (as the good man Company said): My old good lords and friends, . . . I swore because you swore and went that way that you went; do likewise for me now. Let me not go alone. If there be any good fellowship with you, some of you come with me. By my truth, Margaret, I may say to you, in secret counsel, here between us two (but let it go no further, I beseech you heartily): I find the friendship of this wretched world so fickle that for those whom I could entreat or pray for good fellowship to go to the devil with me, among them all I think that I should not find one. And then by God, Margaret, if you think so too, best it is, I suppose, that for any respect of them all, were they twice as many more as they be, I have myself a respect to my own soul."[26]

Good debater that she was, Meg conceded that her father should not swear simply for fellowship, and then proposed instead that he had an obligation to change and reform his conscience so as to be in conformity with the other leading men of England, especially since Parliament had passed this law.[27] More's response was swift and clear: No one is "bound to swear that every law is well made, nor bound upon the pain of God's displeasure to perform any such point of law as were indeed unlawful." Only on a clear point of Christian faith is one obliged to conform one's conscience—not on a point on which Christendom is not in agreement.[28]

Meg then tried a somewhat different tactic, suggesting what prudence would generally recommend: that a private citizen should obey the laws, since the nation's lawmakers see more than any one citizen can see. More replied that although he agreed with this as a general principle, he had "very well weighed" the issues involved. He also pointed out that lawmakers can at times be unduly influenced by such concerns as keeping the prince's favor or avoiding his anger; they might be unduly afraid of losing wealth or overly anxious about their own family and friends. Such concerns might induce "some men either [to] swear otherwise than they think or [to] frame their conscience afresh to think otherwise than they thought." Any such motives as these, More said, he would "not conceive" of his fellow Englishmen. Not only did he have "better hope of their goodness than to think so of them," but he also knew few people so fainthearted as himself. "Therefore will I," he said, "by my will, think no worse of other folk in the thing that I know not, than I find in myself."[29]

Furthermore, he did not see himself as the lone dissenter in the face of an otherwise unanimous consensus. In fact, he saw himself on the side of the majority, if all of Christendom was taken into account. "Of those well learned and virtuous men who are alive," he pointed out, "they are not the fewer part who are of my mind." And that was to say nothing of all those "holy doctors and saints" from the past who also were of More's mind, as evidenced by the books they wrote that "yet to this day remain here in men's hands."[30]

As far as More was concerned, there was no point to further argument. "But as concerns my own self," he said, "for your comfort I shall say to you, daughter, that my own conscience in this matter (I damn no other man's) is such as may well stand with my own salvation. Of this I am, Meg, as sure as that God is in heaven. And therefore, as for all the rest—goods, lands, and life . . . —I verily trust that God shall strengthen me to bear the loss, rather than swear against my conscience and put my soul in peril."[31]

At this point in the conversation, as Meg reports in her letter, her only response was to sit sadly, "full heavy for the peril" of her father. More then smiled and gently teased her, saying, "How now, daughter Margaret? What now, mother Eve? Where is your mind now? Sit not musing with some serpent in your breast upon some new persuasion to offer father Adam the apple once again."[32]

Meg admitted that she was out of reasons, except for a very personal one. "Why should you refuse to swear, Father?" she asked. "For I have sworn myself." But at this, More just laughed and replied, "That word was like Eve too, for she offered Adam no worse fruit than she had eaten herself." Then, overcome with emotion, she simply blurted out, "But yet, Father, by my truth, I fear very greatly that this matter will bring you into marvelous heavy trouble. You know well that as I showed you, Master Secretary sent you word that as your very friend, to remember that the Parliament lasts yet."[33]

"Margaret," he answered, "I thank him right heartily. But as I showed you then again, I left not this gear unthought on. And . . . I know well that if they would make a law to do me any harm, that law could never be lawful, [and] I trust that God shall keep me in that grace that, concerning my duty to my prince, no man shall do me hurt if he does me wrong. And then, as I told you, this is like a riddle, a case in which a man may lose his head and have no harm. . . . I also have good hope that God shall never suffer so good and wise a prince to reward the long service of his true, faithful servant in such a way. Yet since there is nothing impossible, I do not forget in this matter the counsel of Christ in the Gospel: that before I should begin to build this castle for the safeguard of my own soul, I would sit and reckon what the cost would be. During many a restless night, Margaret, while my wife slept and thought that I slept too, I counted what peril could possibly fall to me, so much so that I am sure that nothing more could come. And in considering this, daughter, I had a full heavy heart. But yet for all that, I thank our Lord that I never thought to change, even though the very worst should happen to me that my fear conceived."[34]

Still moved by fear born of daughterly affection, Meg objected that it would soon be too late for More to change his mind.

He replied, "Too late, daughter Margaret? I beseech our Lord that, if I ever make such a change, it may be too late indeed. For well I know the change cannot be good for my soul. . . . And therefore I pray God that in this world I never approve of such change. For as much as I take harm here, I shall have at least that much less therefore when I go from here. . . .

"Mistrust Him, Meg, will I not, even though I feel myself faint. Indeed, although I should feel my fear even to the point of overthrowing me, yet shall I remember how St. Peter, with a blast of wind, began to sink for his faint faith, and shall do as he did—call upon Christ and pray Him to help. And then I trust He shall set His holy hand unto me, and in the stormy seas, hold me up from drowning. . . .

"And finally, Margaret, this I know well, that without my fault He will not let me be lost. . . . Therefore, my own good daughter, never trouble your mind over anything that ever shall happen to me in this world. Nothing can come except what God wills. And I make me very sure that whatsoever that be, even if nothing has ever appeared so bad, it shall indeed be the best. . . .

"Serve God and be merry and rejoice in Him. And if anything happens to me that you would not approve, pray to God for me, but trouble not yourself: as I shall full heartily pray for us all that we may meet together in heaven where we shall be merry forever. . . ."[35]

Chapter Twenty-one

Another David

DAVID WAS THE LEADER OF HIS PEOPLE, a devoted husband and father, a poet and musician, an ardent lover of God, and a man who suffered greatly and sinned greatly. From the wealth of his experience, David wrote many of the psalms, poems of such power and beauty that today, three thousand years later, they are still central to the prayer life of millions of people, both Jewish and Christian.

Certainly they were central to the prayer life of Sir Thomas More. He prayed the psalms for most of his life, and called the psalter "the very sum of clear and lightsome [illuminating] prophecies."[1] As a young man, he carefully studied and translated Pico's "Commentary on Psalm 15" and included it in his first spiritual handbook; later, he undoubtedly knew well that best-seller written by his good friend Bishop John Fisher, *The Fruitful Sayings of David the King and Prophet in the Seven Penitential Psalms*; and at the end of his life, he himself wrote an extended commentary on Psalm 91, as an integral part of *A Dialogue of Comfort against Tribulation*.

More recommended that "special psalms . . . be drawn out of the psalter" as a help in times of trial.[2] We know the selections he made for four different times or situations in his own life. These selections are highly revealing.

For his daily, personal prayer, More chose the seven penitential psalms (6, 32, 38, 51, 102, 130, 143). That he considered himself a sinful person is obvious, and made even more so by the marginal notations he entered into his psalter.[3] Next to the first of these psalms, he wrote: "a prayer imploring pardon for one's sins"; next to the second, "confession of sin"; and next to the third, "a good psalm for obtaining pardon." He also recited these seven psalms with Meg whenever she visited him in prison.[4]

For the family prayer, which he led whenever he was at home, he chose four psalms. The first of these, Psalm 51, might seem a surprising choice; this is, after all, the prayer of repentance that David wrote after he committed adultery with Bathsheba and had her husband murdered. But a consideration of the inherent beauty and power of this prayer readily suggests the kind of impact it could have had on the More children.

The first part begins with a moving petition for pardon and ends with an affirmation of the importance of sincerity and truth.

> Have mercy on me, O God, in your goodness; in the greatness of your compassion wipe out my offense. Thoroughly wash me from my guilt and of my sin cleanse me. For I acknowledge my offense and my sin is before me always: "Against you only have I sinned, and done what is evil in your sight." . . . In guilt was I born, and in sin my mother conceived me; behold, you are pleased with sincerity of heart, and in my inmost being you teach me wisdom.

That More had his children join him in this praise of sincerity and inner wisdom resonates with his primary goal in educating them. As we have already seen, he considered the goal of education to be "the testimony of God and a good conscience." Only if these were attained, he wrote, could one achieve an inner joy and peace that would not be "stirred by praise of flatterers or stung by the follies of unlearned mockers of learning."[5]

In the second part of Psalm 51, the psalmist, acknowledging that only a "clean heart . . . and a steadfast spirit" can bring true "joy and gladness," asks that his soul be cleansed and strengthened. This part of the psalm recalls a theme of central importance to More: that the greatest earthly joy comes from a clear conscience. It is no wonder, therefore, that he recited this psalm (commonly known as the *Miserere*) on the scaffold, as his last prayer on earth.

The second psalm More selected for his family, Psalm 25, begins with a confident offering of oneself to God: "To you I lift up my soul, O Lord my God. In you I trust." From there it moves into a humble request for guidance and for pardon: "Your ways, O Lord, make known to me; teach me your paths, guide me in your truth and teach me, for you are God my savior. . . . The sins of my youth and my frailties remember not; in your kindness remember me, because of your goodness, O Lord." Like Psalm 51, this psalm is a plea for God to inform, guide, and purify one's conscience.[6]

As a sequel to this comforting prayer, More chose Psalm 67, a hymn of praise and thanksgiving for God's generous blessings: ". . . May the peoples praise you, O God; may all the peoples praise you! The earth has yielded its fruits; God, our God, has blessed us. . . ."

Especially in light of the generous love praised in Psalm 67, the final psalm in the series More chose for his family serves as a fitting conclusion. Psalm 130, widely known as the *De Profundis,* is a confident prayer for pardon and mercy, but one that emphasizes deep love and longing for a God of great kindness.

> I trust in the Lord; my soul trusts in his word. My soul waits for the Lord more than sentinels wait for the dawn. More than sentinels wait for the dawn, let Israel wait for the Lord, for with the Lord is kindness and with him is plenteous redemption; and he will redeem Israel from all their iniquities.

This longing for God is one of the major themes which More highlights in his psalter. He marks, for example, the first two verses of Psalm 42 ("As the hind longs for the running waters, so my soul longs for you, O God. Athirst is my soul for God, the living God. When shall I go and behold the face of God?") and writes next to them, "Happy the man who can say this from his soul." In a similar way, he also marks and annotates these lines from Psalm 84: "How lovely is your dwelling place, O Lord of hosts! My soul yearns and pines for the courts of the Lord. My heart and my flesh cry out for the living God."[7]

During his imprisonment, More chose another sequence of psalms to help him in this intensely trying time.[8] The first of these, Psalm 22, gives voice to deep anguish and suffering in the very words Christ uttered on the cross: "My God, my God, why have you forsaken me?" And it continues in language deeply expressive of what More was suffering with and for his Lord: "I am a worm, not a man; the scorn of men, despised by the people. All who see me scoff at me; they mock me with parted lips; they wag their heads. . . . Rescue my soul from the sword, my loneliness from the grip of the dog" (Ps 22:6–7, 20).

Anguished as he is, the psalmist nonetheless expresses complete confidence in God: "You have been my guide since I was first formed, my security at my mother's breast. To you I was committed at birth, from my mother's womb you are my God. Be not far from me, for I am in distress; be near, for I have no one to help me." Then, reflecting upon God's greatness as shown in the past, the psalmist cries out, with confident joy: "The lowly shall eat their fill; they who seek the Lord shall praise him: 'May your hearts be ever merry.' All the ends of the earth shall remember and turn to the Lord. . . . For dominion is the Lord's, and he rules the nations" (Ps 22:9–11, 26–28).

After this psalm expressing the personal experience of suffering, More then prayed one of the many psalms he notes as being "for the king."[9] Psalm 20, his "Prayer for the King in Time of War," calls attention to the ultimate source of a king's power: "Some are strong in chariots; some, in horses; but we are strong in the name of the Lord, our God. Though they bow down and fall, yet we stand upright and firm."

Next, More chose Psalm 74, as a prayer "for the people."[10] This psalm has broad applications to any national catastrophe. In relation to that of sixteenth-century England, verses 21 and 22 must have seemed particularly appropriate: "May the humble not retire in confusion; may the afflicted and the poor praise your name. Arise, O God; defend your cause; remember how the fool blasphemes you day after day."

More's prison psalm-sequence concludes with two prayers of thanksgiving. The first, Psalm 98, is a victory song: "Sing to the Lord a new song, for he has done wondrous deeds; his right arm has won victory for him, his holy arm. . . . He will rule the world with justice and the peoples with equity." The second, Psalm 111, begins with the declaration, "I give thanks to Yahweh with all my heart," and ends with a verse that More flags for emphasis: "The fear of the Lord is the beginning of wisdom; prudent are all who live by it."

One striking feature of the sequence More chose for his prison ordeal is that only one of the five psalms pertains to his personal sufferings—and even this one leads him to thanksgiving and praise.

In addition to this sequence, More collected verses from thirty-one psalms to form one powerful prayer he could lift up to God from his prison cell. In this prayer, entitled "Imploring Divine Help against Temptation, While Scorning Demons through Hope and Confidence in God,"[11] More did what he had always taught his children to do: he used mockery and scorn as weapons against the devil.[12]

This collection of psalms gives voice to a triumph of spirit over fear and suffering. It is the testimony of a confidence developed through long reflection and interior struggle. To read this prayer is to listen to a soul fashioned in the forge of fear, discouragement, betrayal, loneliness, and abandonment, and consequently convinced of its frailty and sinfulness—a soul acutely conscious of living in a dangerous world, of being constantly surrounded by the devil and all his helpers.

First and foremost, however, "Imploring Divine Help" is the prayer of one who knows he is loved and cared for by a wise, loving, and all-powerful God. Well he knows that the world, dangerous as it is, belongs to God. And so these dangers serve only to draw him closer to God. In the end, he is so close to God that he can say, "Even though I walk in the dark valley, I fear no evil, for you are at my side with your rod and your staff that give me courage" (Ps 23:4)—for "only in God is my soul at rest . . .; he only is my rock and my salvation, my stronghold" (Ps 62:1–2).

These four psalm collections reveal a great deal about More's state of mind. Yet we have two other compositions which are even more revealing windows to his soul. The first of these is his own extensive commentary on the psalms; the second, the psalm he wrote himself.

There is a wealth of insight to be gleaned from the many annotations that he made in the margins of his psalter. Through hundreds of markings and comments,[13] More indicated what he was thinking and feeling, and what he found most helpful in his prayer, during the terribly trying months of his imprisonment. These notes reveal his deepest thoughts and aspirations.

The annotations show a soul bearing the full weight of suffering and affliction. "Demons" and "tribulation" are the words that occur most frequently. "Demons," used some forty times, refers to evil human beings, dangerous situations, actual devils, and all those elements of life that conspire to divert the soul from the just way. "Tribulation" is the severe suffering that one encounters, often on account of these various demons.

One form of suffering that More experienced acutely was that of abandonment. He was, after all, the most sociable of men: he loved his family deeply; his favorite recreation was the witty conversation of friends. It is not surprising, therefore, that many of his notes have to do with the pain of abandonment.

At Psalm 38, for example, he makes his longest annotation next to verses 11 through 17:

> My friends and my companions stand back because of my affliction; my neighbors stand afar off. Men lay snares for me, seeking my life; they look to my misfortune, they speak of my ruin, treachery they talk of all the day.
>
> But I am like a deaf man, hearing not, like a deaf man who opens not his mouth. I am become like a man who neither hears nor has in his mouth a retort. Because for you, O Lord, I wait; you, O Lord my God, will answer when I say, "Let them not be glad on my account who, when my foot slips, glory over me."
>
> For I am very near to falling, and my grief is before me always.

Next to the middle section of this passage, More wrote: "A meek man ought to behave in this way during tribulation; he should neither speak proudly himself nor retort to what is spoken wickedly, but should bless those who speak evil of him and suffer willingly, either for justice' sake if he has deserved it or for God's sake if he has deserved nothing."

This was just how More acted throughout the ordeal of his imprisonment, interrogations, trial, and execution. He maintained heroic silence and composure. Nonetheless, we do know that he suffered greatly from his confinement and from the injustice of the accusations made against him.

Several times, More makes reference to the disgrace he is suffering.[14] He marks, for example, the text, "Insult has broken my heart, and I am weak. I looked for sympathy, but there was none; for comforters, and I found none" (Ps 69:20). Another marked passage reads, "You made me the reproach of my neighbors, the mockery and the scorn of those around us. You made us a byword among the nations, a laughingstock among the peoples. All the day my disgrace is before me, and shame covers my face" (Ps 44:13–15). More was, as we have seen, a man who appreciated full well the importance of reputation; it must have taken quite a struggle for him to accept its loss.[15]

One unexpected suffering that More had to endure was a "temptation of the devil into which he had almost fallen," the temptation of the suffering good to envy the prosperous evil. This admission is made next to these words of Psalm 73:

> How good God is to the upright; the Lord, to those
> who are clean of heart! But, as for me, I almost lost
> my balance; my feet all but slipped because I was
> envious of the arrogant when I saw them prosper
> though they were wicked.

In the next two verses, the psalmist explains why he became envious of the wicked. "They are in no pain," he says. "Their bodies are sound and sleek; they are free from the burdens of mortals, and are not afflicted like the rest of men." And that leads him to wonder: "Is it but in vain I have kept my heart clean?"

As More points out, however, prosperity is not necessarily a sign of favor. In fact, he notes in the margin, "prosperity hinders conversion and causes vices to increase." Continuous prosperity can be inebriating,[16] and it can signify that a person has "far fallen out of God's favor."[17] After all, "God chastises all those that he loves and scourges every child whom he receives," and "we cannot . . . come to heaven but by many tribulations."[18]

The way to avoid this temptation to envy, More notes, is to trust in God.[19] But this is not at all easy when one sees the good suffer and the wicked prosper. Psalm 73 continues with this confession: "Though I tried to understand this, it seemed to me too difficult, till I entered the sanctuary of God and considered their final destiny." Only by meditating upon eternity can the psalmist sing, "Yet with you I shall always be; you have hold of my right hand; with your counsel you guide me. . . . For indeed, they who withdraw from you perish; you destroy everyone who is unfaithful to you. But for me, to be near God is my good."

More draws attention to many passages that speak of the importance of justice. Among these is Psalm 5:8: "Guide me in your justice; make straight your way before me." He recited every day those words of Psalm 51: "Free me from blood guilt, O God, my saving God; then my tongue shall revel in your justice." And the following verses are marked with special flourish: "Well for the man . . . who conducts his affairs with justice; he shall never be moved. . . . An evil report he will not fear; his heart is firm, trusting in the Lord" (Ps 112:5–7).[20]

As if to remind himself of this truth, More marks these two passages as well: "Turn from evil and do good . . . for the Lord loves what is right, and forsakes not his faithful ones" (Ps 37:27–28), and "Cast your care upon the Lord, and he will support you; never will he permit the just man to be disturbed" (Ps 55:22).

In fact, More points out, remembering God's justice in times of adversity is an important part of the spiritual struggle. He sets off in a special way Psalm 77, which specifically addresses this issue. This psalm begins with a cry of lament from one who is suffering greatly:

> Aloud to God I cry; aloud to God, to hear me; on
> the day of my distress I seek the Lord. By night my
> hands are stretched out without flagging; my soul
> refuses comfort. When I remember God I moan;
> when I ponder, my spirit grows faint. . . . I am
> troubled and cannot speak.

Here, the just person turns to God, but finds no comfort. This
apparent abandonment leads to a reflection about one's whole
life and its meaning:

> I consider the days of old; the years long past I
> remember. In the night I meditate in my heart; I
> ponder, and my spirit broods.[21] Will the Lord
> reject forever and nevermore be favorable? Will
> his kindness utterly cease, his promise fail for
> all generations? Has God forgotten pity? Does
> he in anger withhold his compassion? And I say,
> "This is my sorrow, that the right hand of the
> Most High is changed." I remember the deeds
> of the Lord; yes, I remember your wonders of
> old. And I meditate on your works; your ex-
> ploits I ponder.

The psalmist knows from past experience the goodness and
power of God; but has God changed? How is he to make sense
of his present affliction? After much reflection, he concludes: "O
God, your way is holy; what great god is there like our God?
You are the God who works wonders; among the peoples you
have made known your power" (Ps 77:13–14).

What can the just person do so as not to forget God's wonderful power? Meditate often. As the psalmist says, in another
passage that More flags for emphasis, "I will remember you
upon my couch, and through the night watches I will meditate
on you: that you are my help, and in the shadow of your wings
I shout for joy. My soul clings fast to you; your right hand up-
holds me" (Ps 63:6–8).

Meditation alone, however, is not enough. Twice in his annotations, More points out that fasting and other forms of
penance are also needed if one is to conquer in times of great

trial.[22] Only the wicked (see Ps 50:16–17) hate the discipline
and detachment needed to live up to God's laws.

Although this theme of detachment is not given great
prominence in More's annotations (for the simple reason that it
is not emphasized in the psalms themselves), it is the subject of
the psalm that he composed in the margins of his prayer book.
That More wrote about a subject not well developed in the
psalms is typical of the man and of all that he wrote.[23] It was
characteristic of him to draw heavily and freely upon the full-
ness of the tradition which he had inherited, and to add his own
modest contributions to it.[24]

More's psalm has been called "A Godly Meditation," but it
could just as well be titled "A Meditation on Detachment." As
the time of his death approached, More developed in different
ways the theme of detachment, indicating that one must be willing to give up everything, even one's body, to save one's soul.[25]

More begins his psalm by asking for the grace to be de-
tached from earthly goods so that he can be securely attached to
God.

> Give me Thy grace, good Lord,
> To set the world at nought;
>
> To set my mind fast upon Thee,
> And not to hang upon the blast of men's mouths.

These lines recall his primary objective in the education of his
children: the "testimony to God and to conscience" that ensures
that one's peace of mind will not be dependent upon the opinions of others.

More goes on to pray for the grace

> To lean unto the comfort of God,
> Busily to labor to love Him;
>
> To know my own vileness and wretchedness,
> To humble and meeken myself under the mighty
>   hand of God;

> To bewail my sins passed;
> For the purging of them, patiently to suffer adversity;
>
> Gladly to bear my purgatory here;
> To be joyful of tribulation;
>
> To walk the narrow way that leads to life,
> To bear the cross with Christ.

As indicated here and in some of his other Tower works, More clearly identified himself at the end of his life with the crucified Christ. He accepted his many sufferings as a way of making up for his sins, of gladly serving his purgatory on earth, and, ultimately, of imitating Christ's love.

The last and most surprising part of the psalm is More's request for the grace "to think my greatest enemies my best friends":

> For the brethren of Joseph could never have done him
> so much good with their love and favor
> as they did him with their malice and hatred.

This part of his prayer shows his appreciation for the way that Providence works to bring all things to the good. More is, of course, referring to the Joseph of the Old Testament, Jacob's favorite son, who was sold into slavery by his jealous brothers. In time, God used this act of injustice to save Israel, by saving Joseph's whole family from famine.

More must have seen his own situation in a similar light. Though he could not have foreseen the outcome of his personal plight, he was convinced that his own enemies "could never have done him so much good with their love and favor as they did him with their malice and hatred." As he explained to Meg, "Nothing can come except what God wills. And I make me very sure that whatsoever that be, even if nothing has ever appeared so bad, it shall indeed be the best."[26]

More, like David, was convinced that "my courage is the Lord."[27]

Chapter Twenty-two

The Power of Artful Conversation II:
From Cowardice to Courage

WHILE IN THE TOWER OF LONDON, More composed what some consider to be his greatest masterpiece: *A Dialogue of Comfort against Tribulation*. This book, which is about courage,[1] explains the value of all suffering, but especially suffering that is exceptionally oppressive.[2] It may well have been inspired by concern for Margaret, and written with her in mind.

The *Dialogue of Comfort* is a conversation between an old man named Anthony, who is lying sick in bed, and his nephew Vincent, who is about to lead their country in a time of extreme peril. They live in Hungary, under imminent threat of invasion by the dreaded Turks. Vincent is terrified, not only for himself, but especially for his family and for all those he must lead. This rich and honored leader of his people knows that all he need do to preserve his privileged status in life is to compromise a few of his beliefs. Will he stand firm or not?

Anthony is well experienced in all that Vincent will soon have to face. In his day, he himself twice confronted the Turks; he has also had wide experience with the doubts and fears now assailing the youth.[3] Respecting his uncle's wisdom and experience, Vincent has come to get a good supply of counsel and comfort before the Turks come, and before Anthony dies.

After three long conversations, Vincent finds that he has overcome his fears and is prepared to face any and all dangers. How does this transformation from cowardice to courage come about? What does old Anthony do to cure this soul overcome with the passion of fear?

Few if any of More's other works reveal as much about his own personality and understanding of human nature as does the *Dialogue of Comfort*. In *A Dialogue Concerning Heresies*, More had likewise portrayed himself in conversation with a youth, but that youth did not share his deepest convictions. In the *Dialogue of Comfort*, on the other hand, the two men are close relatives who are in basic agreement about fundamental beliefs.

It would also be hard to find among More's other works one that reveals so much of his humor. And rightly so. As we will see, humor has an important role to play in bringing about Vincent's eventual cure.

Throughout, Anthony is a thin guise for More himself,[4] and Hungary is a thin guise for England. In choosing this setting, More masterfully calls upon the sense of danger and horror associated with the takeover of Hungary in 1526.[5] Memory of the Turkish sultan, cruel tyrant that he was considered to be, invites readers to consider other tyrants of other countries.[6]

Most importantly, however, the *Dialogue of Comfort* reveals the curative potential of a conversation guided by a master. Through the open and friendly conversation of book one, wise old Anthony discovers the reasons for Vincent's lack of courage: Vincent does not understand the nature of suffering, he doubts certain vital truths of his faith, he is inordinately attached to his riches, and he is repelled by the thought of suffering. Based on this diagnosis of character which takes place in book one, Anthony devises the necessary conversational strategy to bring about Vincent's cure—a cure that will take all of the long conversations of books two and three to accomplish. Through these conversations, Anthony gradually helps Vincent discover the false images and opinions that have been coexisting with his true beliefs. Only after Vincent clarifies his thinking can he be rid of his paralyzing fear.

Early in their first conversation, Anthony discovers that young Vincent does maintain that all suffering can be beneficial. He holds to this view only reluctantly, without clarity or conviction; nevertheless, despite the weeds of doubt, it is obvious that the seed of faith is firmly embedded in his soul. Most of this first conversation is devoted to clarification of the principle that all suffering is either medicinal or something better than medicinal.[7] Anthony even argues convincingly that suffering is better than prosperity, and that it is therefore an especially gracious gift from God. This supernatural perspective is the foundation for all that follows; it is the foundation for unshakable courage. Vincent replies that he can accept this theoretically, but he still finds it "somewhat obscure and dark" and "somewhat hard."[8]

As the second conversation begins, Anthony insists that Vincent do more of the talking. After enough of this friendly prodding, Vincent does agree not to take such a passive role in the conversation. But Anthony not only insists and prods, he also works hard to find ways of actively engaging Vincent more fully in their exchange. He tells some "merry tales" to help his nephew relax and take his fears less seriously. He tells other stories as well, and asks the young man's opinions about them. At one point he even asks Vincent to defend a position which the young man supposedly rejects. This entire approach proves effective in getting Vincent to think through his own positions more fully, to the point where he can see the contradictions within himself.

By helping Vincent articulate his true thoughts, Anthony soon succeeds in bringing to light the "false fantasies" that lie behind his paralyzing fear. Gradually he reveals that when people are dominated by fear, it is because they fail to see things as they are; instead, they see fantasies, vain imaginings, which are rooted in the "cowardice of their own conceiving."[9] To confirm this point, Anthony gives three examples of misperception caused by fear.

The first example is a story about an army encamped within Turkish territory. As Anthony recounts the tale:

> So it happened that in our camp about midnight there suddenly rose a rumor and a cry that the Turk's whole army was secretly stealing upon us. Therefore, our whole host was warned to arm in haste and set themselves in array to fight. And then were our runners, who had brought these sudden tidings, examined more leisurely by the council, as to what surety or what likelihood they had perceived. And one of them said that by the

> glimmering of the moon he had espied and per-
> ceived and seen them himself, coming on softly
> and soberly in a long range, all in good order. . . .
> His fellows, being examined, said that he . . . came
> back so fast to tell it to them that they thought it
> rather time to make haste and give warning to the
> camp than to go nearer to them. For they were not
> so far off but they had yet themselves somewhat
> an imperfect sight of them, too.[10]

As a result, they were "on watch all the rest of the night," ner-
vously listening for the attack. The next morning, however,
brought a surprise:

> But when the day was sprung, and we saw no one,
> out was our runner sent again, and some of our
> captains with him, to show whereabout the place
> was in which he had perceived them. And when
> they came near the spot, they found that the great
> fearful army of the Turks, so soberly coming on,
> turned (God be thanked) into a fair long hedge
> standing even stone-still.[11]

Young Vincent can hardly fail to see that if fear can lead an
entire army to mistake a farmer's hedge for a band of fearsome
Turks, then it can certainly lead anyone's imagination to make
mistakes less spectacular.

The second example is a story, which we have already mentioned, about an ass who is so scrupulous that he fears doing anything.[12] Paralyzed by the fear that his slightest action may cause
grave offense to others, not to mention the loss of his own soul, he
finds himself utterly unable to judge accurately or to get any
peace of mind. Only with the help of his confessor, a worldly-wise
fox, does he develop the capacity to live a normal life.

Vincent laughs at these first two examples. But the third
causes wonder because of its strange and horrible character.
This one is the "most horrible" example of what ungoverned
fear can do: namely, tempt a person to suicide.

Anthony introduces this subject by asking Vincent if he
thinks that such a destructively fearful state of mind can be
cured. (Significantly, this question bears more or less directly on

the temptation Vincent is facing in his own spiritual life: he is strongly tempted to commit spiritual suicide by giving up his faith out of fear of the Turks.) Vincent, inexperienced in such matters, doubts if anyone in this frame of mind can be fully cured.[13]

As one might expect, Anthony disagrees. In the conversation that follows, he sets about proving the contrary position—that there is no unconquerable fear—by opening up to Vincent some dimensions of life that have never occurred to the young man.

To help people debilitated by fear, Anthony begins, one must come to know those persons and their situations well—a knowledge possible only if one succeeds in getting them to speak their true mind. Then, having gained their confidence, the friend, as a "cunning physician," must gradually and pleasantly reveal to them the difference between their realistic and erroneous perceptions.[14] Only after they have achieved a sure knowledge of their own mind can a cure be effected.

To bring about such a cure, says Anthony, two distinct steps are needed: first, counsel; then, comfort. The counseling stage consists of helping the person to see, by the light of true principles, what particular fantasy is the root of the problem. This is a process requiring skill and tact. Anthony compares it to the act of waking someone from deep sleep: it is something to be done gently, not abruptly.[15] Such a process—involving, as we have mentioned, a real knowledge of the person's situation and a securing of trust in genuine conversation—is, of course, precisely the one Anthony has been using all along in his dialogues with Vincent.

Granted, there are people who simply will not be counseled, because they suffer from a "frantic fantasy" born of malice and hardened pride.[16] Anthony gives two examples: a woman who deliberately provokes her husband to such anger that he kills her;[17] and a rich, proud widow who plans her own death and subsequent canonization.[18]

Most people, though, are open to counsel and can profit from it. Yet it may take great ingenuity and patience to find a suitable way of helping an individual distinguish true and false imaginings.

By way of illustration, old Anthony tells the bizarre tale of an overly zealous man who wanted to kill himself so as to immolate "himself for Christ as Christ did for him."[19] After several unsuccessful attempts at dissuasion, his wife finally came up with a devious but highly effective plan. She agreed to help him be killed like Christ. Of course, she added, one must keep in mind that Christ was not killed "by His own hands, but by the hand of another." Furthermore, he "was bound to a pillar and beaten first, and afterwards crowned with thorns." This clever woman then tied up her husband and beat some sense into him. After that, as she was working on the crown of thorns, "he said he thought this was enough for that year" and he would wait for the rest "till Good Friday came again." But when the next Good Friday came, "then was his desire past; he longed to follow Christ no further."[20]

In attempting to cure a suicidal person, says Anthony, it is sometimes necessary to "bind" that person "fast in bed" until the temptation passes.[21] And in any case, friends must "fall to prayer" for that person, for as long as it takes.[22]

Once the attraction to suicide is recognized as a temptation, it is time to administer the second part of the cure: comfort. Comfort is simply help to bear present difficulties. It can take different forms, all of which might be necessary: loving encouragement, prayer, the sacrament of Penance, frequent meditation on the truths of the faith, and the expertise of doctors (both medical and spiritual).

While the first two books deal with fear and suffering basically by way of discussion, book three presents a dramatic enactment of the suffering Vincent most fears. The Turks are close at hand! Trying to find a way to remain calm, Vincent asks whether he should even think about his imminent peril; surely he will just be fearing twice as much, and all in vain. Anthony emphatically disagrees. The best comfort and the best medicine, he says, is to meditate long and often upon the true nature of the sufferings involved. One thus acquires "such a sure habit of spiritual faithful strength that all the devils in hell, with all the wrestling that they can make, shall never be able to wrest it" out of one's heart.[23] Unless we are "well armed . . . beforehand with substantial advice and good counsel," we will have little chance of success in this all-important battle.[24] Only "through grace working with [our own] diligence" will a "strong, deep-rooted habit" be engendered and set sure in our souls; a habit "not like a reed ready to wave with every wind, nor like a rootless tree scantly set up on end in a loose heap of light sand that will with a blast or two be blown down."[25]

In the first half of this last conversation, Vincent mostly listens. He raises no major objections to Anthony's counsels about why he has nothing to fear. He seems to accept quite readily, for example, Anthony's counsel that the comforts of the world are all fleeting and can actually "be deadly destructive of the soul."[26] A little too readily, in fact. To help him reflect on this truth and take a more active role in this important part of the conversation, Anthony asks Vincent to defend the position of a prosperous man who is willing to hold on to his earthly possessions by denying just a small part of his faith. In this dialogue-within-a-dialogue, Vincent defends the rich man's position energetically; it is one with which he can easily identify. After a hearty defense, however, he comes to recognize the many inconsistencies involved, and he concedes defeat.[27]

This exchange has further clarified his thinking; yet his cure is still not achieved. In the next segment of the conversation he is brought to realize that a lack of rational consistency is not the greatest obstacle to clear thinking, but that fear and pride pose much greater difficulties. Unchecked fear and pride give rise to delusions that displace even knowledge we recognize as true. When Vincent finally perceives this important fact, his cure is nearly complete.

He says he can be strong in the face of tribulation—if only he can "remember" in the midst of suffering what he and Anthony have been discussing.[28] The difficulty of remembering good counsel in the face of danger is the only remaining obstacle to Vincent's achievement of true courage. At the beginning of their first conversation, he acknowledged the helpfulness of good counsel, but lamented that he could not remember it. He said to his uncle:

> While you tell me this, I cannot but grant it as true,
> yet if I had not now heard it from you, I would not

have remembered it, nor would it have occurred to me. And furthermore, since our tribulations will only increase in weight and number, we will not need only one or two [comforting counsels], but a great heap of them to stable and strengthen the walls of our hearts against the great surges of this tempestuous sea.[29]

In response to this plea, Anthony promised to give Anthony a "store of comfort" from his lifetime of reading, experience, and reflection. But now, after receiving three books of such counsel, Vincent is still lamenting his inability to remember his uncle's good advice in times of distress.

Anthony now gives his most important counsel, the one that will eliminate his nephew's last obstacle to genuine courage. He reminds Vincent that what we remember depends upon "the affections that are beforehand fixed and rooted in the mind."[30] Unless one deliberately cultivates the loves one has chosen, he says, the mind and imagination will turn traitor. The best way to cultivate these affections is to "deeply ponder the example of our Savior himself."[31] For Anthony (who speaks for More himself), the crucified Christ is the ultimate example of courageous love. In one of the longest and most artfully constructed sentences of the entire book, Anthony articulates as an old man what More had expressed as a youth:

> If we could and would with due compassion conceive in our minds a right imagination and remembrance of Christ's bitter painful Passion—of the many sore bloody strokes that the cruel tormentors gave Him with rods and whips upon every part of His holy tender body; of the scornful crown of sharp thorns beaten down upon His holy head, so strait and so deep that on every part His blessed blood issued out and streamed down; of His lovely limbs drawn and stretched out upon the cross, to the intolerable pain of His sore-beaten veins and sinews, feeling anew, with the cruel stretching and straining, pain far surpassing any cramp in every part of His blessed body at once; of

the great long nails then cruelly driven with the hammer through His holy hands and feet; of His body, in this horrible pain, lifted up and let hang, with all its weight bearing down upon the painful wounded places so grievously pierced with nails; and in such torment without pity, but not without many dispites [much scorn], suffered to be pined and pained the space of more than three long hours, till He Himself willingly gave up unto His Father His holy soul; after which yet, to show the mightiness of their malice, after His holy soul departed, they pierced His holy heart with a sharp spear, at which issued out the holy blood and water, whence His holy sacraments have inestimable secret strength—if we could, I say, remember these things, in such a way as would God that we would, I verily suppose that the consideration of His incomparable kindness could not fail so to inflame our key-cold hearts, and set them on fire with His love, that we should find ourselves not only content but also glad and desirous to suffer death for His sake who so marvelous lovingly forbore not to sustain so far passing painful death for ours.[32]

Once Vincent discovers why he should and how he could remember the example of Christ, he is now capable of living up to his name as "one who conquers."[33] This discovery that More made in his youth became the single most important idea in all of his spiritual writings. As Pico had put it, "If a man had God always before his eyes as a ruler of all his works . . . , he would shortly be perfect."[34] Or, as put by the inspired poet More loved so dearly, "Only in God is my soul at rest. . . . He only is my rock and my salvation, my stronghold; I shall not be disturbed."[35]

Chapter Twenty-three

Spiritual Handbook III:
The Last Word on Statesmanship

AFTER A LIFE SPENT AT THE CENTER of one the most tumultuous periods of history, Thomas More addressed the future leaders of society about the characteristics most needed in statesmen. Having experienced for years the weight and sorrows of office, he knew how easily they could "so grip the mind that its strength is sapped and reason gives up the reins." He therefore warned his fellow leaders to be specially on guard against the "heavy-hearted sleep" that can lead one to "neglect to do what the duty of his office requires."[1]

A neglectful leader, he said, is "like a cowardly ship's captain who is so disheartened by the furious din of a storm that he deserts the helm, hides away cowering in some cranny, and abandons the ship to the waves."[2] Here he echoed those famous lines of *Utopia*: "You must not abandon the ship in a storm because you cannot control the winds."[3] The captain of state must not only know how to command, he must also have the courage to remain with his ship, regardless of the weather.

For his last work, More chose to comment upon that scene of the Gospel that shows Christ suffering under the full weight of the task he was born to assume. There, as he agonizes in the garden of Gethsemane, Christ is overwhelmed by sadness, fear, and weariness. This part of the Gospel had special importance to More. He had, over many decades, frequently contemplated its meaning. In it he saw a "clear and sharp mirror image" of what occurs in every age.[4]

More's last book deals with "the story of that time when the apostles were sleeping as the Son of Man was being betrayed."[5]

As the commentary unfolds, More indicates that the apostles represent Church leaders who fall asleep at their post, while the leaders who commissioned Judas represent "other governors and other caesars"—such as, we can surely infer, Thomas Cromwell, Thomas Cranmer, and Henry VIII.[6]

Ever the good lawyer, More opens his commentary by posing a perplexing problem, one suggested in the very title of his book: *On the Sadness, Weariness, and Fear of Christ*. If Christ wanted us to stand up courageously for our convictions, why did he allow himself to be overcome by fear and sadness? Christ had, after all, "taught His disciples not to be afraid of those who kill the body only." So "how can it be fitting that He Himself should . . . [have been] very much afraid of those same persons?" When we think of all those martyrs who "rushed to their deaths eagerly and joyfully," how can we find it appropriate "that Christ Himself, the very prototype and leader of martyrs, the standard bearer of them all, should [have been] so terrified at the approach of pain, so shaken, so utterly downcast?"[7]

The answer More suggests is thought-provoking: Christ allowed his human nature to rebel so strongly in order to teach the rest of us *how* to bear courageously our own all-too-human reactions to adversity. Experiencing these reactions is not a sin. Christ in his humanity felt their full weight, even to the point that his sadness and fear led to the "unprecedented phenomenon" of sweating blood.[8]

The best and bravest of soldiers regularly experience fear before battle. Such fear is perfectly normal, especially for those who know full well the extreme dangers and horrors of warfare. Only the reckless and foolish will experience no fear. Christ "wished His followers to be brave and prudent soldiers, not senseless and foolish."[9] It must be kept in mind that "before the actual engagement, fear is not reprehensible as long as reason does not cease to struggle against fear—a struggle which is not criminal or sinful but rather an immense opportunity for merit."[10]

Everyone experiences, from within, the rebellion and frailty of human nature. For this reason, everyone "has sufficient grounds to be afraid that he may grow weary under his burden and give in."[11] This realization, however, should simply lead us "to rouse ourselves and wake up to virtuous living"; it should make us more and more convinced of our absolute dependence on God.[12]

The burdens mentioned in this commentary are generally the ones associated with the bearing of heavy responsibilities— burdens experienced in the form of sadness, fear, or weariness. More seems to present these burdens as some of the most dangerous temptations that a good person can face.

Such burdens overwhelmed the apostles, as well as Christ himself. Three times Christ asked his closest apostles to stay awake with him for just an hour. Each time, however, they fell asleep—out of sadness at seeing Christ suffer.[13] Surely it cannot be a sin to fall asleep out of sadness; isn't that only natural? Yes, More admits, it may be natural; but often it is also sinful— so sinful that one can end up in hell because of it.[14]

With this sobering reminder, More shows Christ returning to his apostles, each time appealing to conscience and forcing them to confront their lack of fortitude. "Why did you fall asleep?" This kind but piercing question becomes even more powerful, More marvels, when we reflect that "Judas the traitor at the same time was so wide awake and intent on betraying the Lord that the very idea of sleep never entered his head."[15]

In this context, More proceeds to make some very pointed comments. He asks:

> Does not this contrast between the traitor and the apostles present to us a clear and sharp mirror image (as it were), a sad and terrible view of what has happened through the ages from those times even to our own? Why do not bishops contemplate in this scene their own somnolence? Since they have succeeded in the place of the apostles, would that they would reproduce their virtues just as eagerly as they embrace their authority and as faithfully as they display their sloth and sleepiness! For very many are sleepy and apathetic in sowing virtues among the people and maintaining

the truth, while the enemies of Christ, in order to sow vices and uproot the faith . . . , are wide awake. . . .[16]

What follows this rebuke is an even stronger correction to the apostles' successors.[17] More is not rebuking the bishops only; this criticism is directed to all those in positions of leadership. Nonetheless: "If a bishop does this, I would certainly not hesitate to juxtapose and compare his sadness with the sadness that leads, as Paul says, to hell; indeed, I would consider it far worse, since such sadness in religious matters seems to spring from a mind which despairs of God's help."[18]

Given the weight of such responsibility, what can one do to stay awake while bearing the full measure of its burdens?

More's answer is simple and clear: If one is not to be negligent, if one is not to fall asleep, one must pray. "Again and again He drove home this point to them, that prayer is the only safeguard against temptation and that if someone refuses it entrance into the castle of his soul and shuts it up by yielding to sleep, through such negligence he permits the besieging troops of the devil (that is, temptations to evil) to break in."[19] Christ repeatedly reminds his apostles to get up and pray, warning them "how great the impending danger [is], in order to show that no drowsy or lukewarm prayer [will] suffice."[20]

The apostles fell asleep "even at the very time when such an enormous danger was threatening their loving master" because they had not acquired the habit of prayer.[21] Unless we are constant in prayer, "our minds, no matter how willing to do good, are swept back into the evils of temptation."[22] Christ tells us to pray because this is absolutely necessary if we are not to give in to temptation.[23]

Christ not only tells us, he *shows* us how to pray. In this scene, Christ is "face down on the earth," praying that his "cup" of affliction might pass. Calling attention to how "Christ the commander teaches by His own example," More then addresses the reader directly. "Reader," he says, "let us pause for a little at this point and contemplate with a devout mind our commander lying on the ground in humble supplication."[24]

After making this personal appeal, More shows in one of his artistically crafted sentences how the attentive reader will profit from a prayerful meditation on the scene he has chosen.

> For if we do this carefully [contemplate Christ prostrate in prayer], a ray of that light which enlightens every man who comes into the world will illuminate our minds so that we will see, recognize, deplore, and at long last correct, I will not say the negligence, sloth, or apathy, but rather the feeblemindedness, the insanity, the downright blockheaded stupidity with which most of us approach the all-powerful God and instead of praying reverently, address Him in a lazy and sleepy sort of way; and by the same token I am very much afraid that instead of placating Him and gaining His favor we exasperate Him and sharply provoke His wrath.[25]

What More does in this one sentence exemplifies what he does in the book as a whole. He tries to get his reader to see the real meaning of Christ's "ordinary" human actions. If we truly see what they reveal and if we imitate them, we will not be negligent, slothful, or apathetic; we will not act stupidly; we will not go through life in a lazy, sleepy sort of way.

When we compare our way of praying with that of Christ, we realize how we too often let our "thoughts wander wildly during prayers, frantically flitting about in a throng of absurd fantasies."[26] Unlike Christ, who is prostrate before God and wholly absorbed in his prayer, we let "our actions . . . betray that our minds are wandering miles away."[27] With his earthy and humorous irony, More tries to help us see the absurdity of this way of praying. In embarrassing contrast to the way Christ prays, "we scratch our heads, clean our fingernails with a pocketknife, pick our noses with our fingers, meanwhile making the wrong responses." How can we not be "ashamed to pray in such a deranged state of mind and body—to beseech God's favor in a matter so crucial for us . . . "?[28]

What follows is another brilliant image to help us realize the nature of prayer. More suggests that we imagine we have "committed a crime of high treason" against a prince who is willing to commute or even cancel the death penalty if we show ourselves contrite. His irony then brings into high relief the absurdity of slothful prayer:

> Now when you have been brought into the presence of the prince, go ahead and speak to him carelessly, casually, without the least concern. . . . Then yawn, stretch, sneeze, spit without giving it a thought, and belch up the fumes of your gluttony. In short, conduct yourself in such a way that he can clearly see from your face, your voice, your gestures, and your whole bodily deportment that while you are addressing him you are thinking about something else. Tell me now, what success could you hope for from such a plea as this?[29]

More wants us to realize that we would not fall asleep or be slovenly in our prayer if we actually remembered what prayer is, and to Whom we are speaking in our prayer.

Furthermore, if we prayed like Christ, we would also conquer sadness, weariness, and fear as Christ did. As soon as Judas comes and the moment of action is at hand, Christ displays all the "manly courage" that the situation demands. More marvels at the change in Jesus: from one so fearful and sad that he sweat blood, to one who "fearlessly approaches the whole mass of armed men."[30]

If we pray, we too will have the strength and courage to face our tasks in life. Such is Thomas More's advice in his last work, written during his own final agony. The legendary courage, serenity, and good humor he showed in the midst of his many final sufferings were rooted in the advice he gave others in this last testament: "Let us . . . in our agony remember His."[31]

The counsel More gives in this last spiritual testament is the same one he gave in his first: have before your eyes always the picture of Christ, especially Christ in the agony he bore for us. The warning is also the same: beware of cowardly negligence; use heroically all available means to "stay awake" in the face of duty.

More's heroic perseverance and unshakable serenity came from his conviction that God's fatherly providence directs everything, even the temporary triumphs of the powers of darkness.[32] The source of his extraordinary patience and calm was this absolute conviction that good ultimately triumphs over evil. Nevertheless, he recognized that great prudence is needed if one is to play to the full one's part in the drama at hand—all the while seeking to let God's grander, overall plan work itself out. More knew how crucial it is to be wise as the serpent and yet innocent as the dove. Thus he praised those who managed to flee legitimately from the enemy, and insisted that detachment from all material goods is absolutely required for such a flight.[33] More himself used all the resources of the law to save himself and his family; he never courted martyrdom.

One telling example of how to deal with an enemy, he said, is the way Jesus treats Judas at the moment of betrayal. Here Christ gives a remarkable example of prudence and patience. In all that he does, Christ wants to teach us "to bear patiently and gently all injuries and snares treacherously set for us; not to smolder with anger, not to seek revenge, not to give vent to our feelings by hurling back insults, not to find any empty pleasure in tripping up an enemy through some clever trick, but rather to set ourselves against deceitful injury with genuine courage, to conquer evil with good—in fine, to make every effort by words both gentle and harsh, to insist both in season and out of season, that the wicked may change their ways to good, so that if any-one should be suffering from a disease that does not respond to treatment, he may not blame the failure on our negligence but rather attribute it to the virulence of his own disease."[34]

Throughout his dealings with Judas, Christ acts "as a most conscientious physician" who tries two different "ways of effect-ing a cure." First he uses a gentle approach; he asks, "Friend, why have you come?" This kind appeal to Judas's conscience is of no avail. But Christ, as soon as he sees that Judas is not responding, tries again. He "immediately adds in a grave tone, 'Judas, do you betray the Son of Man with a kiss?'"[35] Unfortu-nately, Judas uses his free will to reject what could have healed that conscience of his, so "full of guilty sores."[36]

From even this one example, one can see why More insisted that "nothing can contribute more effectively . . . to the implanting of every sort of virtue in the Christian breast than pious and fervent meditation on the successive events of Christ's Passion."[37]

This counsel is quite similar to one he had given almost thirty years earlier:

> [In a time of temptation,]
> Think on the very lamentable pain,
> Think on the piteous cross of woeful Christ,
> Think on His blood beat out at every vein,
> Think on His precious heart carved in twain,
> Think how for thy redemption all was wrought—
> Let Him not lose thee, whom He so dear has bought.[38]

Chapter Twenty-four

A Trial to Remember

MORE'S TRIAL is one of the most famous since the trial of Socrates. Unlike Socrates, however, More was an experienced judge and lawyer who had prepared himself for his final trial over several years. At this trial, he was determined to bring all of his experience and training to bear—to defend not only himself and his family, but also the Church, the English tradition of law, and the future of Christendom. His keen sense of history assured him that his trial, like that of Socrates, would not be forgotten. Despite the opposition of his king, of all the bishops then in England (except the imprisoned Bishop Fisher), of his entire family, and of most of his friends, More stood fast in his convictions. He knew that, along with these people, the rest of history was waiting to hear his defense.

More's opponents had spent a great deal of time and effort in preparing this trial. It had taken sixteen months, two difficult sessions of Parliament, and considerable manipulation to bring him to court. Finally, on July 1, 1535, he appeared before fifteen judges and twelve jurors. Despite the impressive numbers, however, this trial was not to be impartial. The judges included Lord Chancellor Audley, Royal Secretary Cromwell, and the Duke of Norfolk, as well as an uncle, a brother, and the father of Anne Boleyn—all of whom had strong interests in convicting More. The jury of twelve was no less partial; this high-profile trial would not have been called at all unless success was assured.[1] Henry had already experienced the shame and inconvenience of being thwarted by true trials of law; his new ministers were determined that their leonine sovereign should not suffer such inconvenience while they served.

According to the custom of the times, More did not have counsel or a written account of the charges against him. And prison life had taken its toll on his health. Nevertheless, he conducted his own defense with extraordinary adeptness, though he had so little strength that he had to sit rather than stand.

Before the actual trial began, the Duke of Norfolk offered him the King's pardon if he would repent and revoke his "willful, obstinate opinion."[2] More graciously declined the offer and simply expressed his hope that God would grant him the grace to maintain his "good, honest, and upright mind . . . even to the last hour and extreme moment" of his life.[3] He prayed in this way because he was well aware of human frailty, and because he had long ago learned to distrust his own abilities in favor of God's.

The government charged More with four counts of treason: that he had maliciously refused on May 7, 1535, to accept the King's supremacy over the Church in England; that he had conspired against the King by writing treasonous letters to Fisher; that he had stirred up sedition by describing the Act of Supremacy as a two-edged sword (that is, a law that if disobeyed would mean bodily death, and if obeyed would mean spiritual death); and that he had "maliciously, traitorously, and diabolically" denied Parliament's power to declare the king to be head of the Church in England.

More argued against the first three charges with relative ease, showing that no offense was involved in any of them. In the first place, silence is not a crime; in fact, according to English precedent, silence means consent.[4] Secondly, none of his letters to Fisher had touched upon matters of state. Besides, since none of those letters existed any longer, and since no one else but Fisher had read them, where was the evidence of treasonous activity? Thirdly, More denied ever having said that the Act of Supremacy was a two-edged sword. When, on June 3, he had been asked his opinion about this formulation, he had answered hypothetically and without malice. He had said that *if* the statute was like a two-edged sword forcing a person to make a choice between physical and spiritual life, then the statute might at a later time be considered illegitimate. How could such a hypothetical statement be considered malicious?

More also argued that he had committed no offense related to the fourth count. The judges rejected this fourth argument, but apparently concurred with the previous three. In any case, the trial focused only upon this last count of treason.

The charge was based entirely on a single conversation, between Sir Thomas More and Solicitor General Richard Rich, which had taken place on June 12, 1535. Rich had been sent to More's prison cell to remove his writing materials and books.[5] At that time, according to Rich's testimony, More had explicitly denied Parliament's authority to make Henry the supreme head of the Church in England.

More strenuously denied having said anything of the kind. In fact, he stated flatly that Rich was committing perjury. To counter this libelous testimony, More took the most solemn step possible: he took an oath, calling God to be his witness. He said:

> If I were a man, my lords, who did not reverence an oath, I need not, as is well known, stand here as an accused person in this place, at this time, or in this case. And if this oath of yours, Master Rich, be true, then I pray that I never see God in the face, which I would not say, were it otherwise, to win the whole world. . . . In good faith, Master Rich, I am sorrier for your perjury than for my own peril.[6]

Next, as any other accomplished lawyer would have done, More demonstrated Rich's lack of credibility as a witness.

> And you shall understand that neither I nor any other man to my knowledge ever took you to be a man of credit in any matter of importance that I or any other would at any time deign to communicate with you. And I, as you know, for no small while have been acquainted with you and your conversation. I have known you from your youth since we have dwelled in one parish together. There, as you yourself can tell (I am sorry you compel me to say so), you were esteemed to be very light of tongue, a great dicer, and of no commendable fame. And so in your house at the

Temple, where has been your chief bringing up, were you likewise accounted.[7]

More appealed to the good sense of the judges and members of the jury, and then made a particularly clever appeal to those judges who had interrogated him earlier in the Tower.

> Can it therefore seem likely to your honorable lordships that I would, in so weighty a cause, so unadvisedly overshoot myself as to trust Master Rich, a man by me always reputed for one of very little truth, . . . that I would utter to him the secrets of my conscience touching the King's Supremacy?— the special point and only mark at my hands so long sought for, a thing which I never did, nor never would, after the Statute [of Supremacy] was made, reveal either to the King's Highness himself, or to any of his honorable Councilors, as it is not unknown to your honors, at sundry several times sent from His Grace's own person to the Tower unto me for no other purpose? Can this in your judgments, my lords, seem likely to be true?

After demonstrating Rich's lack of credibility, More went on to show that even if he had made the alleged remarks, those remarks could not be termed malicious.

> And yet, if I had so done indeed, my lords, as Master Rich has sworn, seeing it was spoken only in familiar, private conversation, without affirming anything, but only putting forth cases without other unpleasant circumstances, it cannot justly be taken to be spoken maliciously, and where there is no malice, there can be no offense.

The word "malice," More explained to the jurors, has a very precise meaning in the context of law. In the statute in question it would be equivalent to the "term 'forcible' . . . in the statute of forcible entries, by which statute, if a man entered peaceably and did not put out his adversary forcibly, it is no offense. But if he put him out forcibly, then by that statute it is an offense, and so shall he be punished by this term 'forcibly.'"[8]

More then went on to establish the credibility of his own character. He reminded them that the King had shown him singular favor and trust for over twenty years, from the day he first entered the King's service to the last day he served as Lord Chancellor of the realm. Even after an intense scrutiny of his entire career, no fault had been found. Henry himself had publicly expressed his trust in More, and his gratitude towards him. How could the "slanderous surmise" of Rich's untrustworthy testimony stand up against this long and unmarred record of loyal public service?

Once Rich realized how soundly More had discredited his testimony, he called Sir Richard Southwell and Master Thomas Palmer to be witnesses to what he had said. Both of these men had gone to the Tower with Rich on June 12 and were present during the conversation in question. Neither would have any part in Rich's perjury, however. Palmer "said that he was so busy putting Sir Thomas More's books in a sack that he took no heed of their talk."[9] Southwell gave an excuse that was even more lame than Palmer's; he claimed that "because he was appointed only to look to the conveyance of his books, he gave no ear" to their conversation.[10]

The total lack of viable evidence against More proved to be totally irrelevant. The jury took only fifteen minutes to render its verdict: "Guilty."

Yet More was not about to admit defeat. Well he knew that the thickets of the law could provide a good deal of protection against blatant injustice—as long as the thickets were allowed to stand.

Just at the point when Lord Chancellor Audley began to pass sentence, More introduced an ingenious legal maneuver that forced his learned and highly experienced judges to question the legality of what they were doing. He made a direct, courageous appeal to the conscience of each of these fifteen judges. This he accomplished by calling for an arrest of judgment.[11] By introducing this motion, he compelled his judges to confront the question of the legitimacy of the law they were using to condemn him—the very law that Henry and Cromwell were using to bring about their revolutionary coup d'état. By introducing this motion, he was also reminding his judges to consider the personal responsibility each of them had as a guardian of England's law.

The climax of this famous courtroom drama had now arrived.

Interrupting Audley, More calmly stated: "My lord, when I was toward the law, the manner in such a case was to ask the prisoner before judgment why judgment should not be given against him."[12]

Audley was undoubtedly anxious about the role he was now playing in the condemnation of an old friend and honored colleague. This unease may well explain the departure he had made from established procedure. But that anxiety would have been even greater had he known what More was about to do.

Aware that his words would echo throughout England, throughout Europe, and throughout subsequent history, Sir Thomas More now brought into full play all of the rhetorical power and legal expertise that a lifetime of training had placed at his disposal. Challenging the very ground on which Audley and the rest of the judges intended to condemn him, he said:

> Inasmuch, my lord, as this indictment is grounded upon an Act of Parliament directly repugnant to the laws of God and His Holy Church, the supreme government of which, or of any part thereof, may no temporal prince presume by any law to take upon him, as rightfully belonging to the See of Rome, a spiritual preeminence by the mouth of our Savior Himself, personally present upon the earth, only to St. Peter and his successors, bishops of the same See, by special prerogative guaranteed, it is therefore in law among Christian men insufficient to charge any Christian man.[13]

To prove this claim, he explained that "this realm, being but one member and small part of the Church, might not make a particular law [that was] disagreeable with the general law of Christ's Universal Catholic Church any more than the city of London, being but one poor member in respect of the whole realm, might make a law against an Act of Parliament to bind the whole realm."[14]

Specifically, More showed that provisions in the Act of Succession and the Act of Treasons went against many other "laws and statutes of our own land" that had not been repealed. Preeminent among these was the Magna Carta, the first clause of which states that "the English Church shall be free, and shall have its rights undiminished and its liberties unimpaired." After citing other such laws, More then cited scriptural texts proving that no layman could be head of the Church.

At this point Audley broke in to dispute his argument. How could More, alone, presume to challenge so stubbornly what "all the bishops, universities, and best learned of this realm" had agreed to support?[15]

The response More now gave was one he had made several times before, but never with such rhetorical and dramatic force.

> If the number of bishops and universities should be so material as your lordship seems to think, then I see little cause, my lord, why that should make any change in my conscience. For I have no doubt that, though not in this realm, but of all those well learned bishops and virtuous men that are yet alive throughout Christendom, they are not fewer who are of my mind therein. But if I should speak of those who are already dead, of whom many are now holy saints in heaven, I am very sure it is the far greater part of them who, all the while they lived, thought in this case the way that I think now. And therefore am I not bound, my lord, to conform my conscience to the council of one realm against the General Council of Christendom.[16]

So powerful were these and the other arguments that More made that Chancellor Audley was "loath to have the burden of that judgment wholly to depend on himself." His conscience having indeed been touched, he "openly asked advice of the Lord Fitz-James, then Lord Chief Justice of the King's Bench, . . . whether this indictment was sufficient or not."[17]

Fitz-James and the rest of the judges looked at each other for some time.[18] Here was a moment of conscience that was undoubtedly acute. They knew that what More said was true; but they also knew that Henry, powerful lion that he was, would brook no opposition to his will.

Chief Justice Fitz-James finally broke the silence. With a clever quibble he took upon his shoulders the immense responsibility for what would occur. But the very ambiguity of his answer shows clearly that More had struck the core of his conscience. What he said was:

> My lords all . . . , I must confess that if the Act of Parliament is not unlawful, then is not the indictment in my conscience insufficient.[19]

One has to stop and reflect on the conditional clause and the double negative in this response to understand clearly what Fitz-James said. He did not say More was wrong in his legal opinion. Instead, he posed a hypothetical statement to his fellow judges: *If* this Act of Parliament is lawful, then the indictment is sufficient according to his conscience. Yet this statement wholly avoids More's challenge. More argued that this Act of Parliament was not lawful, because it stood in conflict with the entire weight of tradition and with the most revered laws of the realm.

With the help of Fitz-James' ambiguous justification, however, Audley overcame the scruple of his own conscience and proceeded to complete his assigned task. He "said to the rest of the lords, 'Lo, my lords, you hear what my Lord Chief Justice says,' and so immediately gave judgment against him."[20]

If Fitz-James or any other of the judges had been another John Markham,[21] King Henry's tyranny could have been checked, or at least deprived of legal justification. Once again, however, tyranny succeeded not through war, but through law.[22] It succeeded not through the force of evil, but through the simple negligence of those who considered themselves good.

Chapter Twenty-five

Death with Good Humor:
"All to the Good"

AFTER A TRIAL OF SUCH SPECTACULAR INJUSTICE, what stood out above everything else was More's unshakable serenity and good humor. Even at the close of his trial, when he was asked for his final statement, he prayed that all who opposed him at this trial might continue as his "friends forever" and that they might "yet hereafter in heaven merrily all meet together."[1] We find this same gracious sentiment interspersed throughout the prayers and instructions which he wrote at the end of his life.

In one of these final instructions, More presents a logical argument for treating enemies well:

> Bear no malice or evil will to any man living. For either the man is good or wicked. If he is good and I hate him, then I am wicked.
>
> If he is wicked, either he will amend and die good and go to God, or live wickedly and die wickedly and go to the devil. And then let me remember that if he be saved, he will not fail (if I am saved too, as I trust to be) to love me very heartily, and I shall then in like manner love him.
>
> And why should I now, then, hate one for this while who shall hereafter love me forever, and why should I be now, then, an enemy to him with whom I shall in time be coupled in eternal friendship? And on the other side, if he will continue to be wicked and be damned, then is there such outrageous eternal sorrow before him that I may well think myself a deadly cruel wretch if I would not now rather pity his pain than malign his person.[2]

This frame of mind was not new to More. For quite some time he had prayed for the grace "to think my greatest enemies my best friends." Why? Because "the brethren of Joseph could never have done him so much good with their love and favor as they did him with their malice and hatred."[3] Here, as we have seen, More refers to the famous story in Genesis where Joseph, the favorite son of Jacob, was sold by his own brothers into slavery. As a result of this malicious act of jealousy, Joseph eventually arrived at the pharaoh's court in Egypt and became the pharaoh's chief minister. In this position Joseph was later able to provide abundantly for his family when they were suffering from famine, thus promoting the growth of the Jewish nation.

This same magnanimous outlook is evident in More's "A Devout Prayer [before Dying]," written sometime after July 1, the day of his trial, and before July 6, the day of his execution. The ending of this lengthy and moving prayer includes several petitions "for enemies."

> Almighty God, have mercy on N. and N., etc., and on all that bear me evil will and would harm me. And by such easy, tender, and merciful means as Your infinite wisdom can best devise, grant that their faults and mine may both be amended and redressed; and make us saved souls in heaven together, where we may ever live and love together with You and Your blessed saints. O glorious Trinity, grant this for the sake of the bitter Passion of our sweet Savior Christ. Amen.
>
> Lord, give me patience in tribulation, and grace in everything to conform my will to Yours, that I may truly say: "Thy will be done on earth as it is in heaven."
>
> The things, good Lord, that I pray for, give me the grace to labor for. Amen.[4]

More's unusual composure was further tested by two events that occurred as he was being led back, after his trial, to the Tower. The first involved Sir William Kingston, "a tall, strong and comely knight, Constable of the Tower, and [More's] very dear friend." It was Sir William's task to accompany More from

Westminster Palace back to his prison cell. But he was so overcome with emotion that before they arrived, he broke down in tears. As he would later explain it to Will Roper, "I found my heart so feeble and [More's] so strong that he had to comfort me who should rather have comforted him." When More saw Kingston so overwhelmed, he said to him: "Good Master Kingston, trouble not yourself, but be of good cheer, for I will pray for you and my good Lady your wife that we may meet in heaven together where we shall be merry for ever and ever."[5]

The ultimate test involved the person he loved best, the one who shared his deepest interests, sorrows, and joys. Though Meg did not attend the trial, she was waiting for her father on his way back to the Tower. She had, of course, already heard the news of his conviction. As her husband later told the story: "As soon as she saw him, after receiving his blessing on her knees reverently, she hastened towards him and, without consideration or care of herself, pressed in among the midst of the throng and company of the guard who surrounded him with their halberds and bills. She hastily ran to him and there, openly in the sight of all, embraced him, took him about the neck and kissed him. He, well liking her most natural and dear daughterly affection towards him, gave her his fatherly blessing and many godly words of comfort besides. After she parted from him, she . . . like one who had forgotten herself, being all ravished with the entire love of her dear father—having respect neither to herself or to the press of the people and the multitude who were about him, suddenly turned back again, ran to him as before, took him about the neck and divers times together most lovingly kissed him, and at last, with a full heavy heart, had to depart from him. The beholding of this was to many of them who were present so lamentable that it made them for very sorrow mourn and weep."[6]

At his execution, More's good humor startled and even scandalized many. The contemporary historian Edward Hall, commenting upon More's death, said that he himself could not decide if More was "a foolish wiseman or a wise foolishman."[7] To explain his perplexity, he mentioned five of More's jests. "Undoubtedly [More] had," he says, "besides his learning, a great wit, but it was so mingled with taunting and mocking that it seemed to them that best knew him, that he thought it nothing to be well spoken unless he had ministered some mock in the communication. For example, when he was coming to the Tower, one of the officers demanded his upper garment for his fee, meaning his gown, and he answered that he should have it, and gave him his cap, saying that it was the uppermost garment that he had. Likewise, even going to his death at the Tower gate, a poor woman called to him and asked him to declare that he had certain evidence of hers from the time he was in office (which, after he was apprehended, she could not get) and that he would ask that she might have it again or else she was undone. He answered, 'Good woman, have patience a little while, for the king is good unto me that even within this half hour he will discharge me of all business, and will help you himself.' Also when he went up the steps of the scaffold, he wanted one of the sheriffs to give him a hand to help him up, and said, 'When I come down again, let me shift for myself as well as I can.' Also the hangman knelt down, asking forgiveness for his death (as the custom is), to whom More said, 'I forgive you, but I promise you that you will never have glory for striking off my head since my neck is so short.' Also even when he should lay down his neck on the block, he, having a great gray beard, stretched out his beard and said to the hangman, 'I pray you let me lay my beard over the block lest you should cut it'; thus with a mock he ended his life."[8]

How could a wise man be such a fool at his own execution—especially when the execution was so clearly unjust? Yet how *should* one act in the face of injustice? Is anger the best response? Or sadness? Or would stoic resignation be most appropriate? But in any event, who would argue that comedy is the most appropriate response?

These questions lead us back to the one Hall asked: Were More's final actions signs of wisdom or folly? If what they showed was folly (one of More's favorite themes),[9] then it was a Christian folly that saw redemptive meaning in the cross. Following the traditional Christian understanding, More considered it to be true wisdom not to rage against the cross, but to glory in it.

So well did More understand this fundamental Christian paradox of the cross, and so long had he trained himself to live it, that he was consistently able to rise above the moment and above his own feelings. He had also learned, from the Greek and Roman comedians, that humor is one of the most powerful allies available to cultured human beings in their pursuit of justice.

At the end of his life, More frequently expressed his desire to "be merry together in heaven" with those who were set on his destruction. Surely this refrain echoed in their consciences as they later recalled the charm of a man whose happiness could not be shaken in any season.[10]

By the end of his life, More had every reason to be angry and pessimistic. He had been betrayed by some of those closest to him, and only one bishop in all of England had joined him in resisting a tyrannical king. In addition, the universal Church he loved had been outlawed in England, he had lost everything he possessed, his health was broken, and not even the children he had personally educated agreed with his "scruple of conscience."

Yet he was merry to the end. Why? Because his good humor was not simply a matter of temperament; it was deeply theological, rooted in the cultivated virtues of a faith lived in the present moment, a hope that did not depend on appearances, and a charity rooted in eternity. Not only did More believe in God's providence; he also lived in the confidence that it works through *everything. Omnia in bonum,* "All things work to the good for those who love God" (Rom 8:28).[11] This conviction helped him keep everything in perspective. When his children suffered disappointment, as we have seen, he explained in a homey but vivid and memorable way that they could not "go to heaven in featherbeds." When the leading bishops of England tried to convince an impoverished More to join them in attending Anne Boleyn's coronation, he told them in a lighthearted but earthy and extraordinarily pointed way that he would not prostitute himself for any reason or at any price. Lighthearted as it was, this response was as powerful as any that has ever been given to those responsible for public affairs.[12]

To understand merry Thomas More, one has to consider the life-and-death battle he fought throughout his life. First and foremost, his fight was an internal one: against moods, passions, whims, and vain imaginings. Although this fight was primarily internal, the external results were abundant: his bright and cheerful home, his life of integrity, his valued and much sought-after judgment, his life as a civic leader who made himself accessible to the people he served. As the evidence shows, his mood was not determined by the success or failure of his personal or professional ventures. After all, in twelve years of public office—during a period of revolutionary change that he strongly opposed—his own family knew him to show anger only twice; and on each of those occasions, this was probably in response to a public attack aimed at destroying himself and those he loved.[13]

His fight also became a political one, waged at the highest level: the level on which matters are judged by the tribunal of conscience. More knew, however, that unless he fought well in the first battle, political matters would never reach that higher tribunal. For if reason did not reign over the passions within himself, how could it reign in matters involving others? If conscience did reign, however, More knew of no stronger human aid to resist temptation and to ease the pain of that resistance.[14]

In other words, More's unusual calm and good humor came from his habitual attention to conscience, which enabled him to assess the particular demands of each situation while keeping his eyes focused upon eternity.[15] Yet he did not rely on his own judgment as the ultimate foundation of his courage.

In one of his last letters to Meg, Sir Thomas responds to his daughter's concern over her lack of courage. Sympathizing with her, he confesses his own lack of courage when confronted with the trials of life. "Surely, Meg," he says to her, "a fainter heart than your frail father has can you not have."[16] He then gives one of his most fundamental counsels—a counsel he gave many times, over many years, in many different ways, going back to the earliest of his poems.[17] In these words can be discovered the ultimate foundation of that courage which so many have admired in the life of Sir Thomas More:

> That you fear your own frailty, Margaret, does not
> displease me. May God give us both the grace to

despair of our own self, and wholly to depend
and hang upon the hope and strength of God. The
blessed Saint Paul found such a lack of strength in
himself that in his own temptation he was twice
obliged to call and cry out unto God to take that
temptation from him. And yet he did not attain
his prayer in the manner that he requested. For
God in His high wisdom, seeing that it was (as he
himself said) necessary for him to keep him from
pride . . . answered, "My grace is sufficient for
you." . . . And our Lord said further, "Virtue is
perfected in weakness." The more weak that man
is, the more is the strength of God in his safeguard declared. And so Saint Paul said, "All is
possible in Him who strengthens me."[18]

Afterword

AFTER AN ECLIPSE of four hundred years, Thomas More was propelled into worldwide prominence just as Adolph Hitler approached the zenith of his power. This was no accident. The darkness of adversity often provides the best test of worth.

When More was canonized (along with John Fisher) on May 19, 1935, the world faced one of the gravest dangers of all time: through unscrupulous manipulations, Hitler had succeeded in gaining control of the resources of the powerful German state and was determined to seek worldwide domination while eliminating the Jews and silencing religion.[1] What were loyal Germans to do in the face of such a flagrant abuse of state power? In answer to this pressing question, Pope Pius XI proposed Thomas More as a model. Why? Because More was a "strong and courageous spirit . . . [who] knew how to despise resolutely the flattery of human respect, how to resist, in accordance with his duty, the supreme head of the state . . . , and how to renounce with dignity the high office with which he was invested. It was for these motives that he was imprisoned, nor could the tears of his wife and children make him swerve from the path of truth and virtue. In that terrible hour of trial he raised his eyes to heaven, and proved himself a bright example of Christian fortitude."[2]

Pope Pius acknowledged that "on a superficial glance it would seem as if God had, as it were, forgotten" Sir Thomas More and John Cardinal Fisher. After all, "so much time has passed since their deaths that, as the world might say, their memory [has] been blotted out."[3] Commenting upon the darkness of

More's own last days and upon the centuries of obscurity that followed, the Pope observed that "Divine Providence is always wonderful; even when it seems to let the darkness fall, it prepares the splendor of the light. The fact that this renewed light and splendor [of More's canonization] has appeared just now is a great reason for confidence on our part, when the whole world has such need, remembering that all things great and small are obedient to a Hand which is not the hand of man, that we are in the hands of God, of God who walks in the ages and whom the ages obey."[4]

Comparing More and Fisher to "grand lighthouses set up to shine upon and enlighten in the ways of God," Pope Pius went on to say: "These holy martyrs come to tell us that God's ways are not as our ways; they are not ways which lead to darkness, but to light. . . . The two great figures which today are upraised before us as objects of our admiration ought also to be the object of our imitation; and, although they are two such grand personalities, yet such imitation is not difficult, but [entirely] possible. . . . There are, in fact, many opportunities for imitating the martyrs without the martyrdom of blood and death. There is a martyrdom which consists in the anguish which each of us experiences in himself in following the ways of God and in the fulfillment of his proper duty. There is a martyrdom which consists in the difficulty of a duty exactly, faithfully, and fully accomplished. There is a martyrdom which occurs in the continual persevering fidelity in little things, in those demands for diligence in the divine service, in the daily duty which becomes a daily cross."[5]

But why did the splendor of such an example take four hundred years to be recognized? As the Anglican scholar R. W. Chambers put it at the beginning of this century, "Public commemoration is not for the leaders of the losing side. And so, though More's name has been widely held in private reverence, there has been a remarkable absence of any public reminder of his place in our history."[6]

Privately, many individuals recognized the greatness of Sir Thomas More. John Donne described him as "a man of the most tender and delicate conscience that the world saw since Augustine."[7] And Jonathan Swift, an Anglican clergyman not known for flattery, characterized him as "a person of the greatest virtue this kingdom ever produced."[8] Yet it must be remembered that the religion More defended was outlawed in England until the Emancipation Act of 1829. Only in 1850 did that church have its hierarchy restored. As soon as it did, the newly appointed archbishop requested that More be given the honor that was his due. This allowed the lengthy process to begin of examining More's life and writings, a process that culminated in his beatification on December 29 (the feast of Thomas Becket), 1886.[9]

To have acted earlier would have invited even worse relations with England. Diplomacy, as More himself would have testified, was necessary in dealing with such matters. Yet, because "time tries truth,"[10] More's importance has begun to emerge. Prophetically, G. K. Chesterton said in 1929 that "Blessed Thomas More is more important at this moment than at any moment since his death, even perhaps the great moment of his dying; but he is not quite so important as he will be in about a hundred years' time."[11]

What Chesterton predicted in 1929 is coming to pass, as events of recent years have shown. Not the least of these events is the appearance of the Yale Edition of *The Complete Works of St. Thomas More*. In retrospect, it seems remarkable that no critical edition of More's work was ever done before, especially given his status as the first major writer of the English Renaissance. Yet thankfully, for the first time, we have ready access to More's complete writings.[12]

One other significant gauge of More's growing importance is the ever-increasing number of societies that honor him. In the world of law and government, Sir Thomas More has become a symbol of integrity; in family and professional life, he has become a symbol of balance, serenity, and good cheer. For people in every walk of life, he has been a portrait of courage.

Appendix 1

Thomas More's Travels

Amiens: In 1527 More accompanied Wolsey to complete peace negotiations with France.

Antwerp: More visited this important commercial center in 1515, during his embassy to Bruges, and again in 1520 and 1521. His *Utopia* opens outside its beautiful church of Notre Dame.

Barnborough Hall, Yorkshire: As a baby, Anne Cresacre became heir to this estate after her parents died in 1512. More became her guardian and assumed responsibility for her lands until she came of age.

Bruges: More made embassies to this city in 1515 and 1521, primarily to negotiate the trade of wool and cloth between England and Flanders. He was appointed by the King, but was probably nominated by the London merchants. In 1520 he was in the

King's retinue for the peace-keeping mission at the Field of Cloth of Gold.

Calais: More went to Calais in 1517 to negotiate with French merchants, and again in 1521 to help Wolsey in peace negotiations between Emperor Charles V and King Francis I.

Cambrai: More considered the 1529 Peace of Cambrai treaty to be the most important achievement of his diplomatic career. It is the only public event he mentions in his epitaph. He rejoiced that peace had finally been restored to Christendom.

Cambridge: More served as High Steward of Cambridge. His friend Bishop John Fisher was its chancellor.

Canterbury: The shrine of St. Thomas Becket was the most popular place of pilgrimage in England. More considered it significant that the date set for his own execution was the eve of Becket's feast. Henry VIII eventually outlawed pilgrimages to this spot. More's head is buried in St. Dunstan's Church in Canterbury.

Coventry: More's sister Elizabeth Rastell lived in this city. On a visit in or about 1506, he met the ignorant friar whom he describes in his "Letter to Dorp." Elizabeth's most famous grandson would be John Donne.

Lancaster, Duchy of: From 1525 to 1529, More served as chancellor of this territory, which encompassed some forty thousand people.

Louvain: More visited Louvain's university around 1508.

Oxford: More attended Oxford for two years and later served as High Steward. In 1518 he wrote an official letter in defense of Greek studies there.

Paris: More visited the University of Paris around 1508.

Rochester: Here More visited his longtime friend Bishop John Fisher.

Southampton: In 1517 More served as counsel and interpreter for the pope's ambassador in a case involving forfeiture of a papal ship that was docked at Southampton.

Woodstock: More often accompanied Henry's royal retinue to Woodstock, where the King loved to hunt. More was here when news of the great fire at Chelsea reached him, on September 3, 1529.

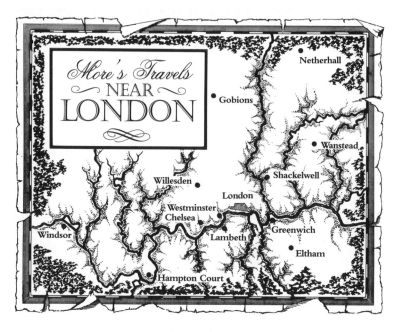

Appendix 2

More's Travels near London

Chelsea: More built his family home on a thirty-four-acre farm, two miles from London. This location gave him easy access downstream to Westminster Hall, where he did much of his business, and upstream to Hampton Court.

Eltham, Kent: More surprised Erasmus in 1499 by having him come along for an unannounced visit to Prince Henry at the royal palace. The Ropers had their family estate here.

Gobions: More's father owned this country estate in North Mimms, Hertfordshire.

Greenwich: The court at Greenwich was one of King Henry's favorites; it was just east of London, on the Thames.

Hampton Court: Cardinal and Chancellor Wolsey built this magnificent palace in 1514, and Henry confiscated it in 1529 upon Wolsey's fall. More was often in this palace to do business with both Wolsey and Henry.

Lambeth Palace: At twelve, More served as page to Archbishop and Chancellor Morton. It was probably here, at a feast in November 1503, that More delivered the comic poem he is thought to have written in honor of his father, who had become a sergeant-at-law, and his maternal grandfather, who had been elected sheriff of London. Later, More would come to this place to see William Warham, Archbishop of Canterbury and former Lord Chancellor of England. Just prior to his imprisonment, More was interrogated in this palace by Cranmer, Cromwell, Audley, and Benson.

Netherhall: More's wife Jane Colt, one of eighteen children, lived on this country estate in Essex.

Shackelwell, Hackney: More became responsible for this magnificent manor and all of its lands when he became the guardian of Giles Heron, in 1523. After More's death, Heron was accused by a disgruntled former tenant of having "mumble[d] certain words touching the King" in the parlor of Shackelwell; he was imprisoned in 1539 and executed in 1540.

Wanstead: This was another estate owned by Giles Heron, a property that Richard Rich acquired after Heron's execution.

Westminster: Here the English Parliament began, and here More practiced law. He served in the Parliament of 1504, which met in the Chapter House of Westminster Abbey. He met with Wolsey frequently at Whitehall; here, during that famous incident of 1523, he tactfully broke off the Cardinal's "displeasant talk" by complimenting him on his beautiful gallery. More was tried and found guilty in Westminster Hall.

Willesden: Giles Alington, husband of Alice (More's stepdaughter), owned an estate near this town. In 1525 a double wedding took place in Alington's private chapel: Elizabeth More married William Dauncey, and Cecily More married Giles Heron.

Willesden, St. Mary: This shrine to our Lady dates back to the tenth century. More walked the seven miles to make his pilgrimage here.

Windsor: At this castle, built as a fortress by William the Conqueror, More served at Henry's court.

Appendix 3

Thomas More's London (see endpapers)

All Hallows Church: More regularly made pilgrimages, always on foot, in and around London. He visited the famous Marian shrine at this church, which was near the Tower.

The Barge: More's first home, where all his children were born, was called "The Barge." This was in an attractive part of London, on Bucklersbury Street, and was aromatic because of the many spice dealers in the area.

Blackfriars: When Parliament met here in 1523, More served as Speaker of the House of Commons. In his opening address, More argued for freedom of speech—the first such appeal ever recorded.

Charterhouse: While studying law, More attached himself to this strict Carthusian monastery to receive spiritual formation. It was Henry II who originally invited the Carthusians to come into England—as part of his reparation for the murder of Thomas Becket in 1170.

Crosby Hall: More bought the lease of this magnificent home in 1523 (Richard III had been a previous resident), but shortly afterwards sold it to his good friend Antonio Bonvisi. In 1910 the great hall of this estate was moved to Chelsea.

Furnivall's Inn: More taught law at this school from 1503 to 1506.

Guildhall: More served as undersheriff and handled a great deal of city business in this grand municipal center.

Lincoln's Inn: Both Thomas and his father studied law at this inn of court and remained active there throughout their careers. Lincoln's Inn was considered the best law school in England.

London Bridge: Both Thomas and his father served on commissions charged with the maintenance of London Bridge. The head of Thomas More was displayed here just after his execution.

Milk Street: More's birth place. Milk Street was a prosperous residential area off the busy commercial district of the city. Sir John More lived here for most of his life; the exact location of his home is no longer known.

Old Swan's Wharf: After his trial at Westminster on July 1, 1535, More landed at this wharf and then walked along lower Thames Street to the Tower.

St. Anthony's School: The school More attended as a child. Just north of Threadneedle Street, St. Anthony's was among the best grammar schools in London.

St. Lawrence Jewry, Church of: This was the Mores' parish church, where young Thomas lectured on Augustine's *City of God*.

St. Paul's Cathedral: More's good friend and spiritual advisor Fr. John Colet was dean of this cathedral.

St. Stephen's, Walbrook: While More lived at The Barge, this was his parish church. It was here that he buried Jane, that he married Alice, and that Margaret married William Roper.

The Tower: More was imprisoned in the Bell Tower of this fortress for more than a year before his public execution on Tower Hill. His body is buried in the Chapel of St. Peter ad Vincula.

Tower Wharf: Margaret's last meeting with her father occurred at this spot.

Appendix 4

A Chronology of More's Life

(More's Age)

1477, Feb. 7 — Born in London to John and Agnes More

c. 1484–1489 — Attends St. Anthony's School, London   (7–12)

c. 1489–1491 — Page for Archbishop and Chancellor Morton   (12–14)

c. 1491–1493 — Student at Oxford   (14–16)

c. 1493–1495 — Pre-law student, New Inn, London   (16–18)

1496–*c.* 1501 — Law student, Lincoln's Inn; called to bar   (18–23)

1499 — Meets Erasmus for the first time   (22)

c. 1501–1504 — Frequents Charterhouse (Carthusians)   (24–27)

c. 1501 — Lectures on St. Augustine's *City of God*; begins Greek   (24)

c. 1503–1506 — Reader at Furnivall's Inn   (26–29)

1504 — Elected to Parliament   (27)

1505 — Marries Jane Colt; Margaret born   (28)

1506 — Studies intensely; visits Coventry; Elizabeth born   (29)

1507 — Financial secretary of Lincoln's Inn; Cecily born   (30)

*c.*1508 —Visits universities at Paris and Louvain   (31)

1509 — Member of Mercers' Guild; John born; Henry VIII crowned (32)

1510 — Elected to Parliament   (33)

1510–1518 — Undersheriff of London   (33–41)

1511 — After Jane's death, marries Alice Middleton;

    Autumn Reader at Lincoln's Inn   (34)

1512 — Governor and treasurer of Lincoln's Inn   (35)

1513 — Henry VIII leads an army against France; to Henry, Erasmus

    dedicates his translation of Plutarch's essay on flattery   (36)

1514 — Elected to Doctors' Commons; serves on sewers commission   (37)

1515 — Embassy to Bruges and Antwerp for commercial treaties;

    Lenten Reader at Lincoln's Inn; refuses royal pension   (38)

1516 — Continues to study history and political philosophy   (39)

1517 — Embassy to Calais; counsel to pope's ambassador in

    England; Evil May Day; Wolsey's Treaty of Universal Peace;

    Luther's "Ninety-five Theses"   (40)

1518 — Joins King Henry's service; Master of Requests   (41)

1520 — Field of Cloth of Gold: peace with France   (43)

1521 — Knighted; undertreasurer; ambassador to Bruges and Calais;

    cautions Henry not to exaggerate the pope's secular authority;

    Margaret marries Roper; Buckingham executed   (44)

1522 — Gives public oration welcoming Emperor Charles V;

    serves as Henry's secretary and cautions against war;

    war with France resumed   (45)

1523 — Speaker of the House of Commons, proposes free speech;
leases Crosby Hall; truce with France (46)
1524 — High Steward, Oxford; moves to Chelsea; war with France
resumes: "If my head could win [the King] a castle in
France, . . . it would not fail to go." (47)
1525 — High Steward, Cambridge; chancellor of the Duchy of
Lancaster; Peasants' Revolt; peace treaty with France;
Cecily marries Heron; Elizabeth marries Dauncey (48)
1526 — Appointed to royal council's subcommittee of four; urges
Erasmus to complete writings against Luther; Turks invade
Hungary; Tyndale's New Testament secretly distributed (49)
1527 — Accompanies Wolsey to France; sack of Rome; Henry
consults More about divorce; More's daughters' dispute
before Henry; Holbein paints the More family (50)
1528 — Tunstall asks More to defend Church in English; Margaret
almost dies; More chosen as alternate Master of Revels,
Lincoln's Inn; More's three great wishes (Roper 13–14) (51)
1529 — Delegate, Peace of Cambrai; fire at Chelsea; appointed
Lord Chancellor; addresses Parliament; John marries
Anne Cresacre (52)
1530 — More almost dismissed for his opposition to Henry;
Cranmer completes his defense of caesaropapism (53)
1531 — Henry declared Supreme Head of the Church in England (54)
1532 — Counters Cromwell's and St. German's attacks on the
clergy; reports universities' approval of royal divorce;
Henry enraged by undiplomatic clerics; Submission of
Clergy (May 15); More resigns his office (May 16) (55)
1533 — Restraint of Appeals to Rome; England declared an
empire (April); Cranmer authorizes royal divorce (May);
Anne Boleyn's coronation (June 1); Pope Clement VII
condemns the divorce (July); to defend his reputation,
More writes to Erasmus (56)
1534 — Henry asks for More's indictment (Feb. 21), but House of
Lords refuses three times; More questioned by royal com-
mission (March), interrogated at Lambeth Palace (Apr. 13),
and finally imprisoned (illegally) for refusal to take
Cromwell's oath regarding the Act of Succession (Apr. 17);
Chancellor Audley sends a warning to More (August) (57)
1535 — Margaret visits while monks are led to execution (May 4);
More interrogated on May 7, June 3, and June 14;
Richard Rich removes writing materials (June 12);
More's trial (July 1) and execution (July 6) (58)

Appendix 4 (continued)

A Chronology of More's Writings

English poems (*c.* 1496–1504)
Correspondence (Latin and English, 1499–1535)
Latin verses to Holt's *Lac Puerorum* (*c.* 1500)
"Letter to John Colet" (*c.* 1504)
The Life of John Picus (*c.* 1504; published 1510)
Translations of Lucian (1505–1506; published 1506)
Latin poems, *Epigrammata* (1496–1516; published 1518)
Coronation ode (1509, published 1518)
Epigrams on Brixius (1513, published 1518)
The History of King Richard III (*c.* 1513–1518)
"Letter to Dorp" (1515)
Utopia (1516)
Poem and letters to his children, and letter to their tutor (1517–1522)
Letters to Oxford (1518), to a Monk (1519), and to Brixius (1520)
Quattuor Novissima [*The Four Last Things*] (*c.* 1522)
Responsio ad Lutherum (1523)
"Letter to Bugenhagen" (1526; published 1568)
A Dialogue Concerning Heresies (June 1529)
Supplication of Souls (September 1529)
A Dialogue Concerning Heresies, 2nd edition (May 1531)
Confutation of Tyndale's Answer I–III (March 1532)
"Letter against Frith" (December 1532; published December 1533)
Confutation of Tyndale IV–VIII (Spring 1533)
The Apology of Sir Thomas More (April 1533)
The Debellation of Salem and Bizance (October 1533)
The Answer to a Poisoned Book (December 1533)
A Treatise upon the Passion; A Treatise to Receive the Blessed Body; A Dialogue of Comfort against Tribulation; "A Dialogue on Conscience" (1534)
"Imploring Divine Help against Temptation"; "A Godly Instruction [on How to Treat Those Who Wrong Us]"; "A Godly Meditation [on Saving One's Life]"; "A Godly Meditation [on Detachment]" (1534–1535)
De Tristitia Christi [*The Sadness of Christ*] (1535, published 1565)
"A Devout Prayer [before Dying]" (July 1535)

Appendix 5

The More Family

From left to right:

1. Elizabeth (21)
2. Margaret Giggs (22) [adopted daughter]
3. Judge John More (76)
4. Anne Cresacre (15) [ward]
5. Sir Thomas (50)
6. John (18)
7. Henry Patenson (40) [family "fool"]
8. Cecily (20)
9. Margaret (22)
10. John Harris (27) [More's secretary]
11. Lady Alice (57)

Appendix 6
Annotated Pages of More's Prayer Book

This first page of More's prayer book has, in More's hand, the following verse from his "Godly Meditation [on Detachment]":

Give me Thy grace, good Lord, / to set the world at nought.

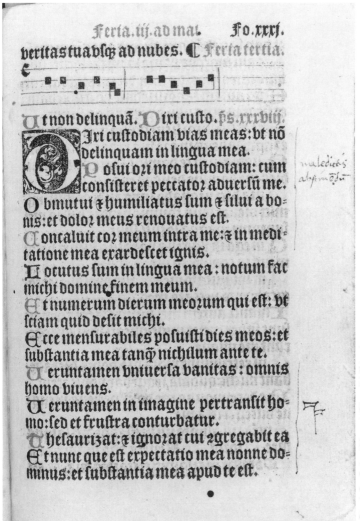

Opposite Psalm 38:2 [39:2], More writes "maledictis abstinendum" ["evil words are not to be used"]. He then marks, with one of his largest and most distinctive marginal flourishes, Psalm 38:6–7 [39:6–7], which reads: "Only a breath is any human existence. A phantom only, man goes his way; like vapor only are his restless pursuits."

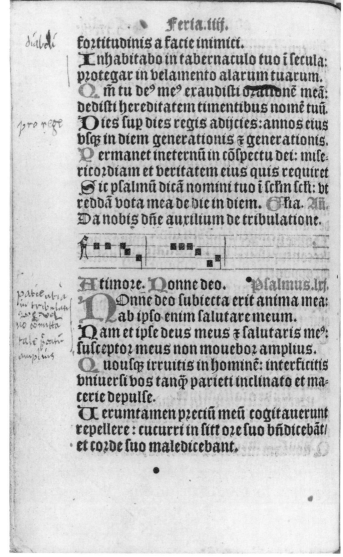

More writes in the margin:
 "diaboli" ["of the devil"] next to Psalm 60:4 [61:4];
 "pro rege" ["for the king"] next to Psalm 60:7 [61:7]; and
 "patientia in tribulacione vel non committam tale peccatum
amplius" ["patience in tribulation, or I shall not commit
such a sin again"] next to Psalm 61:2 [62:2].

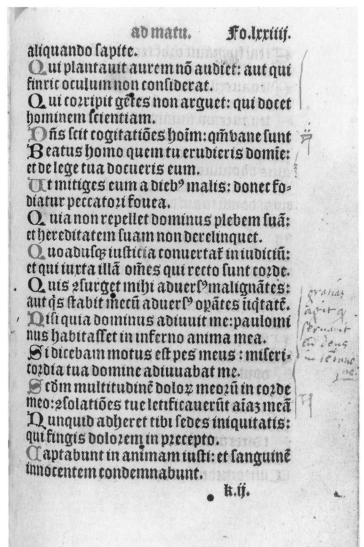

At Psalm 93:16 [94:16] More writes:
"gratias agit quod seruauit eum Deus in tentatione"
["He gives thanks that God saved him from temptation"].

Notes

Epigraph

1. As his epigraph to *The Screwtape Letters* Lewis chose this quotation from Thomas More: "The devil . . . the proud spirit . . . cannot endure to be mocked" [Roper, p. 15].

Introduction

1. SL, pp. 4–5. This is a letter to John Colet, young More's spiritual advisor.
2. CW 3.2, p. 552, n. 1. See also CWE, vol. 7, pp. 276–277.
3. CW 3.1, pp. 5–7.
4. Consider the intensity of the youthful infatuation he describes in epigram no. 263, CW 3.2, pp. 275–279.
5. Instances of this negative use of wit appear in the earliest letter we have from More (SL, p. 2).
6. CWE, vol. 7, p. 19. It is interesting that More's *Life of John Picus* shows Pico suffering from a similar kind of negligence, arising from the same unrestrained passion for learning. Consider especially EW, pp. 358–359. Throughout his life, More warned against the evils that arise from negligence. See, for example, CW 6, p. 369, lines 31–32; CW 9, pp. 53, 145, 158; CW 11, p. 5, lines 25–27, and pp. 92–93; SC, p. 23.
7. In *A Dialogue of Comfort against Tribulation*, a character who resembles More in virtually everything confesses that he often has a hard time controlling his tongue:

    > I myself am by nature even half a gigglot and
    > more. I wish I could as easily mend my fault as I

242

well know it, but scant can I refrain it, as old fool
as I am. However, I will not be so partial to my
fault as to praise it. (CW 12, p. 83)

8. SL, p. 242. A fillip is a small tap with the finger. Pleasure and pain
are among the major themes in More's writings—partly because he
knew their powerful influence upon human beings in general, and
partly because he knew their powerful influence upon himself.

9. Pride is a central and frequently recurring theme in More's writings. He presents it as the root of all other vices. (See chapter 1 of
my *Thomas More on Statesmanship*, Catholic University of America
Press, 1996.)

Chapter 1
Family Foundations in the Heart of London

1. CW 3.2, p. 643. More goes on to qualify this view by insisting that
virtue depends upon personal responsibility and effort more than
upon one's parents. As More puts it, "Who our parents are is
theirs to determine; a good person's only true commendation is
virtue." For this reason the good child of bad parents "deserves
greater praise than the good child of good parents."

2. Stapleton, p. 1.
3. SL, pp. 181–182.
4. Stapleton, p. 4.
5. SL, p. 181.
6. Marius, p. 5.
7. See Marc'hadour, "Thomas More's Birth: 1477 or 1478?"
8. Cresacre More, p. 14.
9. Roper, p. 3.
10. Roper, p. 3.
11. Harpsfield, Reynolds edition, p. 59.
12. CW 2, p. 91.
13. CW 2, p. 90.
14. CW 4, pp. 59–61.
15. Stapleton, p. 3.
16. Stapleton, p. 3.
17. CW 3.2, no. 263.

Chapter 2
Vocational Trials in Revolutionary Times

1. SL, p. 4.
2. EE, vol. 3, p. 394; CWE, vol. 7, p. 21; Stapleton, p. 8.
3. CW 6, pp. 295, 301–302.
4. Chaucer, *Canterbury Tales*, "Prologue," line 187.
5. Lupton, pp. 77–78.
6. CWE, vol. 8, p. 237.
7. CWE, vol. 8, pp. 236–237.
8. CW 6, pp. 107, 298; CW 9, p. 48; CW 10, p. 21; SL, p. 140, lines 1–5.
9. Stapleton, p. 57.
10. Stapleton, p. 57.
11. Roper, p. 4.
12. Stapleton, pp. 7–8.
13. CWE, vol. 5, p. 401.
14. CWE, vol. 7, p. 19.
15. SL, p. 4.
16. SL, p. 4.
17. EW, p. 327.

Chapter 3
More's First Handbook on Spiritual Combat

1. Stapleton says that More's purpose in compiling his *Life of John Picus* "was not so much to bring these [counsels] to the knowledge of others, though that, too, he had in view, as thoroughly to familiarize himself with them" (p. 9).
2. Most of this book is a translation of a work by a nephew of Pico's, but More definitely shapes and adds to this material according to his own purposes. See Lehmberg, "St. Thomas More's *Life of Pico*"; Gabrieli; and especially CW 1.
3. Richard Sylvester calls *The Life of John Picus* a "deftly fashioned spiritual handbook which [contains] a new kind of saint's life, some homiletic letters, a warm illustration of how to read scripture [Pico's commentary on Psalm 15], a series of handy rules for

fighting the good fight, and a sublime hymn lifting the soul to God" ("More's Literary Personality," p. 37).

4. Pico della Mirandola (1463–1494) was a leading humanist thinker of the late Italian Renaissance. Today, the most famous of his works is *On the Dignity of Man*. He was good friends with the Florentine Platonist Marsilio Ficino and with Lorenzo de' Medici.

5. EW, p. 353.

6. EW, pp. 353–360.

7. EW, pp. 359, 369–370.

8. EW, p. 370.

9. EW, pp. 361–362.

10. EW, p. 358.

11. CWE, vol. 7, p. 22.

12. CW 4, pp. 39–41.

13. Copenhaver, p. 176.

14. EW, p. 396.

15. EW, p. 378.

16. EW, p. 367.

17. EW, pp. 367–368.

18. Pico gives a list of these twelve properties, but More develops them into a six-page poem.

19. EW, p. 391.

20. EW, p. 379.

21. EW, p. 379.

22. EW, p. 378.

23. Cresacre More, p. 9.

24. EW, p. 396.

25. EW, p. 381; cf. 1 Tm 6:12 and 2 Tm 4:7.

26. This point about the joy of a clear conscience is a persistent theme in More's writing. See, for example, SL, pp. 235, 250; EW, pp. 365, 384; CW 12, pp. 34, 121.

27. EW, p. 385.

28. EW, p. 360.

29. EW, p. 368.

30. EW, p. 368.

31. EW, p. 386.

Chapter 4
Husband and Father: New Joys, New Sorrows

1. CW 3.2, no. 143, lines 62–65.
2. CW 3.2, no. 143, lines 66–71.
3. CW 3.2, no. 143, lines 76–80.
4. CW 3.2, no. 143, lines 81–101.
5. CW 3.2, no. 143, lines 120, 138ff., 176–177.
6. CW 3.2, no. 143, lines 111–116.
7. Roper, p. 4.
8. Roper, p. 4. John More was probably Roper's source.
9. CW 3.2, no. 143, lines 102–105.
10. Erasmus, "Marriage," p. 120.
11. CWE, vol. 7, p. 21.
12. Although "Marriage" is clearly fictitious, it is commonly interpreted as being about More and his wife. Compare this story with what Erasmus says in his earliest biographical account of More (CWE, vol. 7, p. 21).
13. Erasmus, "Marriage," p. 121.
14. Erasmus, "Marriage," p. 121.
15. Erasmus, "Marriage," pp. 121–122.
16. CWE, vol. 7, p. 21.
17. LP, Addenda I.i., no. 1024.
18. CWE, vol. 7, pp. 21–22.
19. Stapleton, p. 56.
20. DC, p. 183; CW 12, p. 211, lines 19–20.
21. DC, p. 183; CW 12, pp. 219–220.
22. Roper, p. 28.
23. Stapleton, p. 127.
24. See, for example, Stapleton, pp. 68–69; Roper, pp. 13–15, 28–29, 37–38, 47–48, 50; Harpsfield, Reynolds edition, pp. 95–96, 126–128.
25. Harpsfield, Reynolds edition, p. 106; also CW 12, p. 118.
26. CWE, vol. 7, p. 22.
27. SL, p. 109.
28. CW 4, pp. 39–41.

29. Roper, p. 7.

Chapter 5
The Laughing Philosopher: Early Writings

1. Sylvester, "Whittington's Verses," p. 152.
2. CWE, vol. 7, pp. 18–19.
3. Pace, p. 105.
4. Sylvester, "Whittington's Verses," p. 147; CWE, vol. 8, p. 297.
5. SL, p. 16; CW 15, p. 18.
6. CW 6, p. 132.
7. CW 3.1, p. 3, lines 5–6; CW 3.2, p. 644, lines 6–7; CW 4, p. 1, line 4; Horace's *Art of Poetry*, lines 343–344.
8. SL, p. 148.
9. CW 3.1, p. 196.
10. CW 3.1, p. 3.
11. CWE, vol. 7, p. 17.
12. CW 3.2, p. 63.
13. CW 14, p. 349.
14. CW 3.2, no. 128.
15. CW 3.2, no. 133.
16. CW 3.2, no. 262.
17. CW 3.2, no. 42.
18. CW 3.2, no. 57.
19. CW 3.2, no. 221.
20. CW 3.2, no. 72.
21. CW 3.2, no. 73.
22. CW 3.2, nos. 70 and 74.
23. CW 3.2, no. 75.
24. CW 3.2, no. 254.
25. CW 3.2, no. 39.
26. CW 3.2, no. 263.
27. CW 3.2, no. 264.
28. CW 3.2, no. 32.

Chapter 6
Coming to a Statesman's Understanding of Life

1. Stapleton, p. 13.
2. Stapleton, p. 14.
3. CW 2, pp. lxxxvi–xcviii.
4. See the examples cited by Ben Jonson in *The English Grammar* and by Samuel Johnson in his *History of the English Language*.
5. See CW 2, p. xxxiii.
6. Kincaid shows how More makes dissimulation the focal point of Richard's character (p. 378).
7. CW 2, p. 6.
8. CW 2, p. 46.
9. I give an overall interpretation of *Utopia* in part two of *Thomas More on Statesmanship* (Catholic University of America Press, 1996).

Chapter 7
Achieving Professional Success

1. More uses this phrase several times in CW 12, pp. 44–45. "Watch" refers to curbing one's sleep. More continued all three of these practices throughout his life.
2. CWE, vol. 7, p. 23.
3. CWE, vol. 2, p. 113.
4. Roper, p. 5.
5. Roper, p. 5. More did not like these embassies because they took him away from his family for rather long periods of time. They also took him away from his regular work, with detrimental effect to his income. He jokingly said that although he "was no ill husband, no ill father, no ill master, yet he could still not persuade his wife, children or family to fast" until he returned from these foreign missions (Harpsfield, Reynolds edition, p. 64; SL, p. 70).
6. Stapleton, p. 15.
7. CWE, vol. 7, p. 22.

8. CWE, vol. 7, p. 22.
9. Stapleton, p. 13.
10. Roper, p. 29.
11. Roper, p. 29.
12. CW 4, p. 59.
13. CW 9, p. 170.
14. CWE, vol. 7, p. 22.
15. CWE, vol. 7, p. 22.
16. So daring was this 1593 production that it was never staged until 1922. See the introduction to Munday's edition of the play.
17. Roper, pp. 21–22.
18. Stapleton, p. 23; Roper, p. 22.
19. Stapleton, p. 23.
20. Harpsfield, Reynolds edition, p. 65; Stapleton, p. 16.
21. Roper, p. 5.
22. CWE, vol. 2, p. 200, and vol. 3, p. 239.
23. Marius, p. 5.
24. Roper, p. 6.
25. Hall, vol. 1, p. 159.

Chapter 8
"Born for Friendship"

1. CWE, vol. 7, p. 18.
2. CWE, vol. 7, p. 16.
3. EE, vol. 3, p. 391; also CWE, vol. 7, p. 18.
4. CWE, vol. 7, p. 18.
5. CWE, vol. 7, p. 18.
6. CWE, vol. 7, p. 18.
7. CWE, vol. 7, p. 19.
8. Stapleton draws attention to the way in which "humor played a gracious part" in More's general conversation. "Often indeed," Stapleton comments, "[More] would turn aside a matter of grave offense with a joke" (p. 123).
9. Stapleton reports that whenever a dishonorable, disloyal, or

uncharitable conversation began at the More home, Sir Thomas "would interrupt the conversation by saying, 'Let others think and say what they will, but for my part I consider that this gallery is of the greatest elegance and convenience'; and then he would go on to talk of other things" (p. 118).

10. Whenever it became clear that he had the upper hand in a public debate at Oxford or Cambridge, More had the custom of using "some witty device [to] courteously break off into some other matter and give over." He was careful not to discourage or shame those whom he debated (Harpsfield, Reynolds edition, p. 130). More remained courteous to the end, even at his own trial (see Stapleton's assessment, p. 172).

11. Stapleton, p. 124. Here Stapleton also says, "The merriness of his speech and a clever wit were most helpful to More in most difficult circumstances, and were a sure protection to his innocence and his constancy."

12. CWE, vol. 2, p. 163; Sylvester, "Whittington's Verses," p. 147.

13. CWE, vol. 2, p. 163, and vol. 8, p. 297.

14. Pace, p. 105.

15. Bainton, p. 18.

16. CWE, vol. 7, p. 19.

17. CWE, vol. 6, p. 364.

18. CWE, vol. 6, p. 372.

19. SL, p. 16; CWE, vol. 6, p. 392, and vol. 7, p. 114.

20. CW 3.2, no. 21; CWE, vol. 6, pp. 365–367.

21. CWE, vol. 7, pp. 256–257.

22. SL, p. 162.

23. SL, p. 162.

24. SL, p. 254.

25. SL, p. 256.

26. SL, p. 254.

27. SL, p. 256.

28. SL, p. 253.

29. CW 15, pp. 51–53.

30. CW 15, p. 53.

31. CW 15, pp. 53–55.

32. Stapleton gives a fairly lengthy account of their friendship in his biography, pp. 53–59.

33. SL, p. 166.
34. Letter to Cranevelt, April 9, 1521, *Moreana*, no. 117 (March 1994): 17–19.
35. SL, p. 166.
36. Letter to Cranevelt, November 12, 1521, *Moreana*, no. 117 (March 1994): 25.
37. Letter to Cranevelt, February 13, 1521, *Moreana*, no. 117 (March 1994): 9.
38. Letter to Cranevelt, April 9, 1521, *Moreana*, no. 117 (March 1994): 17–19.
39. Letter to Cranevelt, November 8, 1528, *Moreana*, no. 117 (March 1994): 13–15.

Chapter 9
A Reluctant Career Change

1. CWE, vol. 7, p. 22.
2. CW 3.2, no. 19.
3. CWE, vol. 5, p. 401.
4. Stapleton, p. 22.
5. CW 3.2, nos. 243 and 244.
6. SL, pp. 229, 209.
7. SL, p. 94.
8. Roper, p. 7.
9. CSPV 1509–1519, no. 1220.
10. Scarisbrick, pp. 118–119.
11. Scarisbrick, p. 119.
12. This poem is entitled "A King Is Protected, Not by a Corps of Guards, but by His Own Good Qualities." See CW 3.2, no. 120.
13. Scarisbrick, p. 119.
14. Guy, *Public Career*, p. 16.
15. Stapleton, p. 125.
16. Harpsfield, Reynolds edition, p. 72.
17. Stapleton (p. 89) reports that only twice in his life was More known to get angry. He does not say what the two occasions were, but this incident with Brixius and More's confrontation with Richard Rich at his trial seem the most likely possibilities. Roper

reports that he lived with Thomas More for sixteen years and never saw him "as much as once in a fume" (19).

18. SL, p. 74.
19. Marius, p. 249; Fox, pp. 9, 119–122; Elton, "The Real Thomas More?" p. 345.
20. CW 3.2, p. 649.
21. CWE, vol. 7, p. 252.
22. CW 3.2, p. 649; CWE, vol. 7, p. 252.
23. CWE, vol. 7, p. 239.
24. Corr, p. 263, lines 43–44.
25. How More's understanding of free speech fit in with his overall political philosophy is explained in my *Thomas More on Statesmanship* (Catholic University of America Press, 1996).
26. Roper, p. 12.
27. See chapter 13 for further discussion.
28. Harpsfield, Hitchcock edition, pp. 318–319.
29. LP, vol. 5, pp. 187, 46.
30. SL, p. 181.

Chapter 10
Daring Educator, Artful Parent

1. EW, p. 462.
2. CW 12, p. 281.
3. SL, p. 105.
4. SL, p. 105.
5. SL, p. 106.
6. SL, p. 104.
7. SL, p. 106.
8. SL, p. 92.
9. Roper, p. 14.
10. Stapleton, p. 89.
11. Ro. Ba. [abbreviation for an unknown author], p. 129.
12. CW 9, p. 118.
13. CW 9, p. 118.
14. EW, p. 490.

15. Stapleton, p. 67.
16. Guy, *Public Career*, p. 13.
17. CW 12, p. 320, lines 23–26, and p. 5, lines 2–3 and 28–29.
18. *Latin Epigrams*, pp. 230–231; CW 3.2, no. 264.
19. CW 12, p. 312, lines 12–13; cf. p. 198, lines 8–32.
20. Compare this rather philosophical statement of principle to the more imaginative presentation of the same idea in More's spiritual handbooks. Notice especially his easy-to-remember "Twelve Weapons of Spiritual Battle" (chapter 3) and his vivid images in *The Four Last Things* (chapter 11).
21. Stapleton, p. 98.
22. Roper, pp. 14–15.
23. CW 12, pp. 114–119.
24. CW 6, p. 132.
25. CWE, vol. 8, p. 297.
26. CW 15, p. 139.
27. SL, p. 105.
28. SL, p. 106.
29. CW 15, p. 139.
30. CW 15, p. 139.
31. CW 6, p. 132.

Chapter 11
Spiritual Handbook II

1. Stapleton, p. 103.
2. SL, pp. 147–149.
3. EW, p. 459.
4. EW, p. 463.
5. EW, p. 463.
6. EW, p. 461.
7. EW, p. 461.
8. EW, p. 462.
9. EW, p. 462.
10. EW, p. 462.

11. EW, p. 463.
12. EW, p. 464.
13. EW, p. 465.
14. EW, p. 466.
15. EW, p. 467.
16. EW, pp. 467, 476.
17. EW, p. 477.
18. EW, p. 477.
19. EW, p. 478.
20. EW, p. 478.
21. EW, p. 479.
22. EW, p. 479.
23. EW, p. 479.
24. CW 3.2, no. 119; CW 12, pp. 258–280.
25. A "poor-soul priest" was one entrusted with saying daily Mass for the poor souls in purgatory.
26. EW, p. 480.
27. EW, p. 486.
28. EW, p. 493.
29. EW, p. 476.
30. EW, p. 463.

Chapter 12
Reformation over Revolution

1. CW 5, p. 35. More begins this work by printing the whole of Luther's letter of 1522 to Lord Sebastian Schlick. The German text is in *D. Martin Luthers Werke*, vol. 10, Weimar, 1883.
2. CW 5, p. 39.
3. Hillerbrand, no. 1670, p. 192.
4. CW 7, p. 25.
5. CW 7, p. 51; CW 5, p. 501.
6. CW 7, pp. 37ff.; CW 5, pp. 305ff., 617ff.
7. CW 5, pp. 123ff., 183–185. See also CW 8, especially books 2, 3, and 7.
8. More refers quite frequently to the promise recorded in Mt 16:18.

See, for example, CW 5, pp. 161, 172–174; CW 7, pp. 38, 41–43; CW 6, pp. 108, 198–204; CW 8, pp. 410, 412–414, 607, 693, 807, 975; CW 9, p. 158; CW 11, p. 23; CW 14, p. 483.

9. CW 8, pp. 608, 722, 753.
10. CW 5, p. 285.
11. CW 5, p. 285.
12. CW 5, pp. 271ff.
13. CW 5, p. 271.
14. CW 5, p. 279.
15. CW 5, p. 279.
16. CW 5, p. 281.
17. CW 5, p. 263.
18. CW 5, pp. 269, 271.
19. CW 5, p. 207.
20. CW 7, p. 49.
21. CW 7, pp. 59–61.
22. CW 5, p. 143; CW 6, p. 297; CW 8, p. 777.
23. Henry VIII, *Assertio*, p. 458, with adjustments in the translation.
24. For a sampling of the controversy in assessing More's satire, see Boyle, p. 33, and CW 5, pp. 795, 825.
25. CW 5, p. 811.
26. CW 5, p. 1.
27. CW 5, p. 311.
28. CW 5, p. 311; cf. pp. 77, 181, 221, 235, 245.
29. CW 5, p. 21. The same concern is expressed on p. 11.
30. CW 5, p. 11.
31. CW 5, pp. 685, 11.
32. CW 5, pp. 53–55.
33. CW 5, p. 59.
34. CW 5, p. 65.
35. CW 5, e.g., pp. 219, 305, 315, 317.
36. CW 5, pp. 75, 575, 681.
37. At CW 5, p. 45, lines 32ff., More gives his reasons for favoring "a controversy carried on by means of published books, in which neither side can pretend either that any point was falsely kept from the record . . . or that anything had escaped him unforeseen in the heat of a hurried disputation." In More's judgment, "there

cannot be a more level plain for the struggle" than such a disputation in writing.
38. SL, p. 176.
39. More does compare Luther to Achilles, as did Erasmus (CW 5, pp. 225, 365–367; CWE, vol. 10, p. 448).
40. CW 5, p. 45.
41. CW 5, p. 45.
42. CW 5, pp. 689, 271.
43. CW 5, pp. 691–693.

Chapter 13
Wearing the Chain of Office

1. Throughout this chapter and the next, "office" is used in the sense of "duty," "service," or "an act of respect to a person" (from the Latin *officium*). Strictly speaking, this magnificent chain that More wore was given in recognition of services he had already rendered. Hence, he retained this chain even after his resignation.
2. The 1533 Act for Reformation of Excess in Apparel stipulated that "no man, unless he be a knight, [could] wear any collar of gold named a collar of S."
3. Roper, p. 37; Harpsfield, Reynolds edition, p. 147.
4. Regardless of what it meant to More personally, the SS collar was definitely an "emblem of service to the King," believed to refer to the phrase *Souvent me souvien* ("Think of me often"). See Edgar Munhall's *The Frick Collection: A Tour* (The Frick Museum, 1999), p. 48.
5. Guy, *Public Career*, p. 27.
6. Harpsfield, Hitchcock edition, pp. 318–319.
7. Hastings, p. 106.
8. Hastings, p. 109.
9. I agree with Hastings (p. 110) that this rhyme probably originated while More was chancellor of the Duchy of Lancaster and not during the short period of time when he was Lord Chancellor of England. Cf. Chambers, p. 274; Routh, p. 175; Guy, *Public Career*, p. 83.
10. Hastings, p. 118; Guy, *Public Career*, p. 29.

Chapter 14
Chelsea: A Home of International Fame

1. Piper, p. 742. This sketch appears following page 118, above.

2. Morison, p. 18.

3. This would also account for the three daughters' sitting together, with books surrounding them.

4. E. E. Reynolds suggests 1525 (see his 1960 study *Margaret Roper* [London: Burns and Oates], p. 47); Elizabeth Rogers dates the event around 1529 (Corr, p. 403). In his letter to More, John Palsgrave says, "When your daughters disputed in philosophy before the King's Grace, I would it had been my fortune to be present" (Corr, p. 405).

5. See Harpsfield, Hitchcock edition, pp. 318–319.

6. Stapleton, p. 14.

7. Harpsfield, Reynolds edition, p. 132.

8. Roper, p. 14.

9. Roper, p. 15. More also explained that the devil hates staunch opposition because he is so envious that he does not want anyone to gain more merit because of it.

10. Harpsfield, Reynolds edition, p. 97.

11. Although More indirectly asked for his family's support in this way, he did not receive it.

12. Harpsfield, Reynolds edition, p. 96.

13. Roper, p. 27.

14. Roper, pp. 23–24.

15. Stapleton, pp. 144–145.

16. Ro. Ba., p. 189.

17. All were deeply impressed, for example, at the way that Margaret Roper reacted years later when her husband was arrested (Harpsfield, Reynolds edition, pp. 97–98).

18. Heywood, p. 5.

19. Roper says that More usually spent Fridays in this way (p. 14).

20. Roper, pp. 15–16.

21. Harpsfield, Reynolds edition, p. 100.

22. Harpsfield, Reynolds edition, p. 102.

23. Harpsfield, Reynolds edition, p. 102.

24. Stapleton, p. 67.

25. Stapleton, p. 67.

26. Roper, p. 26.

27. Stapleton, p. 64.

28. Roper, p. 12.
29. Roper, p. 18.
30. Roper, p. 19.
31. Roper, p. 19; Harpsfield, Reynolds edition, p. 92. Ro. Ba. adds the qualifier that is in brackets, perhaps to clarify the sense of More's subtle reply (p. 88).
32. Guy, *Public Career*, p. 13.
33. SL, p. 170.
34. SL, p. 169.
35. SL, pp. 170–171.
36. After his resignation from the office of Lord Chancellor, More again decided not to discharge any of his servants without first finding them another place (Stapleton, p. 144).

Chapter 15
The Power of Artful Conversation I

1. More indicates that these long periods of "stooping and leaning" over his desk were responsible for his acute chest pains. See SL, pp. 201, 173; Corr, p. 514; Hernandez Conesa, pp. 27–31.
2. In his 1557 edition of More's *English Works*, William Rastell does use this title, but the sharply polemical character of that edition is well known.
3. Lewis, p. 172.
4. CW 6, p. 30.
5. CW 6, p. 130.
6. CW 6, p. 138.
7. CW 6, p. 246.
8. CW 6, pp. 332–333.
9. More gives this definition of heresy at CW 6, p. 37.
10. CW 6, p. 346.
11. CW 6, p. 369.
12. CW 6, pp. 370–371.
13. CW 6, p. 371.
14. CW 6, p. 373.
15. CW 6, p. 400.

16. CW 6, p. 402.
17. CW 6, p. 406.
18. CW 6, pp. 407–408.
19. CW 6, p. 409.
20. CW 6, p. 416.
21. CW 6, p. 415. Here also More affirms Augustine's position on just war. He agrees with Augustine that a just war is "not only excusable but also commendable" because it is undertaken "in the defense of [one's] country against enemies that would invade it." In such a war "every man fights not for the defense of himself out of a private affection for himself, but out of Christian charity for the safeguard and preservation of all the others."
22. CW 6, p. 423.
23. CW 6, p. 423.
24. CW 6, p. 423.
25. CW 6, p. 432.
26. CW 6, p. 433.
27. CW 6, pp. 434–435.
28. CW 6, p. 435.

Chapter 16
Royal Passion vs. Law and Tradition

1. Dt 25:5 holds that "when brethren dwell together, and one of them dies without children, the wife of the deceased shall not marry to another, but his brother shall take her, and raise up seed for his brother."
2. Shakespeare, *Henry VIII*, 2.2.17.
3. Shakespeare, *Henry VIII*, 2.3.32.
4. Shakespeare, *Henry VIII*, 2.4.11–14, 16–21, 34–35.
5. Later, Catherine appealed to the pope to hear her case, since, as she pointed out, she could not hope to receive a fair trial in an English court.
6. Scarisbrick, pp. 188–189.
7. Today, we would use the word "annulment" or "declaration of nullity" for what Henry called "divorce."

8. If Henry had succeeded in becoming ruler of Germany, how could he have effectively ruled England and the Holy Roman Empire as well? Furthermore, would he not have endangered England's future freedom by setting the precedent that the Holy Roman Emperor should also be the rightful ruler of England?
9. CW 3.2, no. 243.
10. In responding to this book, More repeatedly reminded Henry of his orthodoxy (CW 6, pp. 289, 291, 303, 349–350, 388, 424–425, 431), but only once attacked his propensity for tyranny (CW 6, pp. 370–372).
11. SL, p. 212.
12. CW 3.2, no. 121.
13. CW 7, pp. 111–112.
14. CW 7, p. 116.
15. See, for example, CW 7, pp. 128, 130, 137, 141, 162–163.
16. CW 7, p. 148.
17. CW 7, p. 149.
18. CW 7, pp. 148–149.
19. CW 7, p. 167.
20. CW 7, p. 139, lines 29–30.

Chapter 17
Lord Chancellor of England

1. SL, p. 172.
2. More used this phrase to describe the parliament that bent to the King's will in 1534. "For one parliament of yours, and God knows what kind, I have all the general councils for a thousand years" (*Paris Newsletter*, LP, vol. 8, no. 996, p. 395; Harpsfield, Reynolds edition, p. 163). He also used a similar phrase to describe the court that would condemn him. "Seeing that I see you are determined to condemn me (God knows how), I will now in discharge of my conscience speak my mind plainly and freely touching my indictment and your statute" (Harpsfield, Reynolds edition, p. 161; LP, vol. 8, no. 996).
3. In the 1300s, Parliament passed several statutes concerning the proper jurisdictions of church and state. For a clergyman to be

convicted of *praemunire* meant that he had been found guilty of exercising some spiritual jurisdiction that had not been approved by English law.

4. Guy, *Public Career*, p. 50.
5. Guy, *Public Career*, p. 50.
6. Guy, *Public Career*, p. 79.
7. Guy, "Thomas More as Successor to Wolsey," p. 279.
8. Guy, *Public Career*, p. 87.
9. Roper, p. 23.
10. More discreetly expresses this view in his last work; see CW 14, pp. 261–265.
11. See chapter 6.
12. Much of this account follows Guy's scholarly presentation in *Public Career*.
13. Guy, *Public Career*, p. 147.
14. Hall, vol. 1, p. 279; CSPS 1529–1530, no. 211, pp. 323–324.
15. Scarisbrick, pp. 255–256.
16. On this project Cranmer worked closely with Edward Fox, the King's almoner.
17. Fox and Guy, pp. 156–166.
18. Fox and Guy, p. 157.
19. CSPS 1529–1530, no. 445.
20. CSPS 1529–1530, no. 433; Guy, *Public Career*, p. 139.
21. More and Fisher were not, of course, invited. See CSPS 1530, no. 460; Guy, *Public Career*, pp. 139, 156; Scarisbrick, pp. 261, 292.
22. CSPS 1529–1530, no. 460.
23. CSPS 1529–1530, no. 460.
24. CSPS 1529–1530, no. 460.
25. Guy, *Christopher St. German*, pp. 19ff.
26. CSPS 1531, no. 598; LP, vol. 5, no. 45; Scarisbrick, p. 272.
27. Guy, *Public Career*, pp. 136ff.
28. Hughes, p. 122.
29. LP, vol. 5, no. 171, pp. 83–84.
30. Roper, p. 28.
31. CSPV 1527–1533, no. 754; Kelly, p. 103.
32. LP, vol. 5, no. 898.

33. Cf. More's commentary on Judas's proud reaction to Christ's mild correction at Mt 26:6–16 (CW 13, p. 77).
34. Guy, *Public Career*, pp. 192–193.
35. Hall, vol. 2, pp. 209–210; Guy, *Public Career*, p. 194.
36. Guy, *Public Career*, pp. 194–195.
37. Hall, vol. 2, p. 209; Guy, *Public Career*, p. 192; Scarisbrick, p. 298.
38. Scarisbrick, p. 298.
39. Guy, *Public Career*, p. 211.
40. Kelly, p. 113.
41. Guy, *Public Career*, p. 197.
42. Hall, vol. 2, p. 210; Guy, *Public Career*, p. 196; Scarisbrick, p. 299.
43. CSPV 1527–1533, no. 754.
44. Moyes, pp. 401–414.
45. More uses this metaphor in a particularly striking way at CW 14, pp. 537–543.
46. See Kelly, pp. 109–119.
47. Hughes, p. 162.
48. SC, p. 470; CW 14, p. 265. (See 2 Cor 7:10.)
49. Guy, *Public Career*, p. 201.

Chapter 18
"Wise as Serpents, Innocent as Doves"

1. In 1628 Parliament forced Charles I to recognize their ancient rights (summarized in the Magna Carta of 1215) in that important document of English constitutional history, the Petition of Right. Another restatement and a further refinement of those ancient rights, the famous Bill of Rights, became law in 1689.
2. Fox, p. 186.
3. SC, p. 9; CW 14, p. 59.
4. SC, pp. 112, 9; CW 14, p. 617 [Mt 10:16], 59; see also CW 8, p. 890; CW 15, p. 260; CW 7, p. 45; CW 4, p. 48; CW 3.1, p. 6.
5. CSPS 1529, no. 211, pp. 323-324; Hall, vol. 2, p. 164; Guy, *Public Career*, p. 113.
6. Guy, *Public Career*, p. 113; CSPS 1529, no. 211, p. 323.
7. On the inscription he wrote for his tomb, More presents this as

the most important achievement of his diplomatic career. See SL, p. 181.

8. CW 3.2, no. 243; CW 2, p. 5, line 24; CW 12, p. 224, line 28.

9. Corr, p. 263.

10. Guy, *Public Career*, p. 113.

11. CSPS 1531, no. 683, p. 114.

12. Guy, *Public Career*, p. 114; CSPS 1529, no. 211, p. 324.

13. Guy, *Public Career*, p. 113; Hall, vol. 2, p. 164.

14. More's salary of one hundred pounds a year was cut off at this time. See LP, vol. 7, no. 296, p. 129.

15. More cites the play *Octavia*, which he attributes to Seneca. See CW 4, p. 99; Crosset, p. 578; Kinney, pp. 69–72.

16. CW 4, p. 99.

17. CW 4, p. 101.

18. CWE, vol. 2, p. 249. Erasmus refers to Plutarch as "indubitably the most learned of Greek authors" (p. 251).

19. CWE, vol. 2, p. 250.

20. CWE, vol. 2, p. 250.

21. CWE, vol. 2, p. 251.

22. CWE, vol. 2, p. 252.

23. CW 12, p. 224. More wrote about the harm of flattery several times in his Tower works (e.g., CW 12, pp. 44–46, 212–218, 224; DC, pp. 35–36, 175–181, 185–186). One of his last prayers was that he be given the grace "not to hang upon the blast of men's mouths" (SC, p. 148; CW 13, p. 226).

24. Harpsfield, Reynolds edition, p. 163.

25. Roper, p. 38.

26. CWE, vol. 2, p. 252.

27. Roper, p. 28.

28. Scarisbrick, pp. 117–119; CSPV 1509–1519, no. 1220.

29. Roper, pp. 8–9.

30. Roper, pp. 16–18.

31. See chapter 16 for examples from More's *Supplication of Souls* (CW 7).

32. Fox and Guy, pp. 208–220.

33. CW 2, pp. 6, 45.

34. More uses the word "debellation." See CW 10, *The Debellation of Salem and Bizance*.

35. Several months after More was put to death, Cromwell wrote the following about him in an attempt to justify that unpopular execution:

> When certain laws were passed by Parliament with no opposition as beneficial to the whole realm and in accordance with true religion, these men [Fisher and More] opposed them, pretending that they were entirely given up to the contemplation of divine things, and endeavored to refute and evade these laws by fallacious arguments. (LP, vol. 9, no. 240)

Chapter 19
Imprisonment

1. Roper, p. 28.
2. CW 3.2, no. 120.
3. SL, pp. 179–180.
4. SL, p. 181.
5. See Bradshaw's analysis of the strategy behind More's *Apology*, pp. 552–554.
6. *The Answer to a Poisoned Book* (Dec. 1533); see CW 11.
7. Henry wished to implicate More in action against Elizabeth Barton (commonly known as the Nun of Kent), a visionary who had spoken out strongly against Henry. More had, however, refused to speak with this woman about political matters; he had, in fact, counseled her to refrain from such involvement. Once the lords learned what had actually happened, they "reckoned [More] far worthier of praise than reproof" for his judicious behavior (Roper, p. 35).
8. Roper, p. 32; LP, vol. 7, no. 296, pp. 128–129; Lehmberg, *The Reformation Parliament*, p. 195; SL, pp. 192–215.
9. Chapuys reports the occurrence of this meeting in his letter dated March 7, 1934 (LP, vol. 7, no. 296).
10. Roper, p. 34.
11. Roper, p. 32.
12. Roper, p. 34.

13. Roper, p. 32.
14. Roper, pp. 32–33.
15. Roper, p. 33.
16. Roper, p. 33.
17. Roper, p. 34.
18. Roper, p. 35.
19. Roper, p. 35.
20. LP, vol. 7, no. 296.
21. Lehmberg, *The Reformation Parliament*, p. 197.
22. Roper, p. 38.
23. Roper, p. 38.
24. Lehmberg, *The Reformation Parliament*, pp. 203–205.
25. SL, pp. 215–223.
26. SL, p. 217.
27. SL, p. 218.
28. More himself uses the word "pageant" (SL, p. 219). Contrast this passage with the one in *Utopia* in which the character Morus says that each of us must adapt ourselves to the particular part we have been assigned in a particular play (CW 4, p. 99). As the context of *Utopia* makes clear, Morus is speaking about a good play in which one has chosen to participate.
29. SL, pp. 218–219.
30. SL, p. 219. Elizabeth Rogers translates "quod ille notus erat pontifici" as "that he was known to the archbishop" and "valde familiariter" as "very familiarly." As will be seen, however, these translations do not convey the biblical overtones of the original.
31. See Jn 18:15–16; see also Derrett, "Two Dicta of More's," pp. 68–69.
32. SL, p. 219.
33. SL, p. 220.
34. SL, pp. 220–221.
35. SL, p. 221.
36. SL, pp. 221–222.
37. SL, p. 222.
38. Roper, p. 36.
39. Elton, *Policy and Police*, p. 401.
40. According to this new law, it became treason to deprive the king, or any of his heirs, of any of their dignities, names, or titles. The

previous law, the Treason Act of 1352, had required proof of an overt act against the king.

41. Elton, *Policy and Police*, p. 403.
42. Elton, *Policy and Police*, pp. 402–403.
43. SL, p. 237.
44. Roper, pp. 39–40.
45. I am following Elton's reconstruction of dates (*Policy and Police*, p. 404).
46. SL, p. 247.
47. SL, p. 247.
48. A "bedesman" was someone who prayed, often with rosary beads.
49. SL, pp. 247–248.
50. SL, p. 250.
51. SL, pp. 250–251.
52. SL, p. 251.
53. SL, p. 253.
54. Cresacre More, p. 156.
55. LP, vol. 8, no. 867.

Chapter 20
Between Father and Daughter

1. Corr, pp. 513–514.
2. Roper, p. 41.
3. Stapleton, p. 161.
4. Roper, pp. 37–38: "I find no cause, I thank God, Meg, to consider myself any worse here than in my own house. For I think God makes me a wanton and sets me on his lap and dandles me."
5. Roper, p. 49.
6. Roper, p. 38.
7. Corr, pp. 511–532: letter no. 206, "Margaret Roper to Alice Alington." Scholars generally agree that this letter was written jointly by Margaret and her father.
8. See note 7 to chapter 19.
9. Corr, p. 513.

10. Corr, p. 514. For an interesting medical assessment of More's various ailments, see Dr. Salvador Hernandez Conesa's article "Did Thomas More Have a Cervical Disk Lesion?"
11. Corr, p. 515.
12. Corr, p. 515.
13. Corr, p. 516.
14. Corr, p. 518.
15. Corr, pp. 512–513.
16. Corr, pp. 518–519.
17. *Morus* is Greek for "fool." Sir Thomas liked to joke about his name.
18. Corr, pp. 519–520.
19. Corr, p. 513.
20. Corr, p. 520.
21. Corr, p. 521.
22. Corr, p. 522.
23. Corr, p. 522.
24. Corr, pp. 522–523.
25. Corr, p. 523.
26. Corr, pp. 523–524.
27. Corr, p. 524.
28. Corr, p. 525.
29. Corr, p. 527.
30. Corr, p. 528.
31. Corr, p. 528.
32. Corr, p. 529.
33. Corr, p. 529.
34. Corr, pp. 529–530.
35. Corr, pp. 531–532.

Chapter 21
Another David

1. CW 7, p. 182, lines 3–4.
2. CW 12, p. 156, line 17; DC, p. 127.

3. Martz and Sylvester's edition of *Thomas More's Prayer Book* reproduces the annotated pages of More's psalter. In the back they translate the Latin annotations.

4. Roper, p. 37.

5. SL, p. 106.

6. Neither psalm uses the term "conscience," of course, but the same concept is implied.

7. More writes: "The prayer either of a man who is shut up in prison or of one who lies sick in bed yearning for church or of any faithful man who yearns for heaven." During his year and a half in the Tower, More found himself in each of these situations.

8. Martz and Sylvester, p. 203. The list of these psalms is in More's own handwriting on the inside back cover of his psalter.

9. In his psalter More marks five verses as being "for the king" (20:9, 21:1, 61:6, 72:2, and 89:22), but many other passages must also have led him to think about and pray for King Henry. For example, he marks 33:16 ("A king is not saved by a mighty army"), 103:19 ("The Lord has established his throne in heaven, and his kingdom rules over all"), and 118:9 ("It is better to take refuge in the Lord than to trust in princes"), as well as 47:2, 48:4–7, and 97:1, 10. (All psalm references have been changed to conform to modern usage.)

10. More notes that psalm verses 79:5, 80:3, and 83:1 are also appropriate ones to pray "for the Christian people."

11. The whole of this prayer, along with More's marginal comments, is given in SC, pp. 128–141, and also in CW 13, pp. 214–225.

12. Roper, p. 15.

13. These annotations consist of 151 verbal notations and roughly 278 markings in the margins of More's psalter.

14. See, for example, the annotations at Ps 22:6, 31:11, and 71:6.

15. The first specific request of his own psalm is to be given the grace "To set my mind fast upon You, / And not to hang upon the blast of men's mouths."

16. CW 3.2, no. 224.

17. CW 12, p. 43, line 30; DC, p. 34.

18. CW 12, p. 43, lines 16ff.; DC, p. 34. Here More paraphrases Heb 12:6 and Acts 14:22.

19. See More's marginal note for Ps 73:28.

20. Of all the flags that More draws to mark off special passages, this one and the ones at Ps 71:9, 39:5–6, and 31:24 are the largest and

are given the greatest flourish. Ps 71:9 is "Cast me not off in my old age; as my strength fails, forsake me not." (At this time, More was fifty-seven years old and in poor health.) Ps 39:5–6 reads: "Only a breath is any human existence. A phantom only, man goes his way; like vapor only are his restless pursuits." Ps 31:24 is "Take courage and be stouthearted, all you who hope in God."

21. More flags for special emphasis the phrase "I ponder, and my spirit broods."

22. See Ps 35:13–16 and 69:10–11, and especially More's annotation on the first text.

23. Sylvester notes that More "took special pains not to repeat himself" in his literary work (EA, p. 463).

24. Some of the other contributions More made were these: an explanation of suffering (in the *Dialogue of Comfort*) that was unparalleled for its comprehensive and positive character; an exploration, in light of Christian revelation, of the fundamental issues of political philosophy (see his epigrams, *Utopia*, and *The History of King Richard III*); a style of diplomacy based on humor, irony, truthfulness, and law; and an approach to education (for women, in particular) that became a model for many.

25. SC, pp. 104–112; CW 14, pp. 565–619.

26. Corr, pp. 531–532, lines 661–663. Notice More's provocative use of the active phrase "I make me very sure." This phrase seems to underscore the need of prayer and meditation for keeping this postulate of faith in the forefront of the mind. See *Catechism of the Catholic Church* (1994), no. 313, which quotes these sentences.

27. This phrase (Ps 118:14) is another that More marks for emphasis. Many others like it are also marked.

Chapter 22
The Power of Artful Conversation II

1. "Comfort" comes from the Latin *con* (an intensive) and *fortare* ("to strengthen").

2. "Tribulation" refers to a great affliction that comes from a *tribulum*, or threshing sledge.

3. DC, p. 1; CW 12, p. 3.

4. However, it could also be said that Vincent represents the fearful

will within himself that More struggled against. I am grateful to Stephen Hollingshead for this clarification.

5. For a brief account of these horrors, see CW 12, pp. cxxvi–cxxviii.

6. More may have gotten the idea for this book from his reflections on some of the psalms. See his marginal notes (in Martz and Sylvester) on the Turks and the Hungarians, next to these verses: Ps 16:8, 68:7, 79:4, 79:14, 82:2, 84:2, and 93:2.

7. Following the traditional understanding, Anthony explains that suffering is medicinal in that it can heal the wounds caused by past sins, and can prevent future sins. It is better than medicinal in that it gives one an opportunity to increase the merit for one's good actions.

8. DC, pp. 19, 67; CW 12, pp. 24, 82.

9. DC, p. 91; CW 12, p. 112.

10. DC, pp. 89–90; CW 12, p. 110.

11. DC, p. 90; CW 12, p. 110.

12. DC, pp. 93–98; CW 12, pp. 114–119; mentioned in chapter 10 above.

13. DC, p. 100; CW 12, p. 122.

14. DC, p. 108ff.; CW 12, pp. 132ff.

15. DC, p. 107; CW 12, pp. 131–132.

16. DC, pp. 117, 105; CW 12, p. 143, line 28, and p. 128, line 5.

17. DC, pp. 101–103; CW 12, pp. 124–126.

18. DC, pp. 104–105; CW 12, pp. 127–128.

19. DC, p. 117; CW 12, p. 144, lines 1–2.

20. DC, p. 117; CW 12, p. 144, lines 21–22.

21. DC, pp. 117–118; CW 12, p. 143, line 26, and p. 145, line 13.

22. DC, p. 117; CW 12, p. 145, line 5.

23. DC, p. 164; CW 12, p. 198, lines 30–32.

24. DC, pp. 166–167; CW 12, p. 202, lines 2–3.

25. DC, pp. 169–170; CW 12, p. 205, lines 14–17.

26. DC, p. 186; CW 12, p. 225, line 17.

27. DC, pp. 189–196; CW 12, pp. 229–237.

28. DC, p. 199; CW 12, p. 242, line 14.

29. DC, p. 3; CW 12, p. 5, lines 19–25.

30. DC, p. 230; CW 12, p. 281, line 13.

31. DC, p. 254; CW 12, p. 312, line 8.

32. DC, pp. 254–255; CW 12, p. 312, line 11, to p. 313, line 7.
33. "Vincent" comes from the Latin *vincere*, "to conquer," "to be victorious." See the note at CW 12, p. 3, line 7.
34. EW, p. 391. See chapter 3 above.
35. Ps 62:1–2. See SC, p. 140, or CW 13, p. 225.

Chapter 23
Spiritual Handbook III

1. SC, p. 47; CW 14, p. 263, lines 14–15, to p. 265, line 2.
2. SC, p. 47; CW 14, p. 265, lines 3–5.
3. CW 4, p. 99.
4. SC, p. 46; CW 14, p. 259, line 8.
5. SC, p. 61; CW 14, p. 341, lines 4–5.
6. SC, p. 101; CW 14, p. 543, line 6.
7. SC, p. 8; CW 14, p. 53, line 5, to p. 55, line 5.
8. SC, p. 32; CW 14, p. 191, lines 2–3.
9. SC, p. 9; CW 14, p. 59, line 4.
10. SC, p. 11; CW 14, p. 73, lines 1–4.
11. SC, p. 37; CW 14, p. 217, lines 5–6.
12. SC, p. 36; CW 14, p. 211, lines 11–12.
13. SC, p. 50; CW 14, p. 285, line 1.
14. SC, pp. 47, 50, 34ff.; CW 14, p. 265, line 7; CW 14, p. 287, line 6; CW 14, pp. 199ff.
15. SC, p. 46; CW 14, p. 259, lines 4–6.
16. SC, p. 46; CW 14, p. 259, line 7, to p. 261, line 5.
17. This open rebuke to the bishops seems to be the only one of its kind in all of More's writings. In an indirect and literary way, More does draw attention in his next-to-last work to the evil "bishops" on the Sanhedrin (an obvious and intentional anachronism) who condemned Christ and called for his crucifixion, but there he places special blame upon the "covetice of the kings" who usurped "the right order of the making and choosing of the bishop" (CW 13, p. 72). Earlier, he clearly pointed out that the "Spirituality" had been negligent in their duty to reform abuses, but he did not single out the bishops explicitly (see CW 9, espe-

cially pp. 53 and 145). Other singular or indirect criticisms are given above, on pp. 11, 45–46, 52–53.

18. SC, p. 47; CW 14, p. 265, lines 5–10. (See 2 Cor 7:10.)
19. SC, p. 55; CW 14, p. 309, line 10, to p. 311, line 2.
20. SC, p. 59; CW 14, p. 331, lines 2–4.
21. SC, p. 25; CW 14, p. 159, lines 3–4.
22. SC, p. 27; CW 14, p. 167, line 12, to p. 169, line 1.
23. SC, p. 28; CW 14, pp. 173–175.
24. SC, p. 18; CW 14, p. 113, line 10, to p. 115, line 2.
25. SC, pp. 18–19; CW 14, p. 115, line 2, to p. 117, line 3.
26. SC, p. 19; CW 14, p. 121, lines 4–5.
27. SC, p. 20; CW 14, p. 127, lines 4–5.
28. SC, p. 20; CW 14, p. 127, lines 5–7.
29. SC, pp. 20–21; CW 14, p. 127, line 9, to p. 129, line 1.
30. SC, p. 76; CW 14, p. 419, line 2.
31. SC, p. 45; CW 14, p. 253, lines 14–15.
32. SC, pp. 98–101; CW 14, pp. 531–543.
33. Consider More's reflections, at the end of this work, on the youth who fled naked from the scene when Christ was arrested (SC, pp. 104–112; CW 14, pp. 565–617; see Mk 14:52).
34. SC, pp. 72–73; CW 14, p. 403, lines 1–11.
35. SC, p. 73; CW 14, p. 403, line 12, to p. 407, line 2.
36. SC, p. 83; CW 14, p. 457, line 5.
37. SC, p. 61; CW 14, p. 339, line 17, to p. 341, line 3.
38. EW, p. 388.

Chapter 24
A Trial to Remember

1. At least one of the jurors, John Parnell, had a longtime grudge against More because of an adverse decree he had handed down against him (Harpsfield, Reynolds edition, p. 153; Derrett, "The Trial of Sir Thomas More," p. 455).
2. Harpsfield, Reynolds edition, p. 155.
3. Harpsfield, Reynolds edition, p. 155.

4. Harpsfield, Reynolds edition, p. 157.
5. Roper, pp. 41–42.
6. Roper, p. 43.
7. Roper, p. 43.
8. Roper, p. 44.
9. Roper, pp. 44–45.
10. Roper, p. 45.
11. See Derrett's perceptive analysis of this legal maneuver in "The Trial of Sir Thomas More," pp. 468–475.
12. Roper, p. 45.
13. Roper, p. 45.
14. Roper, p. 45.
15. Roper, p. 46.
16. Roper, p. 46.
17. Roper, p. 46.
18. Derrett, "The Trial of Sir Thomas More," p. 474.
19. Roper, p. 46.
20. Roper, p. 47.
21. See CW 2, p. 70, and the accompanying note. This chief justice emerges in More's assessment as one of the great English heroes. Markham sacrificed his career as chief justice by thwarting the attempts of King Edward IV to manipulate the law.
22. See CW 2, p. 6.

Chapter 25
Death with Good Humor

1. Roper, p. 47.
2. SC, p. 142; CW 13, pp. 207–208.
3. SC, p. 150; CW 13, p. 227, lines 18–22.
4. SC, pp. 154–155; CW 13, p. 231.
5. Roper, p. 47.
6. Roper, p. 48; Harpsfield, Reynolds edition, pp. 164–165.
7. Hall, vol. 2, p. 265.
8. Hall, vol. 2, p. 266.

9. More punned on his own last name, which in Greek means "fool." He was the one who encouraged Erasmus to write his most famous work, *In Praise of Folly*. He also alluded to St. Paul's famous passages referring to the folly of the cross (see 1 Cor 1:17 – 2:2).

10. The effect of this refrain must have been similar to that of the refrain used by Christ in the garden of Gethsemane: "Could you not watch with me for one hour?"

11. The following are only some of the places where More uses or refers to this verse: EW, p. 331; CW 6, p. 400, lines 31ff.; CW 8, p. 527, lines 21ff.; CW 12, p. 248, lines 27–28.

12. Roper, p. 29.

13. See note 17 to chapter 9.

14. See EW, pp. 365, 384; CW 12, pp. 31, 34; Harpsfield, Reynolds edition, pp. 149–150; Stapleton, pp. 127, 144.

15. Stapleton draws attention to this quality repeatedly: see pp. 124, 163, 189.

16. SL, p. 241.

17. For examples, see chapter 3.

18. SL, p. 241.

Afterword

1. That Pius XI had the Nazi danger in mind when he canonized Thomas More is evident from a statement he had made about him in April of 1935: "When we turn our glance to the tremendous crises—economic, political, but above all moral—through which mankind is passing, and when we think of the consequences, still more grievous, which we fear in the future, this is indeed reason for profound grief. And while the evils produced by the last European war have not yet been repaired, behold a dense cloud obscures the horizon once more, from which fresh lightnings proceed so that men hold themselves in fear and trembling . . ." (*The Tablet*, April 13, 1935, pp. 473–474).

2. *The Tablet*, June 1, 1935, p. 694.

3. *The Tablet*, March 16, 1935, p. 337.

4. *The Tablet*, March 16, 1935, p. 337.

5. *The Tablet*, March 16, 1935, pp. 337–338.
6. R. W. Chambers, *The Place of St. Thomas More in English Literature and History* (New York: Haskell House, 1964), p. 21.
7. *Biathanotos*, as noted in *Moreana*, no. 115–116 (December 1993): 168. John Donne was the son of Joan and John Heywood; Joan was the daughter of John Rastell and Elizabeth More, Thomas More's sister.
8. *The Prose Works of Jonathan Swift*, ed. Herbert Davis (Oxford: Basil Blackwell, 1959), vol. 13, p. 123.
9. In *Moreana*, no. 63 (December 1979): 49–55, James Warren gives a brief account of More's beatification and canonization.
10. See CW 7, p. 135, lines 21–22.
11. *The Fame of Blessed Thomas More, Being Addresses Delivered in His Honour in Chelsea, July 1929* (London: Sheed and Ward, 1929), p. 63.
12. This edition is a fifteen-volume set (actually composed of twenty-one books; some "volumes" comprise more than one book). It does not, however, include his complete correspondence.

Works Cited

Abbreviations: Corr   *Correspondence of Sir Thomas More*
               CSPS   *Calendar of State Papers, Spanish*
               CSPV   *Calendar of State Papers, Venetian*
               CW   *The Complete Works of St. Thomas More*
               CWE   *The Collected Works of Erasmus*
               DC   More's *Dialogue of Comfort against Tribulation*
               EA   Marc'hadour and Sylvester's *Essential Articles*
               EE   *Epistles of Erasmus*
               EW   *English Works of Sir Thomas More*
               LP   *Letters and Papers of Henry VIII*
               SC   More's *Sadness of Christ*
               SL   *St. Thomas More: Selected Letters*
               TW   More's *Tower Works*

Bainton, Roland. *Erasmus of Christendom*. New York: Charles Scribner's Sons, 1969.

Bouge, John. "A Letter Sent to Dame Kathryn Manne." *The English Historical Review* 7 (1892): 712–715.

Boyle, Margarie O'Rourke. *Rhetoric and Reform: Erasmus' Civil Dispute with Luther*. Cambridge, Mass.: Harvard University Press, 1983.

Bradshaw, Brendan. "The Controversial Sir Thomas More." *Journal of Ecclesiastical History* 36 (1985): 535–569.

[CSPS]. *Calendar of State Papers, Spanish*. London: Longmans and Co., 1866.

[CSPV]. *Calendar of State Papers, Venetian*. London: Longmans and Co., 1871.

Chambers, R. W. *Thomas More*. London: Jonathan Cape, 1938.

Copenhaver, Brian, and Charles Schmitt. *Renaissance Philosophy*. London: Oxford University Press, 1992.

Crosset, John. "More and Seneca." *Philological Quarterly* 40 (1961): 577–580.

Derrett, J. Duncan M. "The Trial of Sir Thomas More." *English Historical Review* 79 (1964): 449–477.

——. "Two Dicta of More's." *Moreana*, no. 8 (November 1965): 67–72.

Elton, G. R. *Policy and Police: The Enforcement of the Reformation in the Age of Thomas Cromwell*. Cambridge: Cambridge University Press, 1972.

——. "The Real Thomas More?" *Studies in Tudor and Stuart Politics and Government*, vol. 3. Cambridge: Cambridge University Press, 1983.

Erasmus, Desiderius. [CWE]. *The Collected Works of Erasmus*. Toronto: University of Toronto Press, 1974–[still in progress].

——. [EE]. *Epistles of Erasmus*. 3 vols. Trans. Francis Nichols. New York: Russell and Russell, 1962.

——. "Marriage." In *The Colloquies of Erasmus*. Trans. Craig R. Thompson. Chicago: University of Chicago Press, 1965.

Fox, Alistair. *Thomas More: History and Providence*. New Haven, Conn.: Yale University Press, 1982.

Fox, Alistair, and John Guy. *Reassessing the Henrician Age: Humanism, Politics, and Reform 1500–1550*. New York: Basil Blackwell, 1986.

Gabrieli, Vittorio. "Giovanni Pico and Thomas More." *Moreana*, no. 29 (November 1967): 43–57.

Guy, John. *Christopher St. German on Chancery and Statute*. London: Selden Society, 1985.

——. *The Public Career of Sir Thomas More*. New Haven, Conn.: Yale University Press, 1980.

—————. "Thomas More as Successor to Wolsey." *Thought* 52 (September 1977): 275–292.

Hall, Edward. *Lives of the Kings: Henry VIII.* 2 vols. London: T. C. and E. C. Jack, 1904.

Harpsfield, Nicholas. *The Life and Death of Sir Thomas More, Knight.* Ed. Elsie V. Hitchcock. London: Oxford University Press, 1932.

—————. *Lives of Saint Thomas More.* Ed. E. E. Reynolds. New York: Everyman's Library, 1963.

Hastings, Margaret. "Sir Thomas More: Maker of English Law?" In EA, pp. 104–118.

Henry VIII. *Assertio Septem Sacramentorum or Defence of the Seven Sacraments.* New York: Benziger Brothers, 1908.

Hernandez Conesa, Salvador. "Did Thomas More Have a Cervical Disk Lesion?" *Moreana,* no. 83–84 (November 1984): 27–31.

Heywood, Ellis. *Il Moro.* Ed. and trans. Roger Deakins. Cambridge, Mass.: Harvard University Press, 1971.

Hillerbrand, Hans J., ed. *Erasmus and His Age: Selected Letters.* New York: Harper and Row, 1970.

Hughes, Philip, ed. *Saint John Fisher: The Earliest English Life.* London: Burns, Oates, and Washbourne, 1935.

Kelly, Michael. "The Submission of the Clergy." *Transactions of the Royal Historical Society, Fifth Series* 15 (1965): 97–119.

Kincaid, Arthur N. "The Dramatic Structure of Sir Thomas More's *History of King Richard III.*" In EA, pp. 375–387.

Kinney, Arthur F. *Humanist Poetics: Thought, Rhetoric, and Fiction in Sixteenth-Century England.* Amherst: University of Massachusetts Press, 1986.

Lehmberg, Stanford E. "Sir Thomas More's *Life of Pico della Mirandola.*" *Studies in the Renaissance* 3 (1956): 61–74.

—————. *The Reformation Parliament, 1529–1536.* Cambridge: Cambridge University Press, 1970.

[LP]. *Letters and Papers, Foreign and Domestic, of the Reign of Henry VIII.* Ed. J. S. Brewer, James Gairdner, and R. H. Brodie. 21 vols. London: Longmans and Co., 1862–1932.

Lewis, C. S. *English Literature in the Sixteenth Century Excluding Drama*. Oxford: Clarendon Press, 1954.

Lupton, J. H. *A Life of John Colet*. Hamden, Conn.: The Shoe String Press, 1961.

Marc'hadour, Germain. *The Bible in the Works of Thomas More*. Nieuwkoop: B. de Graaf, 1969–1972.

——————. "Thomas More's Birth: 1477 or 1478?" *Moreana*, no. 53 (March 1977): 5–10.

Marc'hadour, Germain, and Richard S. Sylvester, eds. [EA]. *Essential Articles for the Study of Thomas More*. Hamden, Conn.: Archon Books, 1977.

Marius, Richard. *Thomas More*. New York: Albert A. Knopf, 1984.

Martz, Louis L., and Richard S. Sylvester. *Thomas More's Prayer Book: A Facsimile Reproduction of the Annotated Pages*. New Haven, Conn.: Yale University Press, 1969.

More, Cresacre. *The Life of Sir Thomas More, Knight*. Ed. James L. Kennedy. Athens, Pa.: Riverside Press, 1941.

More, Thomas. [Corr]. *The Correspondence of Sir Thomas More*. Ed. Elizabeth F. Rogers. Princeton, N.J.: Princeton University Press, 1947.

——————. [CW]. *The Complete Works of St. Thomas More*. New Haven, Conn.: Yale University Press, 1963–[still in progress].

CW 1   *English Poems, The Life of Pico, The Four Last Things*. Ed. Clarence H. Miller et al. [forthcoming]

CW 2   *The History of King Richard III*. Ed. Richard S. Sylvester. 1963.

CW 3.1   *Translations of Lucian*. Ed. Craig R. Thompson. 1974.

CW 3.2   *The Latin Poems*. Ed. Clarence H. Miller, Leicester Bradner, Charles A. Lynch, and Revilo P. Oliver. 1984.

CW 4   *Utopia*. Ed. Edward Surtz and J. H. Hexter. 1965.

CW 5   *Responsio ad Lutherum*. Ed. John M. Headley. 1969.

CW 6   *A Dialogue Concerning Heresies*. Ed. Thomas Lawler, Germain Marc'hadour, and Richard Marius. 1981.

CW 7   *Letter to Bugenhagen, Supplication of Souls, Letter against Frith*. Ed. Frank Manley, Germain Marc'hadour, Richard Marius, and Clarence H. Miller. 1990.

CW 8   *Confutation of Tyndale's Answer.* Ed. Louis Schuster, Richard Marius, James Lusardi, and Richard Schoeck. 1973.

CW 9   *The Apology of Sir Thomas More.* Ed. J. B. Trapp. 1979.

CW 10   *The Debellation of Salem and Bizance.* Ed. John Guy, Ralph Keen, Clarence H. Miller, and Ruth McGugan. 1987.

CW 11   *The Answer to a Poisoned Book.* Ed. Stephen M. Foley and Clarence H. Miller. 1985.

CW 12   *A Dialogue of Comfort against Tribulation.* Ed. Louis L. Martz and Frank Manley. 1976.

CW 13   *A Treatise upon the Passion.* Ed. Garry E. Haupt. 1976.

CW 14   *De Tristitia Christi.* Ed. Clarence H. Miller. 1976.

CW 15   *In Defense of Humanism.* Ed. Daniel Kinney. 1986.

—————. [DC]. *Dialogue of Comfort against Tribulation.* Ed. Monica Stevens. London: Sheed and Ward, 1951.

—————. [EW]. *The English Works of Sir Thomas More.* Ed. W. E. Campbell et al. Vol. 1. London: Eyre and Spottiswoode, 1931.

—————. *The Latin Epigrams of Thomas More.* Ed. and trans. Leicester Bradner and Charles A. Lynch. Chicago: University of Chicago Press, 1953.

—————. [SC]. *The Sadness of Christ.* Ed. Gerard Wegemer. Princeton, N.J.: Scepter Publishers, 1993.

—————. [SL]. *Selected Letters.* Trans. Elizabeth F. Rogers. New Haven, Conn.: Yale University Press, 1947.

—————. [TW]. *The Tower Works: Devotional Writings.* Ed. Garry E. Haupt. New Haven: Yale University Press, 1980.

Morison, Stanley. *The Likeness of Thomas More.* Edited and supplemented by Nicolas Barker. New York: Fordham University Press, 1963.

Moyes, James. "Warham, an English Primate on the Eve of the Reformation." *Dublin Review* 114 (April 1894): 390–419.

Munday, Anthony, et al. *Sir Thomas More: A Play.* Revised by Henry Chettle, Thomas Dekker, Thomas Heywood, and

William Shakespeare. Ed. Vittorio Gabrieli and Giorgio Melchiori. Manchester: Manchester University Press, 1990.

Pace, Richard. *De Fructu Qui Ex Doctrina Percipitur (The Benefits of a Liberal Education)*. Ed. and trans. Frank Manley and R. S. Sylvester. New York: Frederick Ungar Publishing Co., 1967.

Piper, David. "Holbein the Younger in England." *Journal of the Royal Society of Arts* 91 (1963): 736–755.

Ro. Ba. *The Life of Sir Thomas More*. Ed. Elsie V. Hitchcock and P. E. Hallett. London: Oxford University Press, 1950.

Roper, William. *Lives of Saint Thomas More*. Ed. E. E. Reynolds. New York: Everyman's Library, 1963.

Scarisbrick, J. J. *Henry VIII*. Berkeley: University of California Press, 1968.

Stapleton, Thomas. *The Life and Illustrious Martyrdom of Sir Thomas More*. Trans. Philip E. Hallett. Ed. E. E. Reynolds. New York: Fordham University Press, 1966.

Sylvester, Richard S. "The 'Man for All Seasons' Again: Robert Whittington's Verses of Sir Thomas More." *Huntington Library Quarterly* 26 (1963): 147–154.

—————. "A Part of His Own: Thomas More's Literary Personality in His Early Works." *Moreana*, no. 15 (November 1967): 29–42.

Acknowledgments

Acknowledging with gratitude those who contributed to this book is a task I eagerly take up. Special thanks must go to John Powers, who encouraged this project from the beginning, and to Fr. Germain Marc'hadour and Dr. Tom Jodziewicz, who read through the entire manuscript and gave helpful suggestions. Members of the Thomas More Society of Dallas have provided a wonderful forum for discussing many of the ideas developed here; they have also generously paid for the beautiful color reconstruction of Holbein's sketch of the Thomas More family. Matt Smith undertook the herculean task of composing the maps which grace this book, and he also worked his magic in designing the cover. Alice Puro of the University of Dallas library has been of invaluable assistance over the last decade; she has been unflagging in her efficient and cheerful service. Mary Gottschalk and Bernard Browne have likewise been unusually patient and helpful in the editing of this book. I am also heartily grateful to my colleagues at the University of Dallas for ten years of good conversation and collegial support.

Index